D0903822

Constructing
School
Knowledge

Constructing School Knowledge

An Ethnography of Learning in an Indian Village

Padma M. Sarangapani

SAGE Publications
New Delhi • Thousand Oaks • London

First published in 2003 by

Sage Publications India Pvt Ltd
B-42, Panchsheel Enclave
New Delhi 110 017

Sage Publications Inc
2455 Teller Road
Thousand Oaks, California 91320

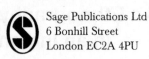

Sage Publications Ltd
6 Bonhill Street
London EC2A 4PU

Published by Tejeshwar Singh for Sage Publications India Pvt Ltd, typeset in 10/12 Baskerville by Star Compugraphics Pvt Ltd, New Delhi and printed at Chaman Enterprises, New Delhi.

Library of Congress Cataloging-in-Publication Data

Sarangapani, Padma
  Constructing school knowledge: An ethnography of learning in an Indian village/ Padma M. Sarangapani
    p. cm.
  Includes bibliographical references and index.
    1. Education, Primary—India—Kasimpur—Case studies. 2. Educational anthropology—India.   I. Title

LA1152.S27   372.954—dc21   2002   2002073432

ISBN: 0-7619-9671-0 (Hb) (US)   81-7829-135-5 (Hb) (India)
        0-7619-9672-9 (Pb) (US)   81-7829-136-3 (Pb) (India)

Sage Production Team: Sarita Vellani, Shahnaz Habib, Amarjyoti Dutta, N.K. Negi and Santosh Rawat

For
Appa and Mata

Contents

List of Figures, Tables and Boxes

Acknowledgements

The children of Kasimpur shared with me their lives and worlds, and patiently and cheerfully entertained my interest and queries. The teachers and heads of the three schools gave me their time, and aided my stay and work in the school by being themselves. All the people of the village, especially the parents, sisters and brothers of the children, and the family with whom I stayed, welcomed me into their homes, gave me time and often fed me with tea and delicious *rotis* which I could never refuse. For their hospitality and affection I will always be grateful. Dr N. Siddiqui suggested the school for study, and his acquaintance with the headmaster made my entry into the school easy.

The Fulbright Foundation provided me with a pre-doctoral fellowship which enabled me to spend nine months at the Eliot-Pearson Department of Child Study, at Tufts University, Massachusetts. The Dudley Wright Centre for Science Education at Tufts provided me with space and work facilities. This was an invaluable opportunity to consult libraries, study and begin my analysis.

Suresh Kumar and Badam Singh of the Teen Murti Traffic Circle, New Delhi, responded to my distress and went out of their way to help me find my lost thesis manuscript and laptop, just a few weeks before it was to be submitted to the Department of Education, University of Delhi, for a PhD. This book is based on that thesis. My debt to them is enormous.

While working on the thesis in Delhi, I enjoyed the supportive presence of many friends, especially Nargis Panchapakesan, Frances Kumar, Deepu, Shefali, Malavika, the Lakshmikumarans, Prof. and Mrs Sharma and the late Father Gregorios and Prof. Shukla. I benefited from the feedback and encouragement received from scholars and friends who read parts of or the whole thesis, and encouraged me in my efforts to turn it into a book— Prof. T.S. Saraswathi, the late Prof. Durganand Sinha, Mohammad Talib,

Prof. S. Anandalakshmy, Baljit and Rekha. Articles based on the research were carried in several issues of *Vimarsh* and *Sandarbh* and helped me rework ideas to make them more accessible.

Evolving a life as an independent scholar in Bangalore would have been impossible but for my sister, Radha, who also drew my attention to the cockroach, and Jane Sahi, who, along with her friendship also generously shared with me much needed criticisms and her insights on reading the drafts of my chapters. Kshama, closet Indologist and mother-in-law, encouraged me with her enthusiasm for the project, interest, assistance in research, editing and proof reading. Sarita Vellani, gentle editor, also generously assisted in preparing this book. Roshan Sahi worked on the various figures included in this book. And Rangaji, Chikki, Jaggi and Badri.

I am grateful to Jaya for her affection, her faith in my scholarship and for being there. Amitabha provided me with just the right kind of editorial inputs I needed to refine the manuscript, and much more. Hari has kept me well humoured and well fed, and attended to most technological glitches, but he is waiting for me to do something more in school education than simply writing about it.

My greatest debt is to Prof. Krishna Kumar, who supervised my PhD work and continues to shape and nurture my intellectual growth with his enduring interest, concern, enthusiasm, faith, friendship and good humour. My parents have anxiously watched over my transition from Science to Education. This book is for them.

Bangalore
16 July 2001

1

Introduction

This book is about children's experience of schooling in a village government primary school in India. Reading this, you might wonder: is there so much to learn and understand about a government primary school that can fill a book? The state of schooling in these institutions is well known. Everyone is familiar with the dreary monotony of teaching–learning where it does occur, the authoritarian, uninterested teacher and the rote memorisation that substitutes for learning. However, these observations are in themselves routine and talking about government schools is pointless if we cannot move beyond such banalities, even if they are accompanied by entreaties to do something for the betterment of these schools.

The attempt here is to re-enter the familiar ground of government schools and use the tools of anthropology to reconstruct our common knowledge about not only the schools themselves but also the process of schooling. The book thus presents the process and meaning of schooling in Kasimpur[1] village as constituted by the children and teachers—insiders of the school. By presenting their view, I am suggesting that the *insider's view* of a government primary school is worth considering. However, since the significance of this, especially in the context of the common government primary school, may not be immediately obvious, it might be worth our while to briefly examine and speculate on the reasons for this claim.

The apparently routinised, ritualised and repetitive nature of everyday activity in a school tends to invite the assumption that this is a world that is simple to understand and easy to enter and to alter. A sociologist or anthropologist will be impatient with such naïveté and remind us that schools are also social institutions—they exist and function not only by virtue of the physical and human infrastructure such as building, blackboard, student and teacher, but perhaps more importantly because of the activity and the discourse through which, each day, life in the school is re-created, relationships are established and learning takes place. Even the routine lasts only as long as everyone cooperates to keep it that way; just one question from a student can threaten the status quo. The viewpoint of the children and the teachers, the everyday participants of schooling, is not only 'opinions and ideas' which educators may be interested in taking into account. It suggests that there is a more elaborate 'world-view' shared by teachers and children. It is from this that they derive the norms, values, attitudes and scripts which support and guide the course of everyday activity and provide the basis to anticipate, to make choices and decisions.

However, in the popular understanding it is not so obvious that in the school there is a world that will become apparent only through patient anthropological study. Especially in the case of government primary schools, there is so little happening, and what we see is so familiar, dreary and monotonous, that even after a brief visit to such a school, we leave with the sense that we 'know' all there is to it. In ordinariness and familiarity it compares with a cockroach; how many of us would suspend our instinct to kill the cockroach on our kitchen counter and pause to observe and notice it as a living creature? The ordinariness of the government primary school invites the attitude that knowledge about the school is common, and we need not make any special effort to pause and gather an understanding about the school. This attitude pervades almost all people and institutions that are associated with the primary school—whether administrators, teacher–trainers preparing teachers for these schools, or voluntary agencies working in these schools. Penetrating through this image to even begin to *see* the school is itself a challenge.

In addition to the apparent ordinariness, the other factor that strongly influences both our perception and discourse of the government primary school has to do with the various degrees of dysfunctionality which plague virtually all these institutions. Whether at the gross level of school building and pupil attendance, or the more nuanced levels of the quality of teaching or the hidden curriculum, things do not seem to be working all right. There is a widespread attempt—supported, if not also driven, by massive foreign aid—to change and reform primary schools. The overarching concerns are articulated in the form of 'how' questions: 'how do we get children to attend school more regularly?', 'how do we motivate teachers to come to the classroom and teach?', 'how do we train them to teach better so that children learn?' As the form of these questions indicates, the orientation is towards *doing* and managing things. It seems imperative to act, to reform and to set things right; it is towards this that present investment and interest in primary education are directed. The dominant discourse is in the form of programmes of action: reorientation, training, motivation, community participation, joyful learning, activity-based education, etc.

Questions such as 'what does education mean to children?', 'why do children submit meekly to the discipline of the school?' or 'why is there a resistance to educational reform that promotes understanding?' are not a part of the discourse.

The urgency to act and change and the magnitude of the task bring with them an impatience with observing, listening and asking, and with understanding that which we have made the object of reform and development activity. I am not suggesting that the concern for how bad schools are, or the attempt to change things, is illegitimate or unwarranted. But I do wish to point out that the orientation towards action influences us to perceive and talk about the field within a frame that is normative and evaluative. It also takes for granted that we know the object of our concern well enough. With the focus being on what needs to be changed, we are only peripherally concerned with what meaning teachers and learners bring in to constitute this institution and their own experience of education. The commonness of the experience, and especially the obviousness of all that is wrong, makes it seem unnecessary to engage in any deeper way with the inner world of the school.

Our familiarity with the ordinary makes us unwittingly arrogant in how we think and act in relationship to it. We forget that it is for cognitive convenience that we reduce the complexity of experience into known categories and habitual response. Resisting the impulse to swat the small cockroach on the kitchen counter, I stopped to observe it. It had its head close to the edge of a tiny water droplet; it was drinking. I added a few more tiny drops and as I watched it drink greedily, I felt humbled by the realisation that my routine response of 'pest' was thoughtlessly self-righteous and unidimensional. The pesky government school may not invite being swatted like a cockroach, but the impulse to evaluate and reform it is in danger of being no less unidimensional and self-righteous a response. Suspending, or at least postponing, the normative frame of the educationist and adopting the frame of an anthropological investigator can be equally humbling and educative.

The Background

The 'knowledge' that children are expected to learn and that teachers are expected to teach—the knowledge that experts in society decide that children at specific grades ought to know, and which becomes included in the school curriculum—how is it organised in the school and how do children come to 'know' it? It was with this question on the nature of learning that I entered the Kasimpur Government Boys' Primary Model School (hereafter KBMS). In education, problems of learning are traditionally dealt with within the ambit of cognitive psychology, and primarily as problems of individual consciousness: for example, the influential Piagetian model of the child as constructing her reality.[2] Influenced by the social constructionist perspective represented by Dewey (1916, 1985b), Berger and Luckmann (1966) and Holzner (1968), I was interested in investigating the problem with a frame that could situate the child in his/her total context and permit questions concerning learning to be asked in relation to the world both in and out of the school. The choice of anthropological tools was a natural consequence of this. The framework was informed by various disciplines and a brief discussion of this is presented in Appendix A.

What began as an ethnography of learning grew into an ethnography of schooling. It was apparent that the child's identity and role as a learner, the activity of learning and the meaning given to it, could be understood only when taken in relation to the totality of the educational experience. This includes, most importantly, pedagogic activity and discourse, roles, teacher and student identities, authority and the joint negotiation of knowledge. But it also includes a more general and abstract experience and understanding of schooling and education, constituted at one level by historical changes in the village and at another by the popular (folkloric) ideology of childhood and education. It includes ideas on 'aims of education', purposes of schooling and how children are to be brought up, and the image of the educated man. Our understanding of the child as a learner, the process of learning and of knowledge deepens as we admit sensitivity to more levels of the locale and tune in to the overtones they contribute to meaning. This construction of knowledge of the school and of learning, although laid out linearly, is in fact a hypertext enriched to the extent that we are able to recognise the interlinkages.

Constructing School Knowledge
from the Child's Point of View

I am concerned with constructing common school knowledge of two kinds. One is the common 'facts' of the government school that I have already referred to—the ethos, the internal structure of authority, the interrelationships of pupils and teachers, pedagogic practice and discourse, etc. These are elements that constitute the familiar, everyday life-world of the children and teachers. The other common school knowledge I am concerned with is that which is included and taught in the school curriculum and which is the object of learning and pedagogic activity. I call this *common* knowledge because by virtue of being included in the primary school curriculum of government schools, there is the implication that this is a selection of what 'everybody should know'.

To bring out the child's point of view, this 'common school knowledge' is constructed, or rather reconstructed, from two perspectives. The first is the viewpoint of the actors themselves, especially the children, but also the teachers and parents: how do children and teachers constitute their school experience? What meaning do they give to the various rituals of schooling and pedagogy that they actively participate in every day? How do they establish and negotiate their activities of teaching–learning and their identities as teachers and learners? What meaning does the knowledge encoded in the curriculum have for them? How does it relate to the world outside the school? The voices and activities that were documented in the form of thick descriptions during fieldwork are presented here.

The second perspective taken is that of the researcher endeavouring to make the institution, the players, their voices and their activities intelligible. For this, I will be drawing on interpretative frameworks provided by theory and related research in philosophy, epistemology, cognitive psychology and the sociology of education and knowledge. While the first point of view is the 'inner world', its significance, depth and 'world-ness' become apparent only when taken along with the second point of view. Both the ethnography and the interpretation are biased towards the child. There is an interest in deliberately foregrounding the child's experience and voice in an effort to comprehend the nature of the child's agency and subjectivity in relation to the school and to school knowledge.

Organisation of This Book

My understanding of schooling and learning in the Kasimpur primary school grew out of an engagement with theory and field observation that can best be described as a dialectically evolving spiral which lasted the entire period—from actual fieldwork right up to writing this book. The chapters that follow are organised more rationally to reflect analytical and thematic unity. Chapter II introduces the village Kasimpur and its ethos. The children and the teachers are introduced in Chapter III, along with the question of why schooling is important in Kasimpur. The ideology of childhood, schooling and failure is examined in Chapter IV. Chapter V focuses on the school as an institution—the construction of pupil and teacher identities and teacher authority are the primary themes of this chapter. The regulation of knowledge in the classroom forms the subject of Chapter VI. Chapter VII is on memorisation and learning. Different aspects of children's epistemology are examined in Chapters VIII and IX. Chapter X, the concluding chapter, has two essays. The first attempts to weave insights of this study into a commentary on the child as a learner or an epistemic subject. The second explores the implications of the findings of the study. Although independent of each other, the order in which the chapters have been arranged is deliberate. An overall understanding of the child emerges from the superposition of several levels: beginning with the ethos of the village and the popular construction of childhood and education, moving through the activities and discourse in the school and the classroom and, finally, an engagement with the child's mind. There is a progressive delimitation and 'nesting' of spaces—first the village, then the school and classroom and finally the child. A psychological nesting is also implied, as often the significance of activity or discourse in an inner space lies outside it.

There is no separate chapter on theory or related literature; instead, in each chapter, I draw on theory and invoke related literature useful in understanding the issue or shaping an interpretation. However, for those who may be interested in the key theoretical perspectives that have shaped the study, a brief note is included as Appendix A. A detailed account of the fieldwork can be found in Appendix B.

Notes

1. Kasimpur is not the real name of the village.
2. The scenario in Indian educational discourse is complex. Piagetian constructivism and even Vygotskian social constructivism are included in education psychology courses and are now being mentioned in government documents [e.g., the National Curriculum Frameworks of 1988 and 2000 (NCERT 1988b, 2000)]. But methodology courses in teacher education and school curricula continue to be conceptualised and discussed in terms of 'behavioural objectives'. Sometimes two, and even all three, perspectives may be found in the same document (ibid.).

2

Kasimpur: Constructing the Ethos

*The interest–evaluative implication of a social structure has been termed
its ethos. Dominant activities (e.g., occupations) determine and sustain
modes of satisfaction, mark definitions of value preference; embodied
in language they make perception discriminatory.*

—Mills 1967: 429

Kasimpur is a large, multicaste village located on the northern fringe of
the metropolitan city of Delhi. It has a census population of almost 10,000.[1]
Located on the state border, just off the Grand Trunk Road on the branch
connecting Delhi to the town of Narela, it is about 18 km away from the
Inter State Bus Terminus. Buses ply almost every 20 minutes to and from
Delhi. The Yamuna river flows about 6 km away. The Block Development
Office for the Kasimpur Block of rural Delhi is located here.

Walking in from the main bus stop along the main road of the village,
which is also the road connecting Kasimpur to Narela, one first passes a
mosque, two government senior secondary schools and the Government
Boys' Model Primary School. Along the road, there are a few modern,
fashionably built, town houses and several small shops and stores where
one can buy not only provisions, vegetables, milk and soap, but also cloth,
trinkets and utensils. There are five fairly large shops selling construction-
related materials such as cement, tiles, implements and hardware. There
is a great deal of vehicular traffic on this road: not only buses plying between Narela and Delhi, but also cars and two-wheelers which seem to
be used for local commuting. Building activity is visible in several places
near the main road. A bank is also being constructed. Fields of mustard

can be seen beyond these areas. The place has the appearance of a village developing into a town.

For the first month of my fieldwork, I was familiar with only the main road of the village. I visited the Kasimpur Boys' Model Primary School every day, observing the classes, talking and listening to the children and making paper toys with them. One day, responding to my curiosity about the village, Navin, a student of Class V, invited me to accompany him home. That afternoon, after school was over, I walked with him and other children returning home; there was some excitement—would I visit other homes too?

About a kilometre from the school, along the main road, past what seems to be the main market area, before the three-storeyed house with P-R-A-D-H-A-N (headman) written on its water tank, if one turns right into the maze of narrow lanes or *galis*, one enters the traditional village. Here, in the cobbled *galis*, children run about playing and older people pull out their *charpais* (wooden cots) in winter to sit in the sun. The houses are whitewashed, single- or double-storeyed, with ornate wooden doors and an occasional simple motif decorating the walls. The lanes are narrow, between 0.5 m and 1.5 m wide, bordered by open sewers on both sides. There are hardly any trees; a few potted marigolds bloom here and there.

Navin seemed suddenly embarrassed as we neared a door. He darted in, beckoning me to follow. We went up a narrow flight of stairs to his house on the first floor: two rooms with a small, open terrace in front. Two young women stood there—his sisters. Even as I greeted them with a *namaste*, Navin said: 'My *didi* from school', and quickly vanished. At first there was some hesitation and they enquired if I had come to complain about Navin. Then they began chatting. Over the next few months I visited Navin's home and the homes of several other children—chatting with their older siblings, parents and relatives, learning about the village from them and sharing their dinners of *bajra-khichdi*, *rotis* and *saag* cooked on dung fires.

Box 2.1 The Village from Census Data

Kasimpur covers an area of 8.55 sq km. It has been a census town since 1981. This means that since then, it has had a minimum population of 5,000, at least 75 per cent of the male workers have been engaged in non-agricultural pursuits, and its population density has been at least 400 people per sq km.

According to the 1991 Census, Kasimpur has a population of 9,256. The sex ratio of 754 females to 1,000 males is one of the lowest among the villages and the urban area included in Delhi. At 19.05 per cent, the proportion of Scheduled Castes in the village is also relatively low.

The 1991 Census records 1,570 families living in 1,438 houses. This indicates an average family size of about six. The details of the employment profile of the village are given in Table 2.1. There are 2,466 main workers, of which about 6 per cent are women. Although this is a village, the number of cultivators and agricultural labourers is small, accounting for 19 per cent of the working population. Service-type employees number 892 and form the largest section of the working population (almost 40 per cent). About 75 per cent of the working women come under this employment category. Private enterprise—manufacturing, transport and trade—account for the remaining employment.

Kasimpur is located in the Indo-Gangetic plain. The soil is good for crops and growing vegetables. In 1971, 70 per cent of the village land was under cultivation. Since then, a lot of land has been colonised, an unofficial estimate being 50 per cent (more recent official figures do not exist). Irrigation is mainly from tubewells, and from July to September by the south-west monsoon. Ploughing is done by tractor. The main *rabi* crops are wheat, mustard, paddy, barley and sunflower. The *kharif* crops are paddy, *bajra*, vegetables and sunflower. Sugarcane and cotton were once grown as cash crops, but have been given up. The staple food is wheat, *bajra* and maize.

Source: Census reports (Government of India 1971, 1981, 1991) and Block Office records.

The account of the village that follows is drawn from conversations, interviews and observations made during fieldwork. I have also made use of census data, factual information from records and earlier anthropological studies, both of the same village and other similar villages on the fringes of Delhi[2] (Lewis 1958, Mann 1979, Rao 1971). The use of data is selective; the aim is not to provide a complete anthropological picture of the village, but to reconstruct the ethos in which children are growing up and going to school. I have followed the socio-anthropological approach of Dube (1955), Rao (1971) and Srinivas (1976) to draw a picture of human and societal lifeways, sensitive to the socio-historical process of change influencing options, choices and motivations.

The traditional village was planned to accommodate different castes in different areas. The upper castes live in the main village in older, larger houses. Some *galis* are occupied only by Jats. In others, there is a mix of castes. The *bania* (business caste group) houses, which are larger and have small gardens in front, are all grouped together in one part of the village. In some houses, one can see buffaloes tied in the *gher* (manger). During the evening, after five, the *galis* bustle with life—women carrying grass on their heads for their milch cattle at home, old men lounging on *charpais* smoking their *hookahs*, old and young women knitting and chatting. Having finished with school and tuition, the children, both boys and girls of all ages, can now be found outdoors in the *galis* or on the roofs, playing cricket or marbles, or flying kites, depending on the season. Later in the evening, it is mainly young boys who are out on the streets. Their mothers and older sisters are occupied at the *chulhas* making *rotis* for dinner, their younger sisters play indoors. The older men once used to gather in the village upper-caste *chaupal*; now they usually drop in on friends and relatives for a chat.

The dalits live in the outer areas of the village toward the east. Here, the lanes are much narrower and the houses more closely packed, without any open spaces. The *galis* are not cobbled. Pigs loll in open sewers. Here, too, children play in the streets. But unlike in the upper-caste areas of the village, women are not seen sitting outside, only moving from here to there. There are also many more men visible at all times of the day; especially during the evenings, they gather in large groups, gambling and playing cards.

The fields are around the village. In the late afternoons, some of the older boys go out to play cricket, either in the fields or in the old Shiva temple which has a large ground. In the last 40 years, the lands lying closer to the village have been built up and come under the *lal dora* (urban land limit). The first new colonies to be built are called *harijan bastis*, as they came up on land given to the dalits as part of the government's land redistribution scheme. But with more migrants coming to live in Kasimpur, and some of the villagers themselves wanting larger, independent accommodation, more fields have come under residential construction. A lot of construction work is under way on the outskirts of the village, though not all of it is legal. The roads here are 5 or 6 m wide, but they are not tarred or cobbled and sewer water collects in ditches.

In the evenings, as one walks through the village, one sees vegetable sellers set up their stalls on the roadside. The market begins to bustle with activity. A few men set up little stalls selling boiled eggs. The *jalebi* and *samosa* stalls are thronged by children, almost all boys. A few older boys and girls can be seen with books in their hands, returning from either tuition or friends they have been visiting—ostensibly to study. In the small Shiva temple near the market, a priest lights up the lamps and begins the evening *puja*, and many young boys, including some who are Muslim, collect there. A few street lamps turn on, but it is mostly the odd tube lights in nearby houses that spill light on to the street. Soon, the old Shiva temple gets deserted, all the children having left the grounds at about sunset, whispering to each other stories about the ghosts that live there. Between nine and ten at night, the village gradually goes to sleep.

The map (Figure 2.1) of the village is based on data gathered from personal observations and conversations with the village residents about its growth over the last few decades. The original village, with the traditional houses, is the kernel of the settlement. As can be seen, the higher castes, mainly Jat but also Brahmin and *bania,* are grouped together, taking up most of the traditional village area. The lower castes—*chipi* (tailor), *nai* (barber), *kumhar* (potter) and others—occupy areas around the upper-caste localities. The harijan castes—*churha* (sweeper/scavenger) and *chamar* (leather worker)—occupy the outermost areas of the original village. The migrants live mainly in the new colonies that have sprung up around the main village.

In the historical memory of its inhabitants, Kasimpur has always been a multicaste village, with a largely agricultural subsistence economy. Old Jat men, and also Mann's anthropological study of Kasimpur in the 1960s (Mann 1979), project Kasimpur as primarily a Jat village or at least as a village where the Jats of the *maan gotra* (non-localised, exogamous, patrilineal clan) have always been the dominant caste. My own conversations with other informants lead me to believe that this may not have always been the case. It seems that before the Partition of India and Pakistan in 1947, there were a few land-owning Muslim families with a significant presence. One of the local *nais* and a few other informants from the artisan castes recalled that there was a time when even a Jat wearing good clothes could not walk down a street where Muslim families lived. While some Jat families owned the land they tilled, most others had *asami* rights, i.e., they hired and cultivated land owned by someone else. It seems that in the period soon after Independence, most of the Muslim families left for Pakistan. Only the *teli* caste (oil crushers) Muslims stayed behind. The houses and land owned by the departed Muslims were appropriated by Jat families.

In pre-British India, Kasimpur was politically autonomous and economically fairly self-contained. It did have ties with neighbouring villages— the *athgama* (eight-village group), of which it was a part, and the larger group of 16 villages whose members were considered brothers and sisters.

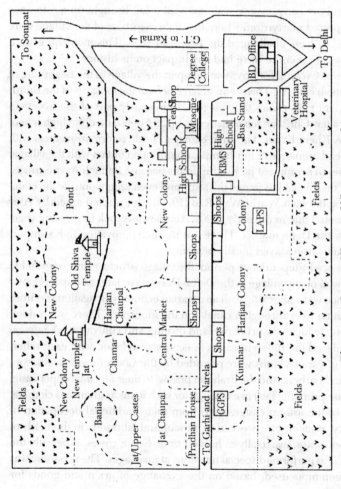

Figure 2.1 Layout of Kasimpur Village (not to scale)

Note: KBMS–Kasimpur Boys' Model School; LAPS–Little Angels Public School; GGPS–Government Girls' Primary School.

Marriages were thus solemnised with villages outside this group of 16, the *solagama*, sometimes even from several hundred kilometres away. The village did not have any particular ties with Delhi in spite of its proximity. Occasionally, itinerant traders, mainly *banias*, from Delhi visited the village. There was a village council composed entirely of male members which judged and arbitrated disputes between members of the village. Mann's study, and my conversation with one senior Jat, brought up a reference to a purported martyrdom where the male members of the village were supposed to have challenged the British in 1856. This incident, even if true, does not seem to have had any impact on its history.

A primary school for boys was set up in the village in the beginning of the twentieth century. This seems to have been at the initiative of the British government rather than the villagers. In the early part of the twentieth century, a few Christian missionaries set up an English-medium high school in nearby Khera Kalan. The Arya Samaj, a Hindu reform movement with widespread influence in north India, established contact with the village. A number of prominent Jat Kasimpurians became staunch Arya Samajis. Some of the village Jats joined the army and even fought outside the country during the First World War. Rao (1971), who studied a nearby Ahir village, noted that in the early 1920s, Ahir farmers took to growing vegetables for the Delhi market. There was no such innovation in Kasimpur, where cultivators stayed mostly peasant.

In the pre-Independence period, the village structure and ways of life were typical of any village in the Delhi–Haryana or larger Punjab region.[3] The village was multicaste, with an agrarian economy. Irrigation was from the Yamuna river through a canal and the monsoon. There was a dominant caste, which was primarily land-owning and cultivating. A *jajmani* system placed the different castes in economic relation with each other; services of various kinds were provided by the *kamin* (lower castes, e.g., potters and barbers, and the Brahmin priests) to their *jajmans* (upper caste, in this case primarily Jats) in exchange for such items as grain and clothing. Several of the artisan castes, apart from their traditional occupation of carpentry, pottery, etc., worked as agricultural labourers in the fields of the upper castes, especially at harvest time. Some castes, especially the barbers, also performed special functions at marriages. The economy was largely non-monetised, based on the exchange of grain and goods for services.

Both the family and the society as a whole were male-dominated. All authority rested typically with the oldest, articulate male member of the family. He took all decisions—from matters of property and inheritance, to marriage and morality. Women never attained any formal position of authority since they were regarded as inferior to men, incapable of supervising their own behaviour or family matters. Children were not expected to exercise any independence and were to be deferential to older, especially male, members on all occasions.

Social Change in the Village[4]

Studies of villages on the fringes of Delhi have noted that proximity to the burgeoning capital city has been the primary source of social, economic, political and cultural change in the village (Lewis 1958, Rao 1971). Early influences of urbanisation came with the ease of commuting, new markets for village produce and opportunities for non-traditional employment which made employment diversification possible. In the 1950s and 1960s, Kasimpur benefited from the Green Revolution. Since the 1970s there has been a growing influx of migrants, and more recently, since the mid-1980s, land value has appreciated considerably. The changing occupational patterns from 1947 onwards form the backdrop of the changes in family, childhood and involvement with schooling (see Table 2.1 and Box 2.2).

Table 2.1 Changes in the Village

Year	1961	1971	1981	1991
Classification	village	town	town	town
Area	2,109	2,112	8.55 km²	8.55 km²
	acres	acres		
Residential houses	–	675	983	1,438
Households	465	715	1,122	1,570
Population				
Total	2,853	4,487	6,735	9,256
male/female	1,527/1,326	2,507/1,980	3,875/2,860	5,277/3,977
0–6 yr.				1,699
male/female				890/809
Scheduled Castes		808	1,310	763
male/female		427/381	718/592	955/822
Scheduled Tribes	0	0	0	0
male/female				
Literates		2,147	3,813	5,004
male/female		1,523/624	2,600/1,213	3,282/1,722
Total Main Workers (I–IX)		1,133	1,906	2,466

(*Table 2.1 continued*)

(Table 2.1 continued)

Year	1961	1971	1981	1991
male/female		1,088/45	1,724/182	2,321/145
Cultivators (I)	1,068	209	245	213
male/female		207/2	211/34	205/8
Agricultural Labourer (II)		171	100	266
male/female		160/11	87/13	257/9
Livestock (III)		16		11
male/female		16/0		11/0
Mining (IV)		0	0	0
male/female				
Total (Va–IX)			1,513*	
male/female			1,379/134*	
Household manufacturers (Va)		1		26
male/female		1/0		24/2
Other manufacturers (Vb)		97		472
male/female		97/0		469/3
Construction (VI)		23		109
male/female		23/0		109/0
Trade & Commerce (VII)		70		260
male/female		70/0		251/9
Transport & Commerce (VIII)		37		217
male/female		37/0		215/2
Other Services (IX)		490		892
male/female		459/31		780/112
Marginal			42	
male/female			10/32	
Non-workers		3,354	4,787	6,790
male/female		1,419/1,935	2,141/2,648	2,958/3,832

Source: Census data for 1991, 1981, 1971 (Government of India 1991, 1981, 1971) and Mann (1979) for 1961.

Note: *Break-up not available.

Box 2.2 Changes Apparent from Census Data

Census data for Kasimpur as a separate unit exist from the 1971 Census onwards (see Table 2.1). The village has been steadily growing, with its population increasing at the rate of about 2,000 people per decade. In the last 30 years, its population has tripled. The ratio of women to men over the last 30 years for which data exist, has been an average of 760 women to 1,000 men.

The number of houses has more than doubled in the last two decades, increasing from 675 in 1971 to 1,438 in 1991. The village continues to grow and there is a lot of construction activity. The average household size has remained more or less constant at six.

The literacy of the village in the 1991 Census is 66 per cent and compares with the average for rural Delhi of 66.9 per cent. It is lower than the average for urban areas, which is about 82 per cent. This is in spite of Kasimpur's relatively longer involvement in education and the presence of several government educational institutions in the village. This suggests that the response to education is more a reflection of the general trends towards education in rural Delhi rather than a specific response to local conditions for education. The proportion of women who are literate has generally been rising, from 29 per cent in 1971, to 31 per cent in 1981 and 34 per cent in 1991.

Between 1971 and 1981, there was a marked increase in the total number of mainstream workers, from 1,133 to 1,906—an increase of 68 per cent. Between 1981 and 1991, the increase of 560 people corresponds to a relative increase of only 26 per cent. On the whole, between 1971 and 1991, the proportion of women mainstream workers increased only slightly, from 4 per cent of total workers to about 6 per cent (1981 saw a maximum of 10 per cent). The proportion of people involved in agriculture and cultivation fell markedly from 33 per cent to 18 per cent between 1971 and 1981. Between 1981 and 1991, the percentage of agriculture-based workers remained more or less the same at 19 per cent. There was also a steady increase in the proportion of agricultural labourers to cultivators, from 1:2 to 5:4. This suggests a shift away from agriculture from the 1970s onwards and a tendency to retain land-ownership while having labourers to till the land.

In 1971, the primary alternative to agriculture was employment in the services. This has been decreasing, from 43 per cent in 1971 to 36 per cent in 1991. Private enterprise as a source of employment has been increasing from 19.5 per cent in 1971 to 37.5 per cent in 1991. The census recorded no marginal workers in either 1971 or 1991. Growth has also been reflected in the village market. In 1971, the village did not have a *haat* or weekly market; since 1981 it has a weekly market on every Saturday.

Source: Census reports (Government of India 1971, 1981, 1991) and Block Office records.

Occupational diversification: In the matter of taking advantage of the opportunities provided by the city, virtually all the native inhabitants of Kasimpur singled out the Satnam Singh Maan household as the one that led the way. Even in the 1920s, this Jat family was important in the village as it owned a lot of land. Of the seven brothers in the family, the first two did not go to school. They, along with the women in the family, shouldered most of the responsibility for agriculture, making it possible for the younger brothers to go to school. The third and fourth brothers, after completing primary school in the village, went on to high school in Khera. This was in the late 1940s. The third secured a job as a primary schoolteacher and continued to live in the village, participating in agriculture as a secondary occupation. The fourth joined the railways as a clerk and moved to live in a residential colony in north Delhi. His two younger brothers came to live with him and were educated in city schools. The feeling seems to have been that it was important to leave the village atmosphere (*mahaul*) in order to not only get a good education but also take advantage of it. The younger brothers then went on to study in Delhi University and later pursued successful careers in the city. In the village, the family had the reputation of being 'model educated men' with great moral authority. They were also staunch Arya Samajis, perhaps the only ones left in the village, and led a somewhat austere, almost Brahminical lifestyle. Their place as elites in the village is today even more entrenched as they are seen as having city connections, and as being able to help young men from the village secure employment in the city.

The earliest and most significant influence of urbanisation in Kasimpur was through the opening up of new, non-traditional employment possibilities that made occupational diversification possible. The story of the Maan family is typical of the process of moving out of agriculture to service-type employment in the city through education. In the 1950s, there was a small group of upper-caste men commuting to the city to work. The process was facilitated by occupational diversification within the family.[5] In the case of the dominant Jat agricultural caste, parents, older brothers, women and girls took on the burden of agriculture, cultivation and cattle rearing, making it possible for some of the younger boys and men to go to school, complete at least high school, and seek employment in Delhi. Many informants said this was not at all easy for the families as, at that time, agriculture was at a subsistence level; there was little surplus available and irrigation and ploughing were more labour-intensive than they are now. Children from the age of 8 years were involved in agricultural work, and by age 16, boys began ploughing the fields. When boys began going to school, even though they continued to help—especially during harvest and sowing—they certainly did not contribute as much as before on a daily basis. Attending high school meant walking to the school in Khera, three miles (about 5 km) away. This made going to school a whole day's business and left no time for other work. Apart from fees, money was needed for books and clothes. Thus, sending a boy-child to school was viewed as an investment by the whole family. Everyone was interested in his success at school. And he was withdrawn at the slightest indication of failure or poor performance.

The question of sending the girl-child to school seems to have not even arisen in the minds of these families. Though both girls and women of the household contributed significantly not only in household work but also in cultivation and other work, their inferiority to the male was taken for granted. In any event, until after Independence, the only primary school in the village was a boys' school. The attitude to educating girls began to change in the late 1980s. Interestingly, as they had done with their sons earlier, now most parents watched the performance of their daughters in school; at the slightest indication of failure, the child was threatened with withdrawal. In contrast to his fate in the 1950s, however, the boy-child was guaranteed to continue in school almost all through childhood and youth, regardless of his performance.

All the villagers identify *harit kranti* or the 'Green Revolution'[6] as being primarily responsible for altering the condition of the cultivators from the 1960s onwards. The older people in the village revered Lal Bahadur Shastri, who was the Prime Minister during 1965–67, more than Nehru. Shastri was seen as having had the cultivators' interests at heart and as having nurtured agriculture, as opposed to Nehru, who was seen as having led industrialisation. Shastri's slogan of '*Jai jawan, jai kisan!*' (hail soldier, hail farmer!) was familiar to all the children and they knew of him as the 'friend of the farmer'. The use of hybrid seeds and fertilisers, growing cash crops, tubewells, tractors and government cooperative and subsidy schemes made it possible to enjoy a surplus. Within one generation the peasant was transformed into a successful profit-seeking farmer. Occasionally, in moments of nostalgia, the villagers observed that the *rotis* used to be more tasty when crops were grown without the use of fertilisers. They also felt that their sons no longer related to the land and thought of themselves more as businessmen than cultivators.

With the monetisation of the village economy and development of new sources of income and consumption needs, the traditional *jajmani* system of economic interdependence of various castes began to wither. In the 1970s, Jat men with meagre land holdings, artisans and *chamars* (leather workers) had begun to find employment in various government undertakings as conductors, bus drivers, gardeners, peons, clerks and electrical linesmen; a few also joined the police, the army and the postal department, or became schoolteachers. After obtaining a certificate of passing Class V or X in school, and in a few cases Class XII, contacts of kinship, caste and village ties were used to find out about and secure these jobs. The biographies of two artisan families that follow illustrate how both *jajman* and *kamin* were equally eager to dismantle the system.

Earlier, both men and women of the *nai* caste attended on the upper castes, visiting them in their homes to cut hair, shave and massage them. At the time of my fieldwork, I found they no longer did so; the upper castes had now taken to other styles and ways of maintaining their hair. Only the tradition of the *nai* as a messenger in marriages was, and is still, observed ritualistically. Kuldip's father was the only member of his community who still worked as a barber. But he did not serve any *jajman*. He pursued his traditional occupation in a new role setting. He had a saloon where he attended to a few customers every day. His wife had begun a small dairy in their home. Kuldip's uncles (father's brothers) had all managed to study till Class X and were employed in class IV government jobs. Neither Kuldip nor his older brother intended to continue with their father's profession. Kuldip was proud that his brother, who had failed his Class X board examination, was training to repair watches at an institute in Jahangirpuri, Delhi.

Metal utensils made the *kumhars* (potters) redundant as suppliers of cooking pots and pans. Pavan's father, a *kumhar*, said that the change took place in his father's generation. His father could use the wheel, and it was still worshipped during marriages, but this activity had not been an important source of income for the family. In other villages the potters had switched to brick making. But in this village, the Jats who owned the clay lands had rented them out to contractors manufacturing bricks. The village *kumhars* had initially switched to their traditional secondary occupation of using their donkeys to transport loads. Pavan's father and his brothers had never learnt to use the potter's wheel although they, along with their mother and sisters, had transported loads on donkeys. Their father had insisted that all his sons get an education, and now all of them had government jobs. Pavan's father now worked as a bus conductor. For the last two years he had also rented a piece of land and had sown and harvested his own family's requirements of wheat for the year. His Jat friend had helped him find the plot and ploughed the field with his tractor. He and his wife had harvested the crop together. This was an accomplishment he was very proud of, as it was still rare in the village for a person from a non-Jat, lower-caste group to try his hand at agriculture.

The *jajman* found new ways of meeting his requirements, either from the city or through migrants, more attractive. The *kamin* adapted by seeking alternative forms of employment outside the matrix of obligations and hierarchies of the *jajmani*. Mann's (1979) study of the village in 1961 reported that the *jajmani* system had been undermined and traditional intercaste dependencies and interactions had changed. By the 1980s, even men and women of the *churha* caste (sweeper/scavenger), the lowest caste of the village, found that employment as sweepers with the municipal corporation, with its steady income, was a better option.[7] In the period of my fieldwork in 1992–93, I found that there was virtually nothing left of the *jajmani*.

In the 1970s, the influx of migrants began, drawn to Kasimpur because of its proximity to Delhi and low rents. With this, opportunities for trade and a market within the village developed. The Keralite couple who established the first private school (English-medium) in the village, also arrived at this time. One group of migrants was from nearby states, and from higher castes/class. The men were educated and had government employment (typically clerks); they settled in the village with their wives and children. The other private schools in the village were established by women from these families. Another group of migrants came from nearby villages of Delhi which were more interior, from villages in the district of Aligarh in the neighbouring state of Uttar Pradesh and also from the far-off state of Bihar. Initially, it was only the men who came in search of work; but many now also brought their families and lived in Kasimpur on a more permanent basis. These migrants—low-caste, rural and uneducated—took up traditional jobs vacated within the village *jajmani*—masonry, whitewashing, menial work and agricultural labour. From the late 1980s they also found daily wage employment in small manufacturing units which were set up in the village. At the time of my fieldwork, the migrant population of the village was demographically significant. The traditional villagers treated migrants as unwelcome intruders and claimed that they had 'spoilt the village atmosphere'. Nevertheless, all caste groups had benefited from the rent and sale of land. The market within the village had grown and was thriving.

From the mid-1980s, the price of land began to sky-rocket and a rapid conversion of agricultural land into housing colonies and farm houses began. Most of this was outside the current '*lal dora*'. Following several disputes, all land dealings were suspended in 1987 and were officially still at a standstill. Everyone gossiped about migrants and land deals. Many were illegal and believed to involve large sums of black money—the official price of Rs 6.25 lakh per acre was about a tenth of the going rate. The two main Jat factions in the village were divided on the issue of land ownership. Children followed the controversies with avid interest.

The first school in the village, a primary school, was established by the British in the late 1890s and functioned regularly from 1907 onwards. By the early 1970s, the village had two primary schools, two high schools (separate for boys and for girls) administered by the Municipal Corporation of Delhi (MCD) and also a degree college affiliated to the University of Delhi.

Family Matters

Embedded in the account so far are biographies of families, providing details, often moving, of sacrifice, struggle, alteration and adaptation to secure a better future for younger siblings and children. The focus on the family unit which emerges in the foregoing account is both natural and deliberate. Traditionally, it was the basic unit of social, economic and political organisation. The new economic (and, to a lesser extent, political) organisation made demands on arrangements within the family, both to ensure that members could take advantage of new opportunities and also as a consequence of these opportunities. It continued as the most significant site in maintaining continuity and mediating social change for children.

The break-up of the joint family and 'nuclearisation' are often cited as a direct fall-out of urbanisation or modernisation. According to census data, however, the average family size, even in 1961, was six. In most caste groups the composition of the basic family unit had not changed— a basic conjugal pair with children and other dependents such as parents and/or unmarried siblings of the husband—i.e., a fluctuating, extended family.[8] Only in the case of Jats, the cultivator caste, did the joint family,[9] which was earlier the norm, give way to either a nuclear unit or a new style of joint living—a group of brothers living together in a complex of small apartments, each with its own kitchen, around a common courtyard where older members met to gossip and children played together. Many of the older informants recalled that in their childhood there had been single-kitchen households; they did not regret the change, saying that this way there was less fighting and less tension.

The discussion on occupational diversification has already shown how women[10] in particular, of all castes groups, adapted and shouldered more responsibilities in the traditional work arena to enable boys to go to school and men to participate in the urban labour market. From the 1980s, the work patterns of the women began changing again. With a number of Jat men selling off their land holdings and turning more and more to either mechanised agriculture or non-agricultural pursuits, many women no longer had agricultural responsibilities.[11] But many families continued to own buffaloes, which the women looked after. One informant told me that these days, without agricultural responsibilities, women have much more spare time. She said they have begun to spend more time on themselves, worrying about their looks and attire. Another old Jat gentleman complained that the younger generation Jats are becoming more like the *bania*: the young men dress foppishly and prefer to sit in offices and start businesses, with their women folk spending more time at home, gossiping and wearing *saris* rather than the traditional *salwar-kameez* or *ghaghra-shirt*.[12] There are a few older educated women who work outside the home as primary schoolteachers. This is a job that younger educated women also hope to find, although some also speak of joining the police force. Women now also seem to have more time to spend on their children—getting them ready for school, taking them there and to their tuitions afterwards. The principals of the two older private schools, who have been in the village for over 15 years, commented on this. They said that earlier, the children looked much more scruffy and unkempt when they came to school and that often they did not bathe in the morning. Now their mothers had more time in the morning to bathe and dress them in clean uniforms.

Relations within the family: Intra-familial relationships and authority remained by and large unchanged. Elderly people still enjoyed their traditional authority over all younger members of their family and caste group, as well as in the village community. They were always addressed in traditional kinship terms. Kasimpur society retained its male-dominated character; women were socialised very strictly to observe the prescribed behaviour of respectability—being suitably deferential to all elders and showing care and concern, especially for their brothers. Interpersonal relations were traditionally governed by factors like kinship, age, sex and status. Mann describes the relations as he observed them in 1961. Villagers considered traditional relationship patterns as still ideal and took care to enforce their observance. If not followed, it could result in lowering the status of the individual and the family. Deviation from the prescribed norms was taken as proportional to social degeneration (Mann 1979: 38–39). I found that traditional norms continued to be regarded as ideal and featured prominently in the commentary of the older villagers. Those villagers who had free access and exposure to the city but continued to strictly observe all traditional norms of social interaction, were singled out for glowing praise—whether it was a highly educated, well-employed daughter-in-law who still took care to veil her face in the presence of older men or a successful man who deferred to his father's opinion. I often heard older people say: 'What use is education if she doesn't know how to serve her guests well?"[13] The women, however, noted that those who were educated, and especially those who were working (mostly in the teaching profession), enjoyed small privileges—they could go out to visit friends and they were exempted from the more labour-intensive household and agriculture/cattle rearing work.

Sons were still considered more desirable than daughters. The census data show that for the last 30 years, the sex ratio has remained heavily skewed towards males at an average of 1,000 to about 750 (though in the 1991 Census, the ratio for the 0–6 years age group is 1,000 to 900). Many traditional and modern rituals are observed for sons from their birth, including celebrating their birthdays—a new custom adopted from the city. Daughters were cherished and seen as far more dependable and responsible than sons. But they were nevertheless regarded as a resource drain on the family as they had to be provided for even after their marriage. The *pir* (father's home) was a special place for all women of the village and they spoke with much longing and affection for their fathers and brothers. They were also proud of not having to depend on their husbands' families for their personal needs, as these were met by their brothers and fathers. I heard some parents express their determination to treat their daughters as being equal to their sons,[14] But many parents were matter-of-fact about their daughters' futures being determined by their in-laws.

Even though child-rearing was left mainly to the mother or older sisters, the father was the ultimate, absolute authority in all other matters of upbringing. A few children spoke of how much their father loved them; all of them said they were scared of doing anything wrong as he would punish them. His authority in moral matters was absolute. On my visits to the children's homes, I rarely saw their fathers as they were often away at that time. Mothers, older sisters and grandparents were the adults with whom children were familiar and intimate. The father was not expected to participate or show much interest in the details of child-rearing. His authority over the child was the subtle authority of the stranger, about whom the mothers would invent myths. Children were especially reminded that he would beat them if they did anything wrong or failed to meet parental expectations. Though young children were intimate and free with their mothers, they occasionally did experience her authority. The parents' position of authority in the family was supported by traditional and customary norms. Children were expected to render them unconditional and unquestioning obedience. They were also expected to observe the same patterns of behaviour with their father's brothers, both older (*tau*) and younger (*chacha*). Paternal uncles generally commanded authority over their nephews. Paternal aunts (*bua*) also commanded authority over their brothers' children and were often consulted in matters related to their nephews and nieces. For the children themselves, grandparents were important as people who loved and indulged them. The young boys, especially, were aware of their power over their grandparents and boasted about it to me, saying they could get what they wanted through them. *Taus* and *chachas* were often referred to with some awe, as close relatives who had their interests at heart (unless of course the relations were strained, in which case disappointment was expressed about their betrayal).

Apart from the father's family, who belonged to the same village, children were very attached to their mother's brothers (*mama*). These were very special people for them. Though they met them rarely—at weddings and during vacations when they stayed with their mother at her father's place—these uncles were important to both nephews and nieces. Perhaps the special affection their mothers felt for their brothers also made the children feel that they enjoyed a special bond with their maternal uncles. They often boasted to each other about their *mamas* and the special treatment they received when they visited them. Today, brothers feel less compelled to continue to support their sisters after they are married. Yet there is enough of folklore and ritual observance during marriage and childbirth to mark the relationship between maternal uncles and nieces and nephews as something special and eternally dependable. Young boys from the primary school who had become *mamas* or *chachas* were very proud of their status, and took care to inform me of it. At home they spent time playing with their nieces and nephews.

Apart from parents, grandparents, uncles and aunts, older brothers and sisters were also important for the child. Older sisters often participated in child-rearing, taking on many motherly responsibilities, especially after the birth of a new baby. Both older brothers and sisters could administer corporal punishment on children. It was not unknown for parents to consult them in matters regarding their younger siblings' future. Many of the adolescent educated sisters I met had very clear ambitions for their brothers, and seemed to often take their parents' place in meeting with the primary schoolteachers and coaching their younger brothers for examinations.

*

The ethos of the village was marked by a heightened sense of the changing structures that regulated employment and income. Studies of urbanisation or modernisation of peasantry in rural Delhi have noted that the process is characterised by a psychic mobility. 'A mobile society has to encourage rationality for the calculus of choice ... People come to see the future as manipulable rather than ordained, and their personal prospects in terms of achievements rather than heritage' (D. Learner, quoted in Mulay and Ray 1973: 2). The occupation of one's parents, which was a part of the caste identity, could not be regarded as a guaranteed or viable employment option. Along with this was an awareness and concern about employment opportunities that are non-traditional and new. This awareness and concern was reflected in the biographies of families. There is today both a material and symbolic surplus which can sustain a period of childhood devoted to schooling[15]—for boys, and increasingly also for girls.

Notes

1. The 1991 Census, which classifies Kasimpur as a census town, includes in its estimate the population of the twin village of Garhi. However, socially and psychologically, the two villages are independent, each with a sense of 'otherness' about the other. Kasimpurians regard Garhi as more backward and rural than Kasimpur. The present study is restricted to the village of Kasimpur. Table 2.1 provides a compilation of census data from 1971 to 1991.

2. The term 'metropolitan-fringe village' is taken from the typology suggested by Rao (1971, 1991) to understand the types of impact of urbanisation on villages. The urban impact on villages surrounding growing metropolitan cities differs, depending on their location vis-à-vis the city. Some villages may get absorbed. Villages that are beyond the built-up suburbs of the city are called the 'urban fringe'. The economy of these villages is more diverse and the presence of the commuting population is an important and unique feature.

3. See Lewis (1958) or Wiser and Wiser (1971) for anthropological accounts of two such villages.

4. In this section, and elsewhere in the book, the terms 'traditional' and 'modern' are used as *historical descriptors* or labels for practices which were prevalent before, and those which arose out of the rapid economic changes that took place from the late 1950s to the 1970s. These changes in practices were related to urbanisation and transformation of the employment profile of the village. This disclaimer is necessary because the dominant usage of these terms in village studies, both in India and elsewhere, draws from modernisation theory, which uses these categories as the basic dichotomy on which the structural description of change rests (Passeron 1986; Dube 1988). The dominant view sees 'internal tensions' or 'conflicts' as the motor and programme of the historical change of a social or cultural system. Institutions and values characterised as 'traditional' are regarded as incompatible with 'modern' ones and as blocking modernisation (e.g., Myrdal 1968). Village studies of the 1950s and 1960s, in India and other parts of the world, dwelt prominently on this theme, claiming that change was possible because of a new 'modern mindset'. The 'modern man' was believed to have personality traits like risk taking, willingness to use technology and a 'scientific rationality' which,

it was claimed, were not a part of the 'traditional mindset' (see, for example, Inkeles and Smith 1974). It must be pointed out that the majority of village studies that I have quoted in the text were conducted within the paradigm of the modernisation theory, and that their use of the terms 'traditional', 'modern', 'progress', 'change' and 'development' is biased by the value orientation of the paradigm.

5. Rao (1971) makes this point in his study of Yadavpur. The biographies of families in Kasimpur which I documented all revealed this adaptation, which is also substantiated in Mann's (1979) study. Rao (1971) and Lewis (1958) also note that the first ones to see the advantages of non-traditional occupations were members of the dominant castes who were already entrenched as elites in the traditional village society and, in principle, had more to lose from the alteration of traditional structures.

6. The 'Green Revolution' was a development programme initiated by the Government of India in the 1960s, with aid from the United States of America. Launched in several parts of the country, including Delhi and the larger Punjab, it came to be known as the 'Green Revolution' in the late 1960s. Hybrid seeds and fertilisers were made available to farmers, tractors were leased for ploughing and tubewells were sunk for irrigation (Byres and Crow 1983; see also Kumar 1996 for a discussion of the Green Revolution in relation to education). The Kasimpur villagers generally clubbed all government-sponsored initiatives in agricultural practices, from the 1950s to the 1970s, under this broad rubric.

7. Rao (1971) noted that urbanisation not only made possible new, non-traditional occupations, but also the pursuit of traditional occupations in modern urban settings. For example, the untouchable castes, who were scavengers and cleaners in the *jajmani* system, now took up employment in the dumps of the municipal corporation, working under a supervisor, with regular hours and pay. As has been observed in other caste groups, here, too, the increased participation of women made it possible for men to move out of their traditional caste occupations. Initially, the *churha* caste women took the place that the men had vacated in the *jajmani*. When women also found government employment, migrants took their place and seemed to form a new untouchable caste.

Of all the *kamin* services that the upper castes lost, this is the only one that annoyed them. It was not easy to find domestic help in the village. The women of the house often had to take on cleaning and washing chores. It was not at all unusual to hear both men and women of the upper castes express their contempt for the *churhas*. They claimed that they were characterless, squandering away the benefits that the government had given them on drink and gambling. They also claimed that their children were useless—they did not study and they brought bad language into the school, spoiling the atmosphere for their own studious children. They also ridiculed the eagerness with which the *churhas* sought out jobs with the municipality, saying contemptuously that there was no real difference in the kind of work they did. Of course, pointing out that this brought them more money immediately elicited another criticism that this, in fact, was bad, because cash is so easily lost in drink and gambling, while the grain they received as payment in the *jajmani* at least made sure their families did not starve.

8. Earlier studies of Lewis (1958), Rao (1971) and Mann (1979) provide the historical detail.

9. 'Joint family' generally suggests a set-up where sons and their families continue to live with their parents—cooking together, often engaged together in work, pooling incomes and expenses, and generally deferring all decision-making to older male figures of authority (Singh 1986; Shah 1998).

10. One can presume that girls shared their mothers' workload, as they do even today. The census data from 1971 to 1991 do not reflect accurately the extent to which women participate in income generation activities. For instance, the 1991 Census reports 11 people (11 men and 0 women) as engaged in livestock rearing (see Table 2.1), but I found that in the village, all livestock was looked after primarily by women.

11. Although grossly underestimated, the census figures also reflect this change. Between 1981 and 1991, the number of women involved in agriculture (cultivation and labour) came down from 47 out of 345 to 17 out of 479.

12. The *sari* is regarded as difficult to maintain and inconvenient if one is to do a lot of manual work. Traditionally, only women of the Brahmin and *bania* castes wore *saris*.

13. Dewey (1957) noted that when values are being eroded, they feature even more prominently and vehemently in commentary.

14. According to census reports, female literacy is increasing.

15. Bikram Nanda makes this insightful observation on the need for material and symbolic surplus to sustain schooling in his study of the experience of schooling among the Bondo Highlander tribe of Orissa: 'It is not only that children cannot be spared but there isn't a concept of "childhood". School cannot be constructed' (Nanda 1992: 4).

3

Going to School

Having explored the village in which children are growing up, in this chapter we enter the portals of their schools. There were several schools in the village but the study focuses on the oldest and largest primary school—the Kasimpur Government Boys' Model Primary School. The Little Angels Public School (a private, English-medium school) and the Government Girls' Primary School are also included, but for less intensive study. The first section of the chapter introduces the three schools. Children who feature several times in this book are introduced in the next section titled, 'Why is schooling important?' (The teachers are introduced in a note at the end of the chapter.) This is the first of several themes explored in the following chapters, where children's voices are foregrounded and interpreted. Here, I look at the reasons children give for believing that *padhai*, i.e., schooling, is very important. I then connect this with the ethos of the village, which was characterised in Chapter II as one marked by a concern for social mobility through new forms of employment. The section that follows presents children's views on the content of schooling in relation to preparing for employment, and choosing a school to study in. In the last section, where the chapter is summarised, the spectra of schooling content and various employment opportunities are synthesised and schematised into a hierarchy. Bourdieu's (1986) conceptions of education as cultural capital through employment are also discussed.

Of course, the episodes reported here and in the chapters that follow have a primarily illustrative function—they do not represent the only data on which the thematic analysis and commentary are based. These episodes are taken from long conversations. In this context, I have avoided extracting only relevant phrases or sentences and have preferred to report the longer exchanges within which these phrases or statements are embedded. This is for two reasons. Often ideas which have been separated out analytically co-occur in conversation and their relevant interlinkages are preserved only in the whole. The meaning and significance of a phrase or statement in a conversation is often linked to something that has been said earlier. But it is not only for the sake of content that I have preferred to report long conversations in several places. It is also because the form and spontaneous articulation of various issues bring out facets of children's own lives: their active interest in making meaning of their own experience, in interpreting the experiences of others, in anticipating the future; their delightful worldly wisdom and their flights of fantasy.[1]

I
The Kasimpur Boys' Model School

In winter, the Government Model Primary School for Boys in Kasimpur begins at 9 a.m. and goes on till 3 p.m. The summer timings are 8 a.m. to 2 p.m. But whether summer or winter, the gates of the school open early in the morning, and children begin coming in by 7:30 a.m., even in winter. Most children arrive on foot from their homes. They usually come in groups of two or three to as many as 10 or 11. The older children usually come along with friends who live nearby and others whom they meet on the way to school. A few come by bus from other villages. Some bring their younger brothers with them—all lugging heavy bags on their backs, chatting with one another. Some younger children are brought by their parents or older siblings. All the children wear their uniform—white shirt and khaki shorts (full trousers are permitted in winter). Most feet are shod in slippers. The ones who wear shoes are very proud of this—it gives their stride a bounce and briskness, visible to the onlooker.

The Kasimpur Boys' Model School (henceforth KBMS) is situated very near the main bus stop (*bus adda*), on the main road linking Kasimpur to Narela and the Grand Trunk (GT) road, next to the girls' secondary school. The school campus is fairly large. It has a single-storeyed, *pakka* main building which houses the headmaster's room and three classrooms. There are several trees around this building and even a small garden in front. Behind this building is a large stage and a large ground. Part of the ground is cobbled with bricks. The rest is a playground. Two sides of this ground are bordered by barrack-like rows of classrooms with asbestos roofs. The third side is bordered by a long municipal garden. There are several large trees, and around some of them are raised platforms to sit on. The barrack-like classrooms also have flower beds in front. The school has only one toilet, which is used only by the staff. Near it are a few taps for drinking water. Behind the school is another walled ground. This is used by the children as a toilet (see Figure 3.1).

In 1992–93, when I did my fieldwork, the school had a total of about 400 children from nursery to Class V. Other than the nursery, of which there was only one section, and Class III,[2] which had three sections, all

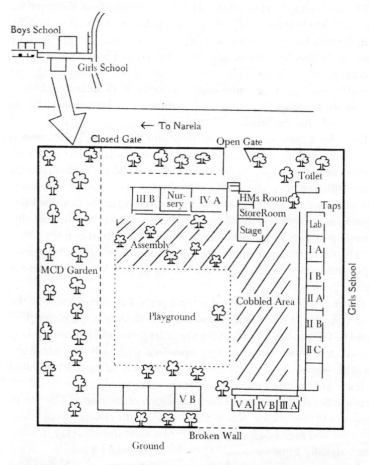

Figure 3.1 Layout of Kasimpur Boys' Government Model Primary School

the other classes had two sections each. The school was managed by a headmaster, Mr Satpal Singh.[3] There were two trained nursery teachers and one teacher each for the remaining classes, making a total of 13 teachers (six women and seven men). One of the women teachers, who was officially the sports teacher, had the additional charge of one section of Class II. Each teacher was a class teacher and taught all the subjects. He/she also moved up each year to the next class with the same group, until the group of students completed Class V and left school. The school also had a sweeper and two chaprassis.

The children who attended the school were mostly from Kasimpur village itself. But as the school had a good reputation, it also drew students from the twin village of Garhi and other neighbouring villages. A group of about 30 boys from the nearby Boys' Home, run by the government, also attended this school. They were accompanied each morning by a caretaker who spent the entire day in school with them and took them back in the evening. He kept an eye on them, to make sure they did not run away during the break.

Each day began with assembly. In winter this was at 9 a.m., and in summer at 8 a.m. By this time, the school was usually fairly full of children, teachers and other adults. At the sound of the bell, all the children, playing in the fields or in their classrooms, would hurry to the assembly grounds. The whole school would gather under the trees near the main building for morning prayer. The students of each class would stand in single file according to their heights. All the teachers would stand in front. Occasionally, the headmaster would also join them. Prayer was led by a group of five children especially selected for the task; they, too, would stand in front.

The prayer was long and had several parts. First there would be the *surya namaskar*, a traditional Hindu religious salutation to the sun. This would be followed by a Hindi hymn about the power of the creator, asking him for protection. The prayer group would sing each line, which the rest of the school would repeat after them. After this, all the children would sit down and assume a meditative posture—they would recite the *gayatri mantra* in Sanskrit and then a Hindi translation of the *mantra*. The prayer group would then ask for '*Maunam!*' (silence); all the children would close their eyes and meditate for a minute or two, until some teacher shouted 'Om!'—signalling that they could open their eyes—which would be echoed by all the students. Next would follow a moral discourse, usually delivered by teachers but occasionally also by students. All the children were expected to listen attentively. Teachers would go around ensuring that no one talked. Announcements, if any, would also be made at this time. The assembly ended with the singing of the National Anthem. Students would then proceed to their classes in single file.

Each class had its own room, with a door on one side and a row of windows on the opposite side. The wall adjacent to the door had a black-board; the opposite wall was decorated with charts that the students and teacher had made, with pictures of patriotic leaders, moral precepts, dia-grams of respiration and photosynthesis in plants, etc. The teacher was provided with a chair and a table, which were set in front beside the blackboard. The children sat facing the teacher and the blackboard. In both sections of Class V and one of Class IV, the children sat on the floor in four or five rows, on long, narrow mats (*tat-pattis*, not durries). Only in one section of Class IV, and in a few of the lower classes, did the children sit in pairs at desk–chair units arranged in four columns.

After assembly, the class teacher usually entered the room a few minutes after the students had settled down. As soon as he/she entered, the whole class would spring to attention, shouting, '*Namaste guruji*/aunty', and remain standing until the teacher indicated that they could sit.[4] Each morning, attendance was taken by the teacher in a special register. Roll numbers, not names, were called out. No other activity could begin without the attendance being taken. (If I happened to enter a class where the teacher was absent, the students would all urge me to take their attend-ance.) After roll call, lessons and other activities would begin.

Every day, each student brought a bag full of books to school. There were several prescribed textbooks, one for each subject they were required to study. In Classes IV and V, these included language (Hindi), math-ematics and 'environmental studies'. There were separate books for science and social studies. English was also a subject, but was rarely taught. Every child had several notebooks—at least one for each subject, a drawing book and a rough notebook. Several children also owned guidebooks, which they would bring every day. These books, published by private publishers, provided answers for all the questions and exercises in their textbooks and also some model essays. Apart from this, their bags usually contained other books and papers that they had collected—photographs from maga-zines, comics, pictures of gods, religious verses, old test papers, small, low-priced books with patriotic verses and songs, and other such materials. All children brought some kind of pen with them; pencils were not common. Some also brought a box of colours and a compass box. Nagpal, a Class IV teacher, insisted that his students bring a slate and slate-pencil with them, as he did not like them to waste their notebooks on solving practice mathematics problems.

The school bell rang only four times a day. The first bell, in the morning, announced the start of the school day. The second, a short bell, marked the end of the morning session and the beginning of a half-hour break. The third bell marked the end of the break and the beginning of the afternoon session. The last, long bell marked the end of the school day. There were no markers for periods. It was entirely up to each teacher and his/her students to decide when to move from one subject or activity to the next. However, most teachers preferred to do mathematics and language in the mornings and environmental studies in the afternoons.

About once a month, on a Saturday, the school would hold a *bal sabha*, or informal gathering of all the students and teachers. On this day, students were expected to present cultural items on their own initiative. They usually sang songs, danced or told jokes and stories. Occasionally, some of the teachers would also perform.

Each new academic year began in April and ended in March/April the following year. There would be a long summer vacation from mid-May to July, and shorter ones for *Dassera* in October and for winter in December. From time to time during the course of the year, the teachers would make the students take tests in each subject. These tests depended entirely on the wishes of the teacher. Three times a year the students also had formal examinations. The children in Classes III, IV and V had examinations in Hindi, English, mathematics, science, social studies and drawing. These were held at the same time for the entire school. A timetable was followed and students were prescribed specific portions on which they would be examined. During the period of my fieldwork, the first set of examinations was held in October, before the *Dassera* break. The second was in December, before the winter break, and the final examinations were held in March.[5] The marks obtained in all three went into determining who passed and who failed in Classes III, IV and V. The first two examinations were set and administered by the class teachers themselves. For the final examination in 1993, the question papers for Class V were set by a board appointed by the Municipal Corporation of Delhi (MCD) for all the government schools under its jurisdiction. But though the students were invigilated by teachers other than their class teachers, their answer scripts were corrected and final marks computed by the class teachers, each for his or her own class.

Little Angels Public School and the
Government Girls' Primary School

In addition to the boys' primary school, the village has a girls' primary school (which is not a model school) and also three private primary schools. What follows is a brief description of two other schools which I also visited for much shorter and less extensive study. There are occasional references to these schools in this and the chapters that follow.

The private school—Little Angels Public School (henceforth LAPS), which was established in the early 1970s, is one of the oldest private schools in the whole area and the oldest in the village. It was run by a couple from Kerala, in a small building which was also their home. This was an English-medium school, from nursery to Class V. The classrooms were very small, but all of them were provided with tables and chairs. There was no space for a playground. The school was very strict about uniforms and right footwear. Almost all the children came from the village. The bell rang often—to mark the beginning and end of the day, the breaks and all the periods. Mr and Mrs Thomas were principal and headmistress, and also taught English and mathematics. There were three other young women teachers. One was from the village and two had come from Kerala. The school was not 'recognised'; all privately managed schools are expected to obtain official recognition from the Commissioner/Directorate of Public Instruction of the region. But LAPS had an arrangement with the missionary school in Khera and its students, after completing Class V, could be admitted to Class VI of the Mission School if they wished. Nursery, Class I and Class II had about 30 children each and the higher classes had about 15 to 20 children. It seemed that often after studying in this school for a few years, children were shifted to the government school. The school was co-educational and seemed to have as many boys as girls.

Mr and Mrs Thomas did not have much capital to invest in their school: it was run like a small entrepreneurship. Understandably, Mr Thomas was very reluctant to provide any exact information on the financial position of the school, and insisted that they were barely able to break even. Nevertheless, not only did the school continue to exist, but by 1984 it had also moved from rented accommodation into its own building. In the last five years the school had begun facing stiff competition from new, large private schools nearby with impressive infrastructure and school buses to transport children. In response, LAPS employed some rickshaws to transport children and introduced typing and computers as additional subjects. The other private schools in the village did not yet constitute too much of a challenge; in one, English was not the medium of instruction, only a subject. Another private school, also run in a house, was only a few years old.

The Government Girls' Primary School (henceforth GGPS) was similar to the boys' school in structure. Each class had two sections with about 30 girls each. Almost all the girls came from the village. The area of the school was much smaller and it had only a small playground. Four of the teachers and the headmistress of the school came by bus from the city every morning. The other teachers were from Kasimpur village itself. While the teachers in the boys' school regarded Kasimpur as a village, distinct from the city of Delhi, the headmistress of the girls' school made it a point to correct anyone who referred to Delhi as different from Kasimpur. 'Isn't this part of Delhi?' she would ask, reiterating that it was. She did not seem to want to think of the school she was in charge of as a village school.

II
Why is Schooling Important?

In Kasimpur, the term most commonly used to speak about the activity that schools engaged in and were concerned with, was '*padhai*'. The verb '*padhna*' means 'to read'. '*Padhai*', the noun, can be variously translated to mean studies, schooling, education, teaching, lessons. Other closely linked terms which were used by the children, teachers and the community in general were: '*padh lena*' (verb)—to be able to read, to get educated; '*anpadh*' (noun–adjective)—illiterate; '*likhai*' (noun)—(hand)writing; '*padha–likha*' (adjective)—schooled, well-educated. The term '*padhai*' seems closer in meaning to 'schooling' than to 'education'. For the latter, the term '*siksha*' may be more appropriate.

Framed by an awareness of being children and the belief that childhood is a time to prepare for adulthood,[6] all children seemed to regard schooling as preparation for the adult world of work. Conversations with children revealed that they all believed that schooling was absolutely necessary. Often their reasons were at first stated simplistically: 'It is necessary for a job.' But a little more probing showed that they were more specifically aware of schooling as a means for *opening up* employment opportunities.

EPISODE 3.1 (LAPS-V)[7]
In earlier times, why didn't they study/go to school?
Amit: There were fewer things they could do. Today there are more things we can do, so we need to study.

Either when answering the question of why schooling is important, or when speaking about the sort of employment they hoped for, children automatically focused on certain specific features that they found attractive. These ranged from simply its non-traditional nature, its steady income or non-manual nature, to the high status that becoming a 'big officer' would bring. A long conversation with some children is reported in Episode 3.2. The conversation opened with Vikas and Ravinder sitting with me under a tree in front of their classroom (Class V). Later, we were joined by other children. Vikas travelled to the Kasimpur school from another, nearby village. According to him, the school in his village was not good as the teachers spent all their time outside the classrooms, smoking and sunning themselves. Vikas had told me earlier that his father had migrated to the village several years ago and had even managed to build a small house there. He had a steady job as a worker in a private factory and was struggling to repay the loan he had taken to build the house. Ravinder belonged to the Jat community and his father owned a little land which he farmed. He also looked after other people's fields. Harish also travelled to school from a nearby village to which his family had migrated. They were *chamars*. In earlier conversations he had told me that his family owed a lot of money. His father had a very unsteady job as a labourer (*mazdoor*), and his mother often sold roasted peanuts and *chana* (gram) at the bus stand.

EPISODE 3.2 (CLASS V)

Why study?
Vikas: Without studies, you can't get a job.
Ravinder: I will leave school and do wrestling (*kushti*).
Vikas: Yes, there is money in that.
Ravinder: You need to stay on to learn English. In the school where I was earlier, they taught English from nursery.
Why?
Ravinder: For a *sarkari* (government) job, you need to study.
Why?
Ravinder: One has to speak in English. It may or may not be useful in reading the bus number.
Vikas: That you can do even now.
Ravinder: I don't know.
But why study at all?
Vikas: You join a company. Someone from outside will come and ask a question/problem (*saval*), you won't know.

Harish: For interviews.

Vikas: Socials, science... it's all information. They may ask us in an interview. We should be able to tell.... We will get promotions. Better pay.

And if not? ˍ

Harish: The Manager... he will give a letter which has come from somewhere else. You won't be able to read it if you aren't educated/schooled (*padha-likha*).

Vikas: They'll put your thumb print, and they'll loot you.

Who?

Vikas: Seth (moneylenders), the rich are clever. They aren't *padha-likha*, but they are clever/sly (*chatur*).

Harish: If you aren't *padha-likha*, you can't get a job easily. You will have to ask here and there and get work (*poochh-poochhke karna padega*).

Vikas: Or you will have to work like Kuldip's father (*who is a barber*). (*Salim and Ajay joined us. Salim's father, a migrant, did masonry work and whitewashing. This is a semi-skilled job. Ajay was a native Chipi. His father had retired from the army and set up a dairy shop in the market, which was doing quite well. Ravinder drifted away from the group.*)

*

Why is it that people who study get better jobs than those who do not?

Salim: In the beginning those who work very hard, can later relax and sit, and those who make merry will have to work.

From among you, who will do manual work?

Salim (pointing to Sanjay[8] who was in the field, picking up leaves and stuffing them in a basket): He will do manual work after the fifth. He may work with his father.

Vikas told the others with an element of surprise: Look, Ravinder's *chacha* got a job in the police after the fifth class!

Why is it so important to study English?

Vikas: These days English is what works (*aajkal English ka chal raha hai*).

Ajay: Even if I leave now, I can work in my father's shop.

Salim: He can do accounts for the milk.

So why study?

Ajay: It's a small job (*chhota kaam*).

What is a chhota kaam?

Ajay: You have to sit on the ground, and you have to repay debts.

So how far will you study?

Ajay: It's the wish of my parents, how far they want me to study.
(To Salim) **What does your father do?**
Salim: He does masonry work.
And you won't do that?
Salim: There is too much hard work in that. And there is too much danger in a mason's job (*kaam khatre ka hai*).

*

(Kuldip joined the group.)
Vikas: No one knows my father's name where he works.
Salim and Kuldip: Everyone knows my father's name.
(To Kuldip) **What will you do?**
Kuldip: I want a *naukari.*
Vikas: Sarkari for me.
Why does everyone want a sarkari naukari?
Salim: There is no anxiety (*pareshani*) in that.
Vikas: Only four to five hours of work every day.
Kuldip: My brother, he failed in 10th, he went to Jehangirpuri, there he is learning to repair watches.
How do they teach there?
Vikas: First they tell you in English. Then if you can't follow, they teach in Hindi.
Salim: If one studies more, one should get a better job.
How is that?
Salim: The man will think: I have studied so much, I should do a better job.
What kind of job is good?
Salim: Government is better. You can sit comfortably on a chair.
Vikas said to Ravinder: A private job is of no use. You get Rs 20–30 a month, can you live on that? And manage a marriage?
(Sunil came out of the class up to the tree and waved a stick at them threateningly. He yelled at them to go back into the classroom.)

Towards steady, secure desk jobs

For Salim, schooling would make a non-manual job with a steady income possible. Whitewashing cannot be done all the year around and without any steady income, life would be difficult. For Vikas, schooling would make a government job possible—a private one would not fetch enough money to manage a household. For Kuldip, the attraction was of getting a job and moving away from his father's traditional occupation as a barber. For Ajay, secure with a job in hand that he could already do, schooling would make a higher status job possible.

In all these cases, one can see that children's employment aspirations are shaped by their awareness of their present socio-economic status as determined by their father's employment and their own desire for mobility. Schooling is seen as being able to open these opportunities. There is also the belief that the higher, better jobs will become possible with more years of schooling. All these children reflect modest aspirations—for respectable, non-manual work that would bring in a steady income. There is also the awareness that a government job will bring more comfort and security.

The *bada admi* aspiration

Ajay, with his observation on the low-status nature of work and the suggestion that continuing with school would make it possible to get higher-status work, takes us to the other kind of aspiration—to become a *bada admi*.

EPISODE 3.3 (CLASS V)
Sunil's father was a chamar *who, after graduating, found a good government job in an accounts office.*
Why do your parents send you to school?
Sunil: So their honour will increase ... and I can become a *bada admi*.

EPISODE 3.4 (CLASS IV)
Will you go to the big school?
Sudhir: One will have to. Work will increase.
Why must you do it?
Sudhir: One can become a big officer.

Raj Kumar, a teacher's son studying in Class V, wanted to study, pass and get a *babu* (clerk's) job. He wanted to become a *bada admi*. When asked why studies were necessary, all the children in the private school (LAPS) said that it was because they wanted jobs as *bada* officer; they all wanted to be *bade admi*. The *bada admi* symbolised the respectable, rich man. The children had an image of him as working in an office, sitting at a desk, looking at files and speaking in English. His name is known to other people and it carries influence.

Several, though not all, of the children with *bada admi* aspirations had fathers who were high up in either the traditional social status hierarchy or the newly emerging order, or in both. A few children from the government school and all the children from the private schools belonged to this category. Typically, their fathers had well-paid jobs. The fathers of children in the private schools were almost all rich landowners or officers. In the case of the government school, most fathers were employed as government officers or were privately employed and enjoying a steady, comfortable income (see Table 3.1).

Table 3.1 Fathers' Occupations and Children's Aspirations

Name	Father's Occupation	Occupation Desired by Child
Vinod	Bank officer	*bada admi*
Sunil	Govt. clerk	*bada admi*
Rajkumar	Primary schoolteacher	*bada admi*
Ajay	Shopkeeper	*bada admi*
Vikas	*Naukari*	*sarkari naukari*
Ravinder	Jat farmer	*naukari*
Kuldip	Barber	*naukari*
Salim	Painter–whitewashing	*naukari*
Harish	Manual labourer (unorg.)	avoiding the unorganised sector
Sanjay	Cobbler	manual labour/traditional job

Note: Ajay, Vikas, Ravinder, Kuldip, Salim, Harish and Sanjay feature in the conversation reported earlier. Vinod, Sunil and Rajkumar are other schoolchildren.

Naukari vs traditional employment

There was a clear trend of wanting to move away from traditional employment towards *naukari*. *Naukari* is employment which involves fixed hours of work and a fixed monthly salary. At first, this seemed a specific aspiration for a desk job, and this aspect was certainly there. But other jobs that their fathers were in, such as bus conductor, driver or gardener in a government park, also seemed to qualify as '*naukari*'. This indicates that the overriding feature was a regular monthly pay, job security, fixed working hours and minimal manual work. Furthermore, it implied work in the organised sector, not the unorganised one. This is work that becomes possible with access to the labour market of the city—in this case, Delhi. If one drops out of school, if one doesn't learn to read and write, one will not be able to access this. One will have to continue with the traditional employment of the caste group. Salim thought that Sanjay would very likely become a cobbler like his father. The reference to Kuldip's father's job is on similar lines. Kuldip himself wanted a *naukari*. In both these cases, the prospect of having to continue in traditional employment was not favoured, especially because it invariably meant some kind of manual work.

Apart from the fact that most traditional forms of employment involve manual work and are labour-intensive, they seem to have other disadvantages in the child's system of assigning value to different occupations. One is that they can be learnt without the use of any coercive techniques. The fact that they can be learnt easily, often simply by following example, seems to be to their disadvantage: 'That comes on its own. Look, I am so small and I can do farming' (Navin, Class V). In contrast, non-traditional employment requires effort and undertaking difficult tasks in school, such as memorisation for examinations.

EPISODE 3.5 (CLASS V)
Why don't they teach (you) to do things like that at school?
Vikas (deprecatingly): That you can learn at home.
How?
Salim: Parents teach us.
And how do you learn?
Kuldip: By seeing we learn.
What do they ask in the exam?
Kuldip: Mark the following.
Salim: Oh. Yes. You will have to tackle that.
Vikas: The whole book will have to be memorised.
Salim: Those who don't study, they keep warning them.

The reasoning seems to be: 'If one doesn't have to work long and hard for it, then it can't be worth much.'

Another problem with traditional employment seems to be that it does not involve any period of preparation that would clearly separate and distinguish the child from the adult in modern society. The child has the feeling: 'I can already do that.' A perverse extension of this seems to be: 'If I, as a child, can do it, then it can't be worth very much, and the adult who does it can't be worth very much either.' Such an occupation is thus treated as the option for failures: 'Those who are much bigger than us, who cannot read, they can do farming' (Jogi, Class IV).

EPISODE 3.6 (LAPS-V)
Did primitive humans **(adi manav)** *go to school?*
Vinod: No.
So why do you go to school?
Because there is no farming left. They used to farm.
If you want to do farming, why is studying/schooling unnecessary?
Because it comes by itself. You can sow seeds by yourself.

EPISODE 3.7 (LAPS-V)
What are the things we need to study for? (There was no answer, so I prompted) Do we need to study for agriculture **(kheti)**?
Renu: We don't need to study (for that).
Amit to Renu: We need to—for reading and writing the name of fertilisers.
Then why don't they teach you that?
Amit: Oh they will, later.
Renu: Those who fail do agriculture.

Amit responded to the question 'Why don't they teach it now?' with 'They will, later.' This recurred several times on different occasions, reflecting the overall belief that schooling is a protracted period of preparation for employment. It also pointed to the faith in and the unquestioning acceptance of the logic and validity of institutions constructed and conducted by adults. So, if something is necessary, of course it will be taught, if not now then later. By the same logic, if it isn't taught, it must be fit for dropouts and uneducated/unschooled people.

Escaping the unorganised sector

In the first long conversation reproduced, Harish observed that if one did not study/get schooled, one would have to seek employment by asking people. The phrase that he used, '*poochh poochh ke karna padega*', also carries the suggestion that this would have to be done repeatedly, because one would not be given a steady job. For children of the lowest castes—*chamar* and *churha*—and also for children of migrant families, there was no option of being able to fall back on traditional employment if necessary. For these children, the prospect of not passing in school conjured up images of adult life where they would go hungry or have to beg for employment or money. It would mean working in the unorganised sector as labourers or in other insecure, low-status jobs.

'If we won't be able to read and write, we will have to beg' (Bijendar, Class IV). Bijendar's father, a *chamar*, worked in the city in a private factory by day. In the evening he would buy vegetables from the *mandi* at Azadpur and sell them in the village market. Bijendar often joined his father in selling vegetables. The following conversation took place with Sonu and Methram—'failures'[9] in Class IV—children of migrant, daily-wage labourers. Both felt that in today's world it was necessary to study if they were to avoid a life where they would receive blows.

EPISODE 3.8 (CLASS IV)
Earlier they didn't have schools.
Sonu: That was the age of the illiterate *(anpadh ka zamana)*.
Then why is it necessary to study now?
So that we won't have to receive blows *(thokaren nahin khani padengi)*.

Kamal, whose father was an unemployed *churha*, was one of the 'failures' of Class IV. One day, when I was sitting behind him in class, he told me spontaneously: 'My mother tells me, study, get a job, you hardly want to stay at home.' Irshad, a failure from the other section of Class IV, whose parents were migrants from the state of Uttar Pradesh, also spontaneously expressed his concerns:

(One) who cannot read/study, he will have to do masonry work ... I know that. That is my father's job. He fell down and got hurt. In a *naukari* you don't fall. It's a job that you do on the ground. If you manage to get educated (read/study), you can get fixed in a job.

For Bir Singh, whose father was a daily-wage worker from the *chamar* caste, this was not a concern for the distant future. Failing meant joining the labour force with immediate effect—washing vessels and plates at wedding feasts or small *dhabas*. This is one of the lowliest kinds of work possible as it involves handling other people's *jhoota*. Furthermore, it is irregular, brings a very unsteady income and is dependent entirely on the whims of the contractor.

EPISODE 3.9 (CLASS IV)
Bir Singh: If I fail this time, I will have to... *(he mimed rubbing one hand on the other)*. You didn't understand?
I shook my head.

I will have to wash cups in the tea shop. My *mama* told my father—put him in a cycle shop. He can learn repairing. If I fail again, I will run away. To the city. I will work, lift weights, do a labourer's work. And then, when I become big-big, I will join the army. Then after many days are over, I will come home.

Why after many days?

Because then they will give me leave.

In Table 3.2 the children's fathers' occupation has been tabulated against their own concern regarding the consequence of failure—all their fathers had irregular, unreliable employment. The episodes illustrate the aspect of employment that most of the children from families in the lowest social rung—the *churhas*, some *chamars* and migrant families—tended to focus on. It represented the alternative to unemployment, begging, menial work and child labour. Within the school, these children were treated as though they were already earmarked for this future—they received very little attention and were often assigned manual chores. Still, while making them very aware of their future, schooling also seemed to hold out some hope of securing employment, or at least postponing joining the work-force as child labour.

Table 3.2 Fathers' Occupations in Relation to Failure

Child's Name	Father's Occupation	Consequence of Failure
·Harish	irregular	will have to ask repeatedly for jobs
Bijendar	private *naukari*	will have to beg
Sonu and Methram	irregular	will have to receive blows
Bir Singh	irregular	will have to wash *jhoota* vessels
Kamal	unemployed	will have to stay at home

Employment and socio-economic mobility

The employment aspirations of all the children reflect the importance of social mobility. In almost every case, the children aspired for jobs which enjoyed a higher status than the ones their fathers currently held:[10] whether it was moving from the unorganised to the organised sector, from the private to the government, or from a low-status to a high-status job. They believed that schooling would provide them with the necessary access. The mobility of some individuals was sufficient to make the ideology of mobility through schooling credible. There was also the belief that for better jobs one needed to stay on in school longer; the further one studied, the better the job that one could aspire for. Higher status did not always mean only better pay; there was a definite trend away from agriculture, even though it could fetch higher earnings than a government job. This leads to the second feature—the trend of moving away from manual and agricultural employment. Both these forms of employment were seen as fit only for failures. These were jobs for which one didn't need any schooling.

The children's aspirations fit well with the ethos of the village as a whole, reflecting the overall concern for alternatives to traditional employment. An orientation to service-type employment was also evident in the village employment profile. The recent disfavouring of manual employment that was voiced in the village echoed quite clearly in the opinions of the children, whose aspirations were generally quite modest and did not reflect unreasonably high expectations.

The strong link between schooling and employment comes through when we examine the reasons that boys gave as to why, unlike in earlier times, girls are sent to school nowadays.

Surya Prakash, Class IV: They can also get jobs.
Pavan, Class V: (That they may also) read and write. And they can become *bade admi*, like doctors.
Sonu, Class IV: They can also work like us.
Jogi, Class IV: Because they can also get jobs. Today girls are flying planes.

III
Preparing for Work

What specific aspects of schooling did the children believe were important for the job they hoped to get? In what manner did they believe that schooling 'prepares' them? Was it primarily for the certification that school gave, or was it something they believed they would need, that they could learn in school? The children's beliefs about these matters came in response to questions like: 'How will such studies be useful in your work?' or 'Earlier they didn't need schooling but now they do for a job. Why?', or when they answered that schooling is necessary for a job, they were asked to explain 'Why?'

EPISODE 3.10 (CLASS IV)
Sudhir: We can't get a job without studying. Those who study more can also become soldiers.
But what is the use of all the padhai?
You need it.
In what way?
Silence. Then: It is *vidya.*
What is vidya?
It is *siksha.*
What is siksha?
Reading-writing... If you get more schooling (*padhai*), you also get a good job.

EPISODE 3.11 (CLASS V)
(*To Devendar*) **Why are studies necessary for a job?**
It is necessary to do mathematics and writing.
You know those things now.
We know only the Class V level.
Why do you learn social (studies) and science?
Who knows, later we may need it in our job.

In the preceding conversations, three features of school learning stand out. The first is that literacy is fundamental. The second is taking for granted the relationship of more schooling to better jobs. The third is the reference to 'bigger', more complicated things that would be learnt later in the higher classes. These sentiments reflect the faith children had in institutions created and run by adults (including the *sarkar* [government]). They accepted these institutions in good faith, believing in their validity, logic and linkage to the job market.

Literacy

Irshad, Class IV: I will not get a *naukari.* Why, I can't even read. I'll get a beating, what else?

Padhai, as the word for schooling itself suggests, was first and foremost linked to learning to read and write. The label 'fail' meant the child was not yet literate. The certifications 'pass' and 'fail' marked the division between two worlds of work. The 'new' world was associated with passing in school and becoming an educated man (*padha-likha admi*). This world offered respectable kinds of employment such as *naukari* and opportunities for social mobility and becoming a *bada admi*. The 'old world' was not respectable anymore. It was the world of the illiterate (*anpadh*), and it offered only manual work—traditional forms like farming or other irregular, stigmatised, daily-wage jobs. By making children literate, schooling provided the first requirement of accessing the 'new world'. Curiously, learning *ganit* (arithmetic) was not linked to employment opportunity. It was regarded as important for everyone to learn since it would enable one to handle money matters in everyday life, keep accounts and avoid being cheated.

'Bol-chal'

Learning that would enable one to maintain a proper social front seemed to be an important dimension of all school learning. When Sonu (Class IV) explained that he was studying to become literate and get a job, I asked him how it would help. He answered, saying: 'Otherwise, if an educated (*padha-likha*) man comes and asks us something, we won't be able to reply. If he makes us write something, then we won't be able to write.' Sonu felt that in order to successfully handle test situations in which people higher up in the hierarchy could place him, and maintain his own dignity, he would have to at least be literate.

Closely linked with becoming literate to maintain dignity was acquiring *bol-chal*—speech and walk. This was regarded as especially important for the children in KBMS as they came from the village and were '*ganvar*' (rustics). In the village people spoke Haryanvi. Although linguistically Haryanvi is a language with a distinctive vocabulary, idiom, style, etc., which distinguish it from Hindi, both the villagers themselves, and certainly the teachers, treated it as an impure, rude form of Hindi. Speaking Haryanvi outside the intimate circle of home and kin-group was regarded as a sign of lack of education and social politesse, unsuitable for modern settings, including the school. '*Sahi boli*', the right idiom/accent, was associated with the city and school learning. Parents from more interior villages sent their children study in Kasimpur as it was closer to the city: '*bol-chal seekh sakti hai...* There they speak roughly, like they will say "*ki jan*"' (village woman on why her niece had come to live with them and study in Kasimpur).

English

EPISODE 3.12 (CLASS IV)
Neeraj opened his notebook and started flicking pages.
Why do you study so much?
Neeraj: I like to. My heart is in it. (*Man lagta hai.*)
And if your heart didn't get involved?
Then you can't study.
And if you don't study, then?
One will fail, and people at home will beat.
Why will they beat?
They have such fat sticks. They say, 'If you don't pass, we will beat you. You must pass, you must pass.'
Why do they say that?
Studies are very necessary.
Why?
For a job.
Why?
They will ask us to write in English and Hindi.
But you know how to write already.
I cannot yet write big-big things. I cannot yet write English.

Once children had crossed the hurdle of becoming literate and were assured of passing, the next most important reason for studying was learning English. Everyone believed that it was very important to know English, which was essential for any respectable job—within the government and certainly the ones that made one a *bada admi*. As can be seen from the preceding conversation, having mastered reading and writing, the current focus of schooling efforts for Neeraj was to memorise texts and answers, and to learn English. In the long conversation reported at the beginning of the last section on the importance of *padhai*, Vikas expressed surprise that Ravinder's uncle had got a police job with just a Class V pass certificate. His reaction stemmed not only from the belief that for such a government job one needed more years of schooling but also that for *that* job—a respectable government job—a knowledge of English was required. Both Harish and Ravinder also added that they had studied in schools where English was taught right from the nursery level.

Children believed that learning English from an early grade would give them an initial advantage that would eventually translate into a better job.

This was one important reason why private schools were considered better than the government schools. The fact that English is taught after Class IV in government schools also seemed to be perceived as a reason to stay on in school.

Jankari[11]

Another 'object' of attention for those who had become literate was 'jankari' or general knowledge. In the first episode reported, both Vikas and Harish expressed the need to know information, saying that it may be asked in an interview; or that someone may ask a question which they should be able to answer. While language, as a subject, was directly related to becoming literate, science and social studies provided one with information that one 'needs to know'. The longer one stayed in school, the more information one would be able to get.

EPISODE 3.13 (CLASS IV)
Why is all this necessary for a job?
Bijendar: To be able to read and write.
Why socials and mathematics?
Don't know.
Jogi and Satish turned around to face us. I asked them the same question.
Jogi: If they ask, we won't be able to tell. Isn't it?
Satish: If we can't answer the question, will they give a job?

EPISODE 3.14 (CLASS IV)
Deepak: In *samajik* they tell us those things that were there earlier. Like the earth is round.
Why do you need to know these things?
It is necessary to know. Like Rakesh Sharma, it is necessary to know about him...
Or that that tree is a **sadabahar**. *Why must you know?*
It may be asked in the scholarship exam; such short, short questions.
Or why is it necessary to know about Vivekanand... (I continued to mention different things that they are required to know.)
There is only one answer for this. That guru*ji* will ask. The inspector can ask, and it can come in the fifth.

'We need to be able to answer'; 'If some one asks us, we should be able to tell'; 'When we grow up, and if someone asks us how the wheel was invented, we will have to be able to tell.' These were reasons why children were concerned about acquiring information. They felt that both now, as children, and later, as adults, they could be *tested* at any time by a superior or a prospective employer. They believed that to be found not to know an answer would create a bad impression—and that it could mean a loss of face, of promotion, or even of employment.

The possibility that one may need knowledge in order to function in the job itself was treated as secondary or almost incidental. When Ravinder in Episode 3.2 said: 'One has to speak in English. It may or may not be useful in reading the bus number,' he was evaluating English as a social requirement against English as a practical one—and giving the former primacy. Similarly, the failures gave literacy a social, rather than practical, importance. *Jankari* would enable them to engage in social interactions, impress and pass tests. School learning, rather than being perceived as enabling one *to do a job,* was perceived as enabling one *to get a job.*

Choosing a school

Surinder was the oldest grandson of the ex-*pradhan*. He was among the first children of the village to begin commuting to Delhi for an English-medium education.[12] Until Class VI, he travelled every day by bus from the village to a private school in Model Town (north Delhi). Then he joined the Rai Public School, a residential school in Haryana. Speaking of his experiences and feelings when he was a student in the Model Town School, Surinder, now 26 years old, said:

EPISODE 3.15 (IN THE VILLAGE)
I had a bad time as a student...I was lonely and misunderstood. There was no one who thought or talked like me at home. I was better off in a hostel. I feel children from village must go to hostel, otherwise the school and home culture are so different, children have a very tough time. For example, I used to come back from school and play with children, marbles or anything, then they'd beat me and scold me saying, 'We spend so much money on your education, sending you to an English-medium school, and you play with these children and won't study or work!' I felt children need play as much as work, but they never understood. Or my grandmother (*dadi*) would insist I work—cut grass, work in the fields. But I never wanted to do manual work. No one else in my school did it. She would say, 'If you don't work, you will die of starvation.' I would tell her, I'd rather die, I will do some

chaprassi work, but I won't do manual work. Because none of the other children did. My best years of schooling were at Rai (a boarding school).

The villagers' response to English-medium education was very similar to their response to education during the 1940s and 1950s. Sending children to school used to be regarded as a fairly expensive investment. It meant freeing schoolgoing members from household chores and agricultural duties. It also meant a lot of additional expenditure—not on fees, as schools were free, but on books, good clothes and some pocket money. Initially, villagers made such investment only for boys, which they then monitored anxiously. From Surinder's recounting, one gathers that even time spent in play was regarded as wasteful. Children felt a pressure to study and pass. The consequence of failure was withdrawal from school.

By the late 1970s, the villagers seemed to have become more conscious of the better employment opportunities that English made available. There was also, by this time, a more monetised economy as compared with the early 1950s. Clearly, there was an economic niche in the village as far as English-medium education was concerned. The establishment in 1974 and success of the first entrepreneurial venture in this niche—the Little Angels Public School—has been described in the first part of this chapter. LAPS was and continued to be a small school, with no impressive playground or building, unlike the school in Model Town, Delhi, where Surinder studied. But by 1993 there were five such private schools in the village. All these schools made new demands on the villagers' finances: a high monthly fee and more expensive uniforms and books. The villagers seemed to regard this as an investment worth making. And they also seemed to pay more heed, monitoring the affairs of the school and their own children carefully.

As pointed out earlier, several children now in the government school had previously studied in a private, English-medium school. At some point, they had been shifted to the government school: 'My father cut my name there and wrote it here.' The most common reason for this was the high fees. Though the villagers believed in the benefits of English-medium education, the fee, which was about 100 to 1,000 times that of the government schools, was very high for those who had 'Class-IV' government employment. Parents often opted to send only their sons to English-medium schools, educating their daughters in the government girls' school. But they were also anxious that their sons should be worth this high investment. If there was any indication that this was not so, they transferred them to the government school.

The conversation with Surinder reveals that the advent of English-medium education in the 1970s differed from the advent of government schooling in the 1950s in one important aspect. It created a divide within the village along new lines. Surinder's grandmother not only discouraged him from playing, she also implied that by associating with village children—even those of the same caste—who were not going to English-medium schools, he was going to undo something he had got from English-medium education and somehow alter the potential benefits. It was as if the cultural capital being acquired in school had to be protected from the corrupting influence of the village culture that came through other children who did not go to English-medium schools. This divide continued to be very apparent even at the time of my fieldwork, in the children's play-groups. There were as many groups as there were different kinds of schools that the villagers recognised: the government school, the English-medium schools in the village, the English-medium schools outside the village, etc.

EPISODE 3.16 (LAPS-V)
How many kinds of school are there in Kasimpur?
Vineet, Akash and Ajay counted up to nine schools.
Why are there so many kinds of schools?
(*They did not respond to the word 'kind'.*) Because Kasimpur is so big. It needs many schools. It is becoming a city.
How is that?
Vineet: One will have to think a little bit and answer this. It is getting many-many houses and so many shops everywhere.
Should it become a city?
Akash: Yes!
Vineet: No. Then there'll be too much pollution and traffic... My house is the tallest.
Ajay: My father is a bank officer. He is a 'big man'. So is my brother-in-law (*jijaji*).
Why don't you all (children of Kasimpur) study in the same school?
Madam, no. It depends on their father, where they want to send their children.

The difference between various schools of the village, when discussed, was in terms of whether they were English-medium or at least taught English as a subject. The most clear-cut distinction was between the private schools in the village and the government school.

EPISODE 3.17 (LAPS-V)

Amit: If we go to the government school, then we can't learn English. **But they learn the same things in Hindi.**

Ajay: We can understand theirs (i.e., what they learn), but they can't understand ours.

Amit: That is also good, but less good. It is this way that we get more control over the brain.

EPISODE 3.18 (LAPS-V)

Why don't you go to a sarkari school?

Vineet: They don't teach there.

The other three children said they didn't know. Then suddenly Ajay said: They start teaching English, a-b-c-d, from sixth onwards. Here we can learn from now.

Why do you need to know English so early?

It's better. Now everywhere they want English. *Gyan* (knowledge) increases, and we will become *bade admi*.

Harish: If we get more *gyan*, we can get a better job.

Children were also aware that while LAPS was English-medium, Nand Lal School taught English as a subject right from the nursery level. Within the government schools also, the children pointed out that in the boys' primary school, English was taught as a subject from Class IV onwards,[13] while in the girls' school it was not. The girls would have to wait to go to the senior secondary school to start learning English from Class VI.

The fact that English was taught in the high school also seemed to be very significant. The promise of learning English seemed to be, for many children, the reason for staying on in school and continuing to study: 'You need to stay on to learn English' (Sudhir, Class IV). The Class V students eagerly looked forward to this change in their curriculum. Later that year, when they had moved from the primary school to Class VI in the senior secondary school, they continued to regard this as the major change.

EPISODE 3.19 (CLASS V)

Ajay made me write a, b, c, d,... in his notebook.

Why?

Ajay: I will go to Class VI. I will need it. So I am practising (*riyaz*) right from now.

EPISODE 3.20 (IN THE VILLAGE)
In the village Ajay yelled out to his friend walking across the road: Hey
.Pilla *(Ajay's pet name for Pradeep)*, get your father to write your name
quickly. We are already learning English. Later you will find it difficult
to understand.

In addition to being able to learn English, there was also the belief
that there was no proper teaching in government schools. English-medium
schools were generally regarded as being 'good', real schools.[14] Here,
children believed, there was a closer adherence to proper values and
norms. Administrators and teachers were far more strict. They insisted
on the right uniform and on punctuality. They gave children a lot of work
to do, and they taught many things very early. And they punished the
children if they did not satisfy these requirements. It seemed that in these
schools the teacher's eye operated more effectively, regulating morality,
self-identity and instruction; this is what was appreciated.[15] All the villagers
seemed to think that, in comparison, the government/Hindi-medium
schools were lax about these matters. They often complained about their
poor standards.

EPISODE 3.21 (IN THE VILLAGE)
Daughter-in-law of the postmaster: My children go to DAV and LAPS.
Because everyone knows that government schools are bad. No teaching
there. Some teachers are good, but some are bad. We can't tell. And the
people from the village also don't go and ask, 'Is my child studying?'
And then they (DAV School in Narela and LAPS) teach in English,
and now without English one can't get anywhere.

On one occasion, when a child's mother complained about the lack-
adaisical attitude of teachers in the government school where her sons
studied, I asked her why she didn't send them to one of the private schools
of the village.

EPISODE 3.22 (IN THE VILLAGE)
We did go to ask (at LAPS). First, the fees were too much. Then they
punish for everything; uniform, correct books, being late. So I decided
let them study in government school.
What about Nand Lal?
They don't give certificates. That's the main problem.

It was not only the label of 'government school' but of being 'Hindi-medium' that seemed to suggest a lower standard. A nearby reputed private school, after a change of management, had decided to change its medium of instruction from English to Hindi. This became a topic of discussion among the villagers and the children, who discussed it in school as well:

EPISODE 3.23 (LAPS-V)
Vineet mentioned Shambhu Dayal school in Sonipat.
Akash: It has become Hindi medium.
Vineet: It has gone down.

The presence of several kinds of schools in Kasimpur indicates that there was a spectrum of means, not aspirations, that different schools catered to. There was no doubt that all parents and children would prefer to be educated in the large, English-medium, private schools which also had the reputation of being 'better schools'. But the high fees and the fact that many did not provide a Class V certificate made them cautious. The presence of English-medium schools seemed to suggest to the children that Kasimpur was becoming more like a city. There were many more people now in Kasimpur who would be seeking non-manual employment. Learning English seemed to be a big motivating factor to attend school and to stay on.

*

Education as Cultural Capital

The contents of schooling, classified in the manner just described, fall into a rough hierarchy of contents and outcomes with increased years of schooling. This has been represented schematically in Figure 3.2. Schooling marks the basic divide between the traditional and modern worlds—only through schooling/literacy can one escape the stigma of being an illiterate. The figure shows the contents of schooling in relation to the hierarchy of aims/purposes of schooling and the time spent in school. Literacy and numeracy, both more functional skills, are in order to get jobs. Additional skills and knowledge, acquired with increased years spent in school, provide advantages in getting better jobs, in securing promotions and ultimately in becoming a *bada admi*. Anticipating the analysis and findings reported in the next chapter, I have included 'good citizenship, moral

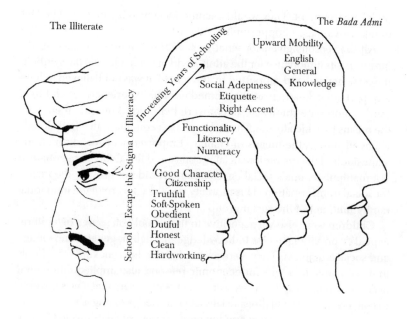

The Illiterate

The *Bada Admi*

Upward Mobility

English
General
Knowledge

Increasing Years of Schooling

Social Adeptness
Etiquette
Right Accent

School to Escape the Stigma of Illiteracy

Functionality
Literacy
Numeracy

Good Character
Citizenship
Truthful
Soft-Spoken
Obedient
Dutiful
Honest
Clean
Hardworking

Figure 3.2 Becoming a *Bada Admi*

character' at the first level as the core outcome of schooling. This outcome was emphasised by the teachers—it included punctuality, obedience, honesty, respect for elders, etc. Children themselves rarely stated explicitly that '*padhai* is for becoming good'. A rare exception was Vipin who, although an ambitious boy, stated rather piously and with circumspection: '*padhai* is for becoming good. Who can say about becoming a *bada admi*? For some, their future (*kismat*) opens up.' Most children focused on the future consequences of being good (students) while teachers focused on being good as an aim in itself.

Whether it was the knowledge of reading and writing, of English, or of knowing information, the children's answers showed that they were responding to a situation that was already predefined by more powerful people. It was but natural that for them, as children, the world they were growing up in was shaped by adults. But they also seemed to envision the adult world as a world where they, even as adults, would have to adapt: 'they'—the *bade admi*—expected them to know English, 'they' would ask questions to test them. Children felt that equipped with literacy, English and information, they would be able to exercise more control over their social environment. They would become socially more adept and be able to take advantage of opportunities.

All the reasons given for what in *padhai* is important related to the future and its importance for the adult world of work. Outside the symbolic universe defined and supported by the school, it was not believed to have any particular bearing on the immediate life experiences of children. Furthermore, the studies at school were believed to provide them with the means by which to adapt to and cope with conditions that had already changed—not as the means of change. Empowerment was through the acquisition of the means for social mobility and the ability to negotiate, if not manipulate, one's social environment. It did not provide the means for social transformation. This mobility was the concern of the individual family unit, not of the social group.

Children were also very sensitive to the school as a source of 'cultural capital',[16] providing access to knowledge of English, general knowledge and social adeptness. They were aware that the different kinds of schools they were able to access for economic reasons, also implied differential access to cultural capital. They were also keenly aware that it was possible to convert cultural capital—especially the knowledge of English—into social capital through government employment. Apple[17] suggests that in the new economic order of liberalisation, English will probably have a different function. This is already being noticed in the Eastern bloc European countries, where American rather than British English is regarded as the language for the market. However, this has yet to find an echo in the voices of the children of Kasimpur village.

Box 3.1 Meeting Teachers: My First Day at School

In the following paragraphs I describe my first day in school in order to introduce the teachers of the KBMS, through their own introductions on our first meeting. A more detailed description of entering and researching the school is included in the appendix on method at the end of the book.

I had met the headmaster of the school, Mr Satpal Singh, in his office about a month prior to beginning fieldwork. He was cordial and modestly proud of his well-maintained school. On being congratulated on his 'best teacher' award—there were pictures of him receiving the award on the wall behind him—he made a short speech telling me about himself and his work. He had passed Class XII with science. He had to start teaching soon after, as his father had died, leaving him with the responsibility of looking after the family. Teaching in school was a patriotic duty and teaching young children was a nation-building task. He had been a teacher for several years and the government had recognised him and given him the award, after which he came as headmaster to Kasimpur, which was also his native village.

When I returned a month later to begin work, children were gathering for morning assembly. I stood behind the rows of boys, waiting to meet Mr Singh and formally inform him that I would be starting my work from that day. Two men in their early 30s came up and enquired what I was there for. They then introduced themselves to me: Surjeet and Ajay Gupta. Both of them taught Class I. Surjeet said he was a graduate of Delhi University. He used to be in the army, but when he found they were posting him far away from home, in the South, he quit and did his BEd. This was the only opening he had found at that time. But it was all right; it left him with time to meet other people. He introduced Ajay Gupta to me, saying that he was a science graduate and that he could speak well in English. Ajay Gupta then added in English that he ran tutorial classes in Narela. He felt that that was his real job and school work kept him busy only in the mornings. He claimed that teaching children here was of no use: you can teach a lot, but these village children don't learn. Surjeet added that Parmesh, who hadn't come in that day, was also a graduate, though the other male teachers in the school were not.

Assembly began. A young woman arrived shortly afterwards, stood near me and introduced herself. She was Asha, who taught Class IV, and travelled to Kasimpur from Narela. She said she was quite eager to be posted out of this village school. Though she was a post-graduate with a BEd, she said she found this job convenient as it did not involve much work. A full-time job would be difficult to manage with the home. When I asked her who the other women teachers in the school were, she pointed out to Krishna Kumari, a Class V teacher, and Sunita, a Class II teacher, adding that they were both graduates with BEd degrees. She dismissed the other women teachers, saying that Santosh was in school for sports and the other two were nursery teachers. She did not seem to consider them at par with primary schoolteachers.

Soon after assembly, the headmaster took me around the school to meet a few teachers. First he introduced me to Nagpal (Class IV), the seniormost teacher in the school. Nagpal was in charge of the school store and helped the headmaster in keeping accounts. Then we met Pavan Kumar (Class III) who, he added, was a state awardee teacher. Both these teachers had their classrooms in the same building as the headmaster's room.

As we walked around the school, Kapil, the Class II teacher, intro-duced himself to me and said that he had got into teaching after a long stint at truck driving. After an accident, when he could no longer continue with truck driving, he did the teacher training diploma and began to teach in the primary school. Within a minute of introduc-ing himself to me, Bhardwaj, a Class V teacher, stated that he was a Brahmin, and that though he had begun to teach soon after he had completed his training, he had studied and privately passed the BA and MA examinations. He stayed on in this job because it gave him time to continue with his religious consulting work. I found both Surjeet and Ajay Gupta together in one room, chatting. Another per-son, whom I had seen briefly in the morning, was conducting a com-bined class of the two first grades. Surjeet introduced him to me as Balbir, the caretaker of the children who came to school from the near-by Boys' Home. Balbir seemed to keep himself busy and sometimes obliged teachers by taking their classes.

A little later, Sunita, the Class II teacher, came up and spent quite a bit of time telling me how, being a postgraduate, she felt wasted in her job. It was her mother, the principal of a school, who had insisted that she should teach, as she felt this was one profession women could take up without sacrificing the home.

Like the headmaster, each of the teachers spontaneously provided some autobiographical details. Only Satpal Singh, the headmaster, Nagpal and Pavan Kumar seemed content with being teachers. The others, in their introduction, included bits of additional information about themselves, which were by and large unconnected with the school. But they seemed to feel that those details were significant. Most of them also felt the need to provide information on the circum-stances that had forced them to become primary schoolteachers although they could have pursued higher status jobs in different cir-cumstances. They had stayed on with this job primarily because of the convenience and security it provided.

This 'presentation of self' (Goffman 1959) reflects the low status that is awarded to primary schoolteaching in Indian society. Many teachers felt the need to 'manage' my perception of them and broaden their identities to include aspects which they felt were more readily recognisable as worthy of respect.

Notes

1. Those who are interested in more details of the research design and method—fieldwork, data collection and interpretation—may wish to first read Appendix B on method at

the end of the book, before reading this chapter and the ones that follow where field data is presented and exposited.

2. In India, the term 'class' refers to grade or level.

3. All names are pseudonyms.

4. This way of saluting was followed for every teacher and official who entered the room, interrupting whatever activity was in progress. It was not done for school peons, sweepers or visiting parents of children. At first, it was also done for me. I returned their salutation but discouraged them from standing up to attention; with my frequent entering and leaving the room, this would have been a serious disruption. The verbal exchange of salutations continued and, as I did not insist, even these were dispensed with later. Initially, the teachers were embarrassed when their students forgot to greet me when I entered their class. I assured them it was perfectly all right, so they too let the matter drop. Eventually, I was able to enter and leave classrooms without disrupting the activity in progress.

5. In the period of my fieldwork from November to May, I observed the conduction of the December and March (annual) examinations.

6. Children's awareness of 'being children' is discussed in the next chapter under Section I: 'Ideology of Childhood'.

7. At the beginning of every episode reported, the information provided within brackets provides details of location and context. For episodes set in the KBMS, only the relevant class of the children is reported, e.g., Class V, without distinguishing between the sections A or B. LAPS-V refers to Class V of LAPS, etc.

8. Sanjay was acknowledged to be illiterate and survived in the class due to the benevolence of the class teacher.

9. The typification 'failure' is elaborated in the next chapter.

10. Harish and Ranpal were interesting exceptions to this. Harish was prepared to earn a living selling peanuts. Ranpal wanted to quit school and to farm. Ravinder and Rigel were exceptions in that they were interested in jobs that involved manual work. The former wanted to be a wrestler and the latter to work in a factory making tractors. Both these jobs, however, are not menial but romantic, involving physical prowess, which was valued among the Jat community to which both belonged.

11. *Jankari* (noun) from the verb *jan-na*, to know: information, things that are known.

12. The Satnam Singh Maan family referred to in the previous chapter was different because there the boys went out of the village to live with their brother in Delhi and be educated there. Surinder Singh, however, continued to live in the village and commute to an English-medium school in Delhi.

13. It is another matter that these classes were never conducted.

14. The only person who voiced a contrary opinion was Ranpal's father who said of English-medium education: 'No, it's all useless—fraud.' He was a driver in the Delhi Transport Corporation (DTC) and an active member of the union.

15. In the next chapter the belief about the importance of discipline to the process of schooling is explored in more detail. The 'teacher's eye' as an instrument of regulation is discussed in Chapter VI.

16. See Bourdieu (1986) on forms and convertibility of 'capital'.

17. 1996, personal communication. I thank Michael Apple for this and the previous insight.

4

The End of Childhood

EPISODE 4.1 (OUTSIDE CLASS V)
During assembly, Surjeet (teacher) had told the children about a freedom fighter and martyr called Lala Hardayal; he had formed the Gadar party to protest against the excessive discipline and restrictions imposed by the British on the Indians. Later in the day, I talked about the strict discipline in the school with Ashok and Vipin of Class V. Both of them concurred that their headmaster was a strict disciplinarian and that they feared him. I tried to instigate them to fantasise about protesting the regime of discipline in their school, reminding them of Lala Hardayal.
Ashok was very shocked by the idea and exclaimed: No! Then school won't remain a school. We will have to shout *gobhi le le, aaloo le le* (buy cabbages, buy potatoes).

To bring out the contradiction in the teacher's personality, Krishna Kumar (1991) has described the Indian teacher as a 'meek dictator'. On the one hand is his low status in the hierarchy of professions and his complete lack of control in curricular matters; on the other is his enjoyment of a dictatorial position over students within the classroom, where he maintains total power and social control. As was evident in their introductions to me (described in Chapter III), the Kasimpur teachers were very conscious of the low status of primary schoolteachers. Yet, within the school they were very authoritarian. All children feared the teachers, but they seemed to believe that such a regime of discipline was essential to the idea of school itself. This was conveyed in Ashok's exclamation, 'Then school won't remain a school', in the episode reported at the beginning of this chapter. The teacher's authority over the student was implicated, justified and reasserted in virtually every aspect of the process of schooling. The present and following chapters will all explore why and how the experience of control and authority acquires the character of being essential for schooling to be successful—not only in behavioural matters but also for learning (i.e., knowledge construction).

In Chapter III we saw that preparation for and access to the world of work was believed to be the purpose of schooling. The prospect of success or failure in school seemed to loom large in the minds of children. In this chapter, I will examine some other consequences of this polarisation of school experience in terms of success and failure. The importance of discipline can be traced to the shared beliefs of teachers, children and the village community regarding the nature of children, and what it takes in order to become good students; this, in turn, could be linked to success in finding a respectable job in the adult world of work. The first section of this chapter explores the ideology of childhood, the opposition of 'play' with 'work' and the socialising functions expected of a good school. This ideology seems to suggest the need to bracket out the present, the here-and-now of the child, and give schooling a future orientation. The second and third sections of the chapter look at how the future manifests itself in the present and controls the children—through the idea of developing the '*pehchaan*' or image of the educated man, and the typifications of 'model student' and 'failure'.

At the end of Chapter II, I suggested that Kasimpur seems to have the symbolic surplus to support the ideas of childhood and school. This chapter and the next one bring out the local/indigenous/traditional character of the frameworks and theories that support the idea of a childhood devoted to schooling.[1] In addition to the data and analysis from school and classroom observation, I also draw on popular literature on childhood and education represented by the articles in two annual volumes of the popular North Indian Hindi periodical, *Kalyan*, published by the Gita Press: the issue on childhood, *Balakank* (Kalyan 1953) and the issue on education, *Sikshank* (Kalyan 1988).

I
Ideology of Childhood[2]

In the village, children were characterised chiefly by their playfulness. It was common to describe all their activities as 'play'. Adults would exclaim indulgently: 'Children keep playing all the time. When they start playing they forget everything.' Children also said this of themselves: 'We are children, we will play.'

This sentiment is echoed in an article[3] in *Kalyan*'s annual volume on Children: *Balakank* (Kalyan 1953). 'Children keep playing all the time. When they are not playing, they are either crying or sleeping. Their whole life's purpose is just this' (ibid.: 65). It is precisely this playfulness that the villagers and schoolteachers of Kasimpur, and the writer of this article in *Kalyan*, identify as the target of socialisation by adults. Here, I will digress briefly and present how this article argues for disciplining children's playfulness.

The proclivity for play is presented in opposition to work. The writer of the *Kalyan* article claims that play has no previous plan or design and it is independent, i.e., without reference to the larger social context. Both these aspects are believed to be undesirable. What Tagore sees in play, as revealing the child's charming innocence, the author of the article sees as actually demonstrating the child's ignorance of the adult world. Hence it is ignorance rather than innocence which prompts the child to equate his collection of shiny pebbles with his father's collection of coins. The author also plays up the so-called dangerous side of children's play—wanton destructiveness. Independence is portrayed negatively as wilfulness, as being destructive rather than constructive. Drawing on the positive and negative connotations of the word 'playful', he suggests that this 'playful attitude' is dangerous:

> Then the question arises, What? Will we treat this world as a plaything, and believe that our primary purpose is to be able to play with it? ... His play is also play, and destruction is also play. Do we want to propagate such a world? (Kalyan 1953: 65).

Obviously, the answer is no. This understanding of play rightly alights on its essentially independent character. Child psychologists point out that play is often a phase where we 'assimilate' the world into our own framework of understanding rather than just 'accommodate' to it (see, for example, Piaget 1951; Garvey 1977). But in this article the playful attitude, which centres on and permits the independence of the child, is seen as potentially anarchist. Thus, since the existing order in society must not be challenged, the playful character of the child should not be encouraged. The author condenses the wisdom contained in his argument in an Indian proverb he quotes: 'Jump and play, you'll become worthless' (Kalyan 1953: 65).[4]

Does this mean that, in spite of his popularity, the playful child-God Krishna cannot be a model for Indian children? Yes, and the article itself presents an argument to contain the contradiction between the cultural tradition of appreciating Krishna's childhood pranks, while at the same time discouraging play in children.[5] Preparing us for the distinction between Krishna and other children, the author writes: 'Krishna's childhood absorbs our mind completely. We cannot say the same of every cowherd's child' (Kalyan 1953: 65). Krishna is said to exhibit the quality of 'child-likeness' (*balvritti*), while ordinary children exhibit the undesirable quality of 'childishness' (*balishta*) which the author equates with ignorance and stupidity. Krishna's play is presented as being purposeful, infused with a 'divine purpose', the welfare of humanity. This divine play is therefore more like adult work and unlike what has already been claimed about ordinary children's play. In fact, the article argues that if work is performed with dedication, a growing sense of its purpose and with expertise, it becomes like divine play. The divine child is thus presented as the ideal adult—as the culmination of successful socialisation into the norms of the adult world: 'Our lives will be our play (*lila*) where duty, work and helping each other, these attitudes, like in play, will be pleasurable' (ibid.: 65).

Such an elaborate rational framework to contain contradictions was not articulated in the Kasimpur community; nor was there need for it. For teachers, adult villagers and the children themselves believed, categorically, that however enjoyable and entertaining, childhood play must be given up and replaced with work. They all believed that, in the school, strict discipline was necessary to discourage play, as were constant reminders of 'good qualities'.

Schooling for growing up

Children in the school seemed to have distinguished the school as a space where they were to be socialised into the norms of adult society, primarily by the teacher. They also felt that their own 'childish playfulness' would not find a place in the world shared by adults; they had to retreat with their playfulness into a private space which they shared with their peers, away from the adult gaze. This was a world characterised by things they enjoyed and laughed at—magic, comics, the absurd, errors of childish clumsiness or misunderstanding, and fights—all of which invited adult disapproval.

One day, when their teacher was not in the room, two children were giggling helplessly over something they were reading—an essay on making tea. I peeped at it and found it was quite a serious essay outlining the procedure of making tea. I asked them why they were laughing. They answered with a slightly aggressive air—'We are children, this is for us'—and went back to laughing. I overheard some of their exchanges and realised that they had not actually read the essay! Having read the title, they had read into and invented the rest of the text as one meant for the entertainment of children: an essay of follies while making tea involving upsetting the water, mixing wrong ingredients, etc.!!

Accounts of magic and fantastic, fearful creatures were exchanged: *vetals* or ghouls and flying snakes with red eyes that struck the forehead and back of the head. Comics were read surreptitiously. The children's emerging sexual awareness also seemed to belong to this world. Some of the boys exchanged meaningful glances and loud sounds on a few occasions when girls of their age group entered their classroom. Of course, the teacher was either not present or out of earshot. Sometimes, during *bal sabha*, their teacher Pavan Kumar, suddenly growing indulgent, would entertain them with a performance of absurd news items: 'In the neighbouring village a woman gave birth to seven puppies; yesterday, a cat drove the bus from Delhi to Narela village....' The children loved this and laughed uproariously.

As in the *Kalyan* articles, teachers seemed to believe that children were naughty and morally weak, unable to resist the seductive enjoyment of things that were taboo and (like infantile adults) incapable of recognising what was good for them.

EPISODE 4.2 (MORNING ASSEMBLY)

Nagpal (teacher): Every day we tell you matters relating to human values (*maanav moolya baten*). Animals are not told animal values. Because man falls out of the path of righteousness, but animals walk on their path. Therefore *haivan* (animal) is better.
He recited a poem which began with, 'Human, become an animal. (Ai manushya, tu haivan ban ja).'

Nagpal was suggesting that humans, unlike animals, need to be reminded about human values all the time. Otherwise they stray from the path of righteousness. It was believed that, while there were some students who were good and could learn things simply by being told about them, most children in the school could not learn unless they were beaten and scolded. The teachers were thus forced to beat them for their own good.

Otherwise, they would not learn anything. It was the responsibility of the school and the teachers to compel them to study by disciplining them. They were so used to listening to the rod that they would not understand words.[6]

EPISODE 4.3 (MORNING ASSEMBLY)

Surjeet (teacher): There are three kinds of students: (those) who are just good, who learn by telling, (those who learn through) beating and (those) who never learn. We teach you every day. We tell you things so well, but still you don't learn.... Many children look very straight, but do bad things quietly.

Like their teachers, children also felt that they were mischievous and needed disciplining. The teacher's authority, though irrationally exercised—sometimes even through student monitors—was experienced as an absolute power that inspired fear. Yet the children, like Ashok in the episode reported in the beginning of the chapter, seemed to think that this was essential for a good school, and for schooling to be successful.

EPISODE 4.4 (CLASS V)

There is compulsion here (*yahan pabandi hai*).
Why is there compulsion?
To make it a good school.
Without compulsion can't it be good?
No.
Why?
If you don't beat, children will become useless.

The English-medium schools, and the other schools that children talked about by name, like the Rai Sports School, had the reputation of being very strict and making students work very hard. It was for this reason that children wanted to study in those schools.

EPISODE 4.5 (CLASS V)

If you had full freedom, which school would you go to?
Navin: Shall I tell you?...
Tell me.
To an English-medium school. There they make you do lots of work, lots of work. From the time you are small. They give big-big letters (of the alphabet) to write. But I can memorise in just two minutes.

And here?
Here they don't make us work every day.

This discipline therefore constituted the school into a discontinuous space within which children could experience a different identity: as 'children-learning-the-ways-of-the-world'. They were conscious of themselves as growing up and preparing for an unknown but desirable adult world, and giving up their identities as children of the village. The discipline that coercively made students conscious of meeting different standards seemed to give the school its agency in secondary socialisation. Those children who responded positively to the discipline could aspire to become *bade admi*. The 'failures' were those who had not given up playfulness and had remained in the state of being children. Failure was taken to imply a lack of moral character—laziness and unwillingness—rather than a lack of intelligence. The stigma attached to the life and work of the illiterate adult also had this immoral element. The future consequences of present role choices were already familiar to the children. If you could become an *adarsh vidyarthi* (model student) in school, then you could aspire to be a *bada admi*[7] when you grew up. If you stayed a playful child, you would be a failure and grow up into an *anpadh* (illiterate).

One perspective suggested by the schematisation presented in Figure 4.1 is that by postponing entry into the adult world of work, a childhood has been created which takes on its distinctive character around schooling and preparation for adulthood. It is a period of learning and growing up, without productive work. In contrast, those who opt out of school, and

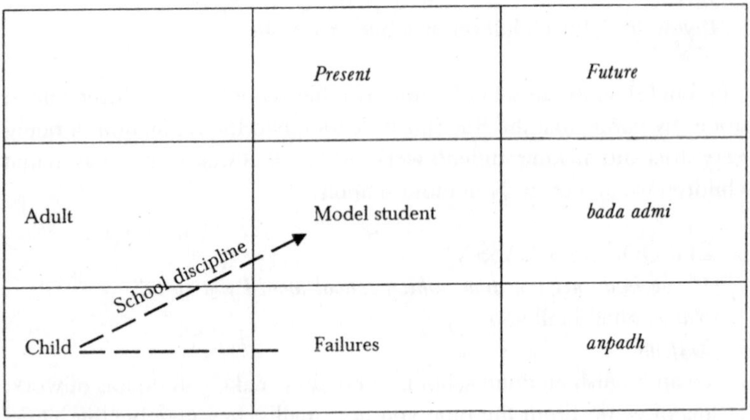

	Present	*Future*
Adult	Model student	*bada admi*
Child	Failures	*anpadh*

Figure 4.1 Schema of Options in Childhood in Relation to Adult Futures

therefore into a world of work that is available to children, do not experience this childhood. It is such a model of childhood—a model of childhood happiness that is conditional on freedom from work—that has inspired much international legislation and, above all, the Convention of the Rights of the Child. By implication, metaphors such as 'living outside childhood', 'losing childhood' and 'being robbed of childhood', which are used in the context of children who work, seem justified (Nieuwenhuys 2000: 45–46).

Looking again at the schematisation in Figure 4.1, when we examine the nature of the categories, we find that the children-as-model-students are actually less like children and more like adults. Ram-Prasad (nd) points out that it is this adult-like quality that is regarded as admirable in Lord Rama's childhood. Of the three divine childhoods he analyses—Krishna, Kartikeya and Rama—he finds that Rama presents the most conservative paradigm of youth. Not surprisingly, the playful Krishna is the most radical. The children in Kasimpur who have a childhood free of 'work' also give up 'play'. The illiterate adult is devalued and childish. The understanding of childhood that we see here is not the ideological basis for either the modern anti-child labour or the child rights rhetoric.

II
Model Students and Failures

The setting is Class V of the Government Boys' Model Primary School. The short break had just ended. I was in the classroom with about 30 boys, teaching them to make paper birds. Their teacher had not yet come in. The children were clamouring for the square newspaper pieces that I was distributing. They completely ignored my calls that I would give them the papers one by one. They crowded around me, pushing and trying to grab the papers, which I held aloft, out of their reach. Then their class teacher entered. Quickly, as the boys realised this, order was restored: they scampered to their places on the *tat-pattis* (long mats) on the floor and the room became quiet. Then their teacher, Bhardwaj, spoke:

EPISODE 4.6 (CLASS V)
Look, this madam, she tries to make you understand, so gently. We are very strict with you. We don't have even 1 per cent of the affection she has. Still you don't want to obey her. Then what is the use of learning?

He asked them if they had seen a recent television programme about Shruti Verma, a famous pandvani *artist.*[8] *Many children excitedly said yes, they had. Bhardwaj began telling them the story of her life, recounting episodes that had been shown on television. Many of the children who had seen the programme excitedly echoed and contributed details, which Bhardwaj ignored completely. He then went on to describe an episode in which a piece of paper is brought to her for her signature. At this point he raised his voice, infused it with shock and contempt, and said:* She used her thumb print to sign! The thumb print is the way to recognise the illiterate man. I am saying this to you, because if you can learn by heart, but you can't write, then there is no measure of your being educated. With difficult words, you still put '*badi ee ki matra*' instead of '*chhoti ee*', and that is very bad for your *pehchaan* (identity). So I am giving you *shrut lekh* (dictation)—that which is heard and written.

In this episode Bhardwaj used a pedagogic strategy that many of us must have experienced in our childhood. This is the ability of the teacher to draw from small episodes of bad behaviour dire moral consequences which are then used to justify tedious and unpleasant pedagogic tasks on hand. In this case dictation was not a punishment; bad behaviour justified the need for dictation. But this episode does more than demonstrate the teacher's consummate skill in such deductive reasoning which draws on a framework that links morality with learning through discipline. Bhardwaj drew on Shruti Verma's story to emphasise the stigma attached to illiteracy. He seemed to suggest that even Shruti Verma, a successful and popular artist, could not escape this stigma, and ultimately *gave away her true identity*—she was not just illiterate, she was 'an' illiterate. Using this as a contrast, he directed them to pay attention to developing attributes that would assist in the formation of their identities as 'educated men'. He used the word '*pehchaan*', which means recognition, and which is loosely translated to mean 'identity'. But this word suggests what commentators have pointed out: that in the Indian context identity is not simply a matter of what you think of yourself; it is more a matter of what others recognise you to be (Vaidyanathan 1989: 153).

Model student (*Adarsh vidyarthi*)

Various attributes of the model student were actively promoted in the school through many different modes. Morning assembly provided occasions for much direct moralising, relating folk stories and recounting biographies of leaders, oath taking, making comparisons with the *'sishya'* as model and rewarding exemplary students.

Direct moralising: Direct moralising involved stating various do's and don'ts, particularly advocating good character, personal hygiene and neat appearance.

EPISODE 4.7 (MORNING ASSEMBLY)
Headmaster: Everyday we tell you some good things, in order to put good habits into you. You will become good citizens. Cleanliness of the body is good. How many of you didn't have a bath this morning?
Many hands went up.
It is a good thing you are honest and have raised your hands, but try and have a bath in the morning and come... How many children's finger nails are overgrown and black?
Hands went up.
... And when you walk on the road, walk on the left and don't talk. Meditate every day. That way your brain (*buddhi*) will grow.

Aspects of general good character such as regularity, honesty and politeness were also emphasised. They were also given the quality of being 'core values'.

EPISODE 4.8 (CLASS V)
Bhardwaj: You can also be a PM.
Manoj: He is also human *ji.*
Bhardwaj (generally addressing the whole class): You can be a *tehsildar.*
Ajay: I will be a magician.
Manoj: Someone like Sanjay, what will he be?
Bhardwaj: Why? He can be anything.
Manoj: But he doesn't study *ji.*
Bhardwaj: So what? That doesn't matter. He can earn money and do something else. It is important that his words be good and sweet.

Speaking about their educated relatives, villagers also observed: 'What is the use of their education when they do not know how to behave?' This suggested that moral character, also associated with good citizenship, was believed to be the heart of education and a core value. Personal hygiene and cleanliness were also a prominent preoccupation. Teachers felt that the villagers did not observe suitable norms and complained: 'Your parents do not even bathe you before sending you to school.' They spoke frankly about the importance of regular bowel movements and cleaning ears.

EPISODE 4.9 (MORNING ASSEMBLY)

Kapil (teacher) made a speech in which he told them about health and about having a bath every day: Because you sweat, and the body gets rid of all kinds of dirt through sweat. Like the ear—dirt keeps coming out of it. Some people put in pins to clean their ears. This must never be done. You must not put things into your ears...
Even as the speech was going on, Surjeet was going around, cuffing the boys and getting them to sit in straight lines. He cuffed even the very young boys in Classes I and II.

Good habits and cleanliness were presented as the marks by which good students could be recognised. They were listed as do's and don'ts: don't read comics, don't watch films, read good books, listen to your elders, obey your elders, study hard, work hard, study every day, be honest, be clean, have a bath every day, don't tell lies, speak softly, use the right pronunciation of words, practise and make your handwriting neat, never make a noise, don't cheat/copy, etc.

EPISODE 4.10 (MORNING ASSEMBLY)

It was the day that all the Class V boys had been waiting for, 31 March. Their results were to be announced. At assembly time, the headmaster first gave a speech. He told them: You are going to a school where no copying will work. There each child will get a different paper.... *He continued to tell them about inculcating good habits, respecting older people, etc. Towards the end of the speech, he said:* So that you may improve your life, we tell you good things.

There were some specific references to school work such as wearing the correct uniform, developing good handwriting and memorising daily lessons. On two occasions, children were made to take oaths to give up practices that were believed to interfere with schooling. Once they had to swear not to see movies or watch television. Some of the children later told me that they took the oath, but they had the fingers of one hand crossed behind their back so that the oath was cancelled. They knew that it wouldn't be possible for them to keep such an oath and did not want the complications and unpleasant consequences of breaking it. The teacher Bhardwaj, too, was critical of the headmaster making the children take an oath which would be so difficult to keep. On another occasion in Class V, each child made his own promise of adopting some good habit that he would henceforth practise.

Folk-tales: Stories about students, folk heroes and mythological heroes such as Rama and Yudhisthira were recounted; following the common belief about the pedagogic importance of stories, morals were always drawn from them for students. These highlighted desirable traits such as complete obedience and perseverance. On another occasion during assembly, after the *gayatri mantra* had been recited, there was a break of nearly three minutes. The teachers seemed undecided about what to do. Then Pavan Kumar announced that he would tell a story:

EPISODE 4.11 (MORNING ASSEMBLY)
'Princess Leban' (a Russian folk-tale). The story was very long, and continued for about 15 minutes. Everyone listened very attentively. It was about a prince who has many adventures while searching for the princess he wants to marry. Every now and then, Pavan Kumar translated a word into English: 'I want to marries (sic) *her* [9]*–hum marriage rachayenge', 'fight–*ladai–*kiya'. At the end, he moralised:* What do we learn from this? That the prince did not lose heart. Now this is not the age for you to go after princesses. Now you must study. Every day, wake up in the morning and till late at night, if you do your lessons, then you will earn sweet fruits (sweet rewards).

On another occasion the story of the honest woodcutter, who would not lie and was therefore rewarded by the gods, was also related. The moral, 'honesty is the best policy',[10] was expounded. Both these stories suggested that it was important, or enough, to pursue immediate concerns with dedication, without worrying about how they connected with the larger scheme of things; if there was enough dedication, it would definitely bring good rewards. Especially in the story of Princess Leban and the prince, dogged perseverance and hard work, even in the face of troubles and 'obvious' dead ends, were portrayed as traits which brought very desirable rewards. The same quality was echoed in a folk-tale about a guru and his *sishya* (student), which is recounted in the section on the *sishya* as an ideal. It seemed that students were being urged not to consider the apparent rationality or irrationality underlying the activities they were undertaking, but to pursue them doggedly and in good faith.

Biographies of national leaders: The lives of great leaders, especially the 'national' leaders, were recounted with the expectation that children would learn something and draw inspiration from them. The 'preachings' of these great people were also supposed to provide maxims by which to live.

EPISODE 4.12 (MORNING ASSEMBLY)
It was Indira Gandhi's birthday. During assembly Nagpal (teacher) eulogised her. He related the story of her life and her prime ministership. Glossing over the Emergency period, he said: Emergency mein unhone kuchh gadbad kiya (she created some confusion/made some mistakes during the Emergency). *At the end, after he spoke of her death as martyrdom, he went on to add that her message was: Kadi mehnat karo...door ki bat socho. Satyameva jayate, shrama eva jayate* (work hard and you will achieve success—think of the future. Truth always wins, hard work always wins). If you work hard, you will become a leader of the nation.
The assembly ended with the children clapping and shouting popular electioneering slogans like 'Indira Gandhi amar rahe!' (Long live Indira Gandhi!).

In the case of Indira Gandhi, the moral to be learnt was 'work hard'—hard work can bring every kind of success. Other leaders whose life stories were recounted during assembly were Maulana Azad, Lal Bahadur Shastri and Lala Hardayal, from whom the main teaching to be learnt was: work hard and you will succeed. In the story reported in Episode 4.13, the moral was: follow rules, and you will succeed.

EPISODE 4.13 (MORNING ASSEMBLY)
Surjeet (teacher): There was a man named Ramamurthy, who wrote books. He did an MA. On a board in his room it was written: 'Do-or-die.' (*He translated this into Hindi: Karo ya maro.*) He did yoga and other exercises and became strong. Many places he showed his strength, breaking ropes, stopping a jeep. He did a PhD and became a doctor. This was when India and Pakistan were one. There was a Muslim, Gama. He was a world champion. Someone else wrote to Ramamurthy and challenged him. He accepted. And he defeated him (*i.e., Ramamurthy defeated Gama in a wrestling match*). It is important to be a scholar and also to be strong. There are rules, for good health there are rules. And to become a scholar, obey your guru*ji* and obey the orders of your parents.

Exemplary students: On a few occasions, the teachers identified some students as model students and referred to specific virtues they had exhibited. One such student was Vipin of Class V. He had won the painting competition at the block level. Announcing this award during assembly, the headmaster gave him Rs 10 as an additional reward: 'His good name will go back home before him and many other people will also come to know.' Another such child was Shankar.

EPISODE 4.14 (MORNING ASSEMBLY)
Shankar was singled out and praised because, through the whole year, he had never taken even a single day's leave. The headmaster decided to give him an award of Rs 10.
Kapil (teacher) observed to the gathering: We need such children who will achieve something in any field.
The headmaster continued, talking about the importance of attendance: Those children who have full attendance, they will be an inspiration. Imitation is a good quality. It is a good attribute to copy, but copy good children.

On the day the Class V children got their report cards and left the school, for high school, Shankar was identified as the student with '100 per cent' attendance and as a diligent, serious student. The children in the school *kho-kho* (a popular game) team had won their matches against the other schools in the block. Following this, they were held up as models of what one can achieve if one practices very regularly and diligently.

The *sishya* (disciple) as an ideal: References were made to the good qualities of *sishyas* or disciples, particularly of complete obedience to elders and teachers, showing respect to them and being attentive. One such story was a folk-tale of a guru and his *sishya* which Bhardwaj told his students (Class V):

Every day a guru worshipped stone idols of gods and made a ritual offering of food to them. Once, he had to go away for a few days and he asked his sishya *to continue the worship in his absence and make sure to feed the idols. The* sishya *did as he was told and worshipped the idols. He made the offering of food and waited for them to eat. When the idols did not eat, he became concerned and begged them to come and eat, so that he would not be in danger of disobeying his guru's instruction of feeding the idols. When the idols still did not oblige him, he became angry and threatened to beat them unless they came and accepted his offering. The gods were so pleased by his innocent devotion that they made an appearance and ate the food.*

The children loved this story. They seemed to have heard it several times before but were not bored. They waited eagerly for the part when the *sishya* threatens to beat the idols with a fat stick. From this story, Bhardwaj drew the moral on the need to obey the guru. In the story, blind obedience to the guru's orders, even when they seemed to be irrational, brought unexpected rewards that the guru himself had not foreseen. On one occasion during assembly, one of the teachers, Kapil, expounded on five qualities of a good student:

EPISODE 4.15 (MORNING ASSEMBLY)
Kapil (teacher): There are five traits of a student (*vidyarthi*): perseverance like a crow, concentration like a stork... do you know why?
Many children shouted: Ji, because that's how the stork catches fish. He stands on one leg, and concentrates and catches fish.
Kapil acknowledged this and continued: If you find good things, immediately internalise them. Sleep like a dog. Then they (*sishyas*) are *alpahari*—those who eat less. If they give you four *rotis*, how many should you eat?
The children shouted: Three.
Kapil: And *sadachari*, one whose behaviour is good. And sleep less. Why should you be like this?
One child shouted and several others affirmed and echoed his answer: Because if anyone throws a stone, we should be alert and dodge it.
Kapil: But why should a student be like this?
Again, one child shouted and several others affirmed and echoed his answer: Because we must be alert. If a thief comes at night, we should be able to catch him. If we keep sleeping, we won't know he has come.

This speech was based on a popular Sanskrit verse on the qualities of a *sishya*:

Svannidra bakula dhyanam, kaka cesta tathaiva cha,
Alpahari sadachari vidyarthi panchalakshanam.[11]

Here, the qualities of good character, perseverance and the more Brahminical traits of self-denial were mentioned. It was amusing to listen to
the children who were all keenly following Kapil's talk; however, instead
of responding to the underlying moral message, they gave the verse a
very pragmatic, everyday-life-oriented interpretation.

An inventory of various traits and attributes of the *adarsh vidyarthi* is
presented in Table 4.1. They have been classified to indicate the mode
used and grouped thematically into three broad areas: personal hygiene,
general aspects of good character and specific aspects identifiable with
school or students. These three areas of concern are also echoed in
Kalyan's volumes on education and childhood: the traits listed refer mainly
to external and behavioural characteristics. *Pehchaan* means recognition:
the use of this word suggests that one's identity is determined by what
others recognise one to be. It is therefore important to signal your identity
through appropriate external marks through which your type can be
recognised. The external and behavioural traits listed under 'the marks of
an educated man', or what the teachers in the school referred to as *'padhe-
likhe admi ki pehchaan'*, are those markers through which students could
signal their identity as *adarsh vidyarthis* and which, in the future, would
enable them to be recognised as educated men.

On several occasions students themselves echoed the sentiments of their
teachers on the role of the ideal student, indicating their own desire to
exemplify that role and aspire for it. Most certainly, acceptability in the
adult world was supposed to hinge on their ability to show how many of
these ideal behavioural traits they had internalised. On 'public occasions',
such as assembly time, *bal sabhas*, or even in their classrooms, where they
knew they were under the scrutiny of their teachers and the headmaster,
they made sure they said things that were 'politically correct'. These
included reciting stories,[12] patriotic songs, poems and essays on the lives
of important people that had been rote-learnt from guidebooks. They often
took great trouble to let their teachers know that they were obedient and
dutiful.

EPISODE 4.16 (CLASS IV)

Deepak: Look, anything starts from the smallest and then we learn the
biggest things. I always note and Guru*ji* also says. Look, 'from the atom
and the molecule the ant was formed. And they took the form of the
entire world and universe' *(lines from their morning prayer)*. Just think,

Table 4.1 Inventory of Traits and Qualities of an *Adarsh Vidyarthi*

Mode	Theme		
	General Good Character	Specific to School/Students	Personal Hygiene
Direct moralising	Be regular/be honest/ don't tell lies/speak softly and politely.	Read good books, no comics or films/ don't copy or cheat/ memorise your lessons everyday.	Bathe every morning/ clean the ears and nose/ regular bowel movements/ dress neatly in clean clothes/comb hair/ clean cut nails and clean hands, wash before eating.
Marks of the educated man: *padhe-likhe admi ki pehchaan*	Be respectful/speak sweetly, with right pronunciation.	Make your handwriting neat/spell correctly/be neat and clean.	
Oath taking	'I will not see TV or films.' 'I will do my duty.'	'I will read good books.' 'I will do what I have to regularly.'	'I will eat fruits everyday.'
Sishya	Obedience/showing respect.	Concentration/alertness/ eating less/sleeping less/ good character/Attentiveness to teacher.	

(Table 4.1 continued)

| | Theme | | |
Mode	General Good Character	Specific to School/Students	Personal Hygiene
Stories: traditional/folk	Honest woodcutter: honesty brings rewards. Princess Leban: persevere and toil and reap rewards. 'Like in the Ramayan they say we should be obedient.' 'Like Yudhisthira we should not lose courage.'	Blind obedience to guru's order brings rewards. Work hard, study hard. Obey elders and succeed, disobey and fail.	
Biographies of leaders	Indira Gandhi: Truth always wins, hard work always wins. Maulana Azad: Work hard. Shastri: Work hard, do your duty. Lala Hardayal: Fearless opposition, perseverance. Ramamurthy: Follow rules for success.	Study hard/obey teachers, parents. Regularity/hard work/practice	
Exemplary students			

from small to big. *Later, he continued:* Like in the Ramayan they say
we should be obedient, like Yudhisthir we should not lose courage.

What does the *adarsh vidyarthi* symbolise?

An article on the guru–*sishya* relationship[13] in *Kalyan*'s annual volume on
education *Siksankh* (Kalyan 1988), claims:

> *Moksha* (emancipation) is the ultimate aim/goal of tradition (*sam-
> pradaya*), and without the guru's guidance it is not possible. This proves
> the importance of the guru... The Mundakopanishad says clearly that
> learning (*vidya*) must be got straight from the guru's mouth (ibid.: 257).

Having thus established the all-important role of the guru, the author goes
on to present the qualities that a good *sishya* must have, according to the
Sarada Tilaka[14]:

> Noble, decent, clean *atma* (soul), engrossed in manliness, at ease with
> the study of Vedas, immersed in work, well-wisher of life-forms, en-
> grossed in religious and social obligations, working for the well-being
> of father and mother with devotion, in complete service of the guru
> with body, mind, voice and wealth, completely unconscious of pride
> of *jati*, following the guru's orders and ready to give up one's own work
> in preference for the guru's, and full of devotion, obedience and well-
> wishing toward the guru (ibid.: 260).

All the qualities that the *Sarada Tilaka* lists emphasise the importance of
obedience to the guru's will. Whatever one knows is because it is revealed
by the guru. 'Not only ordinary knowledge, but even knowledge of Brah-
man can be realised through respect for the guru and following his com-
mand obediently with devotion and respect' (ibid.: 260). The article also
claims that 'like Svetaketu, Prahlad, Nachiketa and Dhruv,[15] everything
can be gained by going to a guru and following him completely' (ibid.:
260).

An article on 'Model Students' presents four stories.[16] Three of them—
Eklavya, Aruni and Upamanyu—involve the *sishya*'s obedience to the
instruction of the guru at great cost to the self. Eklavya lost his archer
thumb, Upamanyu suffered blindness and Aruni lost his life as they placed
their unhesitating devotion to their guru and their determination to carry
out his orders over their personal gain. The narrator is full of admiration

for them, glorifying them as ideal students. These stories, like the folk-tale about the innocent devotion of the *sishya*, place the guru's actions and deeds outside the boundaries of rational enquiry by students—closed to examination, questioning or even understanding. What is important for students is not reflecting on the rationality, content or intention of the guru's instruction, but simple obedience. Obedience in and by itself brings rewards. The traits listed hinge on the importance of accepting the ration-ality of a larger scheme of things. Traits such as questioning, investigating or independent decision-making are conspicuous by their absence. Ulti-mately, as Vaidyanathan (1989) has noted, it is the idea of submission to elders, especially the guru, which governs Indian behaviour and concep-tion of self, and that also forms the cornerstone of the student's identity.[17]

The extent to which the *Kalyan* version of the characteristics of the good student permeates the Kasimpur boys' school is startling. It is clearly reflective of the popular and folkloric construction of teaching–learning and knowledge being brought into the secular–modern institution of school. The good student personifies all those moral values that the trad-itional society cherished and promoted. The theme of 'good character', which stresses the importance of mechanical obedience, doing one's duty for its own sake and proper conduct in the presence of parents and elders, is dominant in Table 4.1. Attention to personal hygiene also compares well with the general 'Hindu' preoccupation with cleanliness and purity. Overall, these traits of the *adarsh vidyarthi* are the same as those of the *sishya*.

Failures

Graubard (1974: 206) observes that 'failure' is the essential nightmare of modern culture, and that in order to be successful one must learn to dream of failure. In stark contrast to the *adarsh vidyarthi*, who seemed destined to become a *bada admi*, the *anpadh* (illiterate or unschooled) was held up to the child as a symbol of failure of a very fundamental kind. It was as if the illiterate lacked the very essence of what made someone a respectable human being. As reported earlier in Episode 4.6, even successful and world-famous Shruti Verma could not escape this stigma. Children were fearful of this future; they would not be able to find any regular job and would have to beg. They would have to face insults and physical abuse. They would have to toil in a traditional job or they would be forced to take up the lowliest kinds of work—like washing other people's *jhoota* vessels—uncertain at every moment of what would come next. Every class had a few aspiring *adarsh vidyarthis* who were given, or themselves created, occasions to demonstrate their good qualities. But there were also the groups of 'failures'—grim reminders for everyone, of those who had remained children, playful and unwilling to learn. In Episode 4.17, Surya Prakash revealed how stigmatising the label of failure, or not passing, was for all children and how tense they all were about passing.

EPISODE 4.17 (CLASS IV)

Surya Prakash: My heart wishes 'let me pass'. Bakri's heart also wishes 'let me pass', but he failed.
Why do they fail people?
Because they can't read and write.
Why is that necessary?
They say, if you can't read and write, what use are you?

Bakri, whose real name was Rajinder, was so called because of his un-canny resemblance to a goat. He was quite severely mentally handicapped, but even he desperately wanted the label 'pass'. Both sections of Class IV had groups of children who were designated by the label 'failure'. Some of them had not been promoted to Class V because they were certain to fail in the examinations and thus lower the result of the school. The extent to which these children were degraded was dramatic. They were physically separated from the rest of the class: grouped together in a row at one end, they were not allowed to sit in other parts of the classroom. Also, almost none of the other children ever sat with them. Surya Prakash told me that earlier, they used to all sit together as a class, but ever since Asha took over as class teacher, she made them sit separately.

Generally, it was believed that these children could not yet read and write. Even after four years in school, they had not picked up these elemen-tary skills. Several children pointed out the row to me, identifying them as failures and adding: 'They cannot read or write.' Whether said contemp-tuously by the teacher or the other children, or said with resignation by the failures themselves, this was the only reason cited for the typification.

EPISODE 4.18 (CLASS IV)

I sat in the failures' row, next to Irshad and Hasan. A social studies lesson was going on. But I carried on a soft conversation with them:
Have you both been in this school from the start?
Both: Yes.
(To Hasan) ***What are you writing?***
Hasan just smiled.

Dharmendar, who was sitting in the row in front of us, turned around:
Ho! Can you read?
There was no reply from Hasan.
(More softly to Hasan) **Can you read?**
Irshad smiled tentatively: (We) can't read.
Why?
Irshad: Thick head (*mota dimag*).
Hasan did not reply, studiously kept copying.
Dharmendar again taunted: Can you read?
Irshad asked him: Can YOU read?
Dharmendar: Of course.
(He pointed to a word in the Hindi text and showed it to Irshad. Irshad could not read it.)
Dharmendar read it out: Neeraj.
Irshad: Then why are you sitting here? Go to the next row.
Irshad (to me): Aunty, ask him how much is 10 and 10. (*He pointed to Dharmendar and his neighbour sitting in front.*)
I asked as directed. There was no reply from them. Irshad looked as if he had made his point and proved to them that they still belonged in the failures' row.
(I asked Irshad) **How much is it?**
Irshad: 20.
And 20 and 10?
Irshad: 30.
Your brain isn't thick.
Irshad (long pause): What else? The brain is thick. Of this whole line.
How did it become thick?
No answer. Irshad got engrossed in his textbook. I repeated the question after a gap.
Irshad: When everyone starts to read, they sing songs and see pictures (movies).
He began copying out question-answers from the guidebook. In between, he and Hasan (pretended to) correct each other's work—putting a dot here and a dot there. Once, Hasan nudged Irshad and told him: Go, Aunty will beat.
Hasan had finished 'writing' the poem and was now reciting it, but following the text with his finger as though he were actually reading. Then suddenly, he stopped reciting/ 'reading' and began participating in the social studies lesson going on, chorusing the tag phrase 'hoti hai' along with the rest of the class.

Irshad was offended by Dharmendar's taunting question: 'Can you read?'. Of course he couldn't. Otherwise, would he be in the failures' row? It was in that sense that he reacted to Dharmendar's demonstration of reading skill: 'If you can read, why are you in this row?' Although he too was sitting in the failures' row, Dharmendar had learnt to read. On a later date I asked him when he had acquired the skill, why and how.

EPISODE 4.19 (CLASS IV)
Why don't they teach farming?
Surya Prakash: Don't know. The HM (headmaster) makes the boys do work. The ones in the *kachcha* line—he makes them do work. Keeps calling them out. Aunty makes them sit separately. Sonu, he's gone out—to do work. Dharmendar, he can read, still Aunty doesn't let them sit in the *pakka* line. I don't know why. They didn't know earlier how to read. We used to all sit together. Then Aunty made them sit separately.
I asked Dharmendar: Why doesn't she let you sit with the others?
Because we can't do problems.
When did you learn to read?
When Aunty made us sit separately.
How?
Surya Prakash: He said to his mother, get me a cycle and I will study. Since he got his cycle, he studies regularly...Shobhraj must be begging now. He used to study a lot. He used to come first. I liked him very much.... *Didi*, the stories of Vikram Vetal are real. They used to happen in front of Dilli Gate.
How do you know?
My *dadi* tells me stories of earlier times.
(To Dharmendar) Why did you learn to read?
To pass.
How did you learn?
By cycling you can learn.
How?
Surya Prakash: I'll tell you. He'll cycle a bit, then come in and his mother will teach him, then again he will cycle and come in and his mother will teach him.
Why is it necessary to pass?
Dharmendar: To save one's pride (*izzat bachane ke liye*).

Surya Prakash thought it was unfair that Dharmendar had to continue to sit in the failures' row after he had mastered reading and writing. Dharmendar, though, did not protest. He had found another reason why he should still be there: his inability to add and subtract. It was this that Irshad had exposed earlier when he asked Dharmendar to add 10 and 10. Dharmendar, when he said it was necessary to pass to save one's pride, was re-echoing the general sentiment that literacy was absolutely necessary for one's self-worth.

Why couldn't the failures learn? Irshad thought it was because he had a thick head; so when the teacher asked them to read, he felt like singing or watching movies. Surya Prakash and Dharmendar seemed to suggest that the failures could learn once they began studying regularly. When Dharmendar, motivated by the acquisition of his cycle, began to spend time studying at home with his mother, he was able to learn reading. The children, and certainly the teachers, felt failure was on account of the child's own inherent incapacity. The 'thick head' or 'low IQ' was believed to make children unwilling to study, unresponsive to discipline and forgetful. Only Sulaiman, a non-failure from Class IV, suggested that something other than the child may be responsible: 'It's *vidya*, comes to some and not to others.'

Surya Prakash's use of the terms *kachcha line* and *pakka line* to respectively describe the failures and others (who would pass) signified the perception of their tenure in school. '*Kachcha*', raw or temporary, suggested that the failures' continuation in school was not confirmed—they could soon expect to leave the school and join the world of work and the illiterates outside. '*Pakka*' indicated those whose membership in the student community was confirmed and permanent. These were children who would most likely be studying further. It was taken for granted that the failures were headed for manual, unskilled jobs that would be physically exhausting:

Jogi (Class IV), pointing to the failures in his class: They won't get jobs. They'll have to lift loads.
Renu (Class V, LAPS): (The one) who fails does farming.

As Surya Prakash observed, even within school, whenever there was manual work to be done the headmaster called upon the '*kachcha*' line. In the first week of February, the whole group of failures was engaged for several days in re-laying the cobbles on part of the school ground. Sanjay, the only failure in Class V, was often called out to the school field to collect dried leaves and paper scraps.

The teachers and other children treated failures as objects of ridicule or contempt. In Asha's class they were virtually ostracised and completely excluded from all the regular proceedings of the class. She only made sure they were busy doing something all the time. They could, if they wished, copy the things she put on the blackboard for the other children, or just copy anything from their guidebooks or other books. She wanted them to be busy and quiet. Almost none of the children in class spoke or played with them (except Surya Prakash and Bir Singh). When I talked to them, I was advised by the children: 'Don't ask them. They are failures. They can't answer. Aunty makes them sit separately. She never asks them anything. They can't read and write even.'

In Nagpal's Class IV, the ostracisation was not so complete. From time to time, Nagpal attempted to include the failures in the lessons by asking them questions that were considered simpler. But they would usually stand mum and abashed, or give random, wild answers that would make the whole class roar with laughter.

EPISODE 4.20 (CLASS IV)
Nagpal was checking the books of the children in the failures' line: This is also wrong... this is also wrong.
Naresh, sitting two rows ahead of me in the same line, turned back, caught my eye and exclaimed amusedly: None of them know!
For the next 10 minutes, the line of failures became a source of amusement for the entire class because Nagpal decided to have one of them, Nawab Ali, stand up and provide answers at every step of the algorithm being done on the blackboard.
Every answer was wrong. For '0 minus 5?', he answered '0'. He failed to recall 7 times 5, 7 times 3, or even answer 'yes' or 'no' as a response to the algorithm question 'will it go?' (can it be subtracted without carry?)
At each point there were other voices prompting him. Nawab Ali's confusion was very apparent; he fidgeted and twisted each time he had to say something. It was quite obvious that he was repeating any answer that reached his ear. Every time he made a mistake, which was every time he spoke, the whole class roared with laughter. And he kept grinning with embarrassment.

Social class of the failures: All the children who were failures came either from Scheduled Caste families native to Kasimpur village, or from migrant families who had come to Kasimpur seeking work. Their fathers were either unemployed or employed in the unorganised sector. Two of the children's mothers also worked in the unorganised sector. Not all children from this socio-economic group were failures. But no child who was not of this socio-economic group was a failure. That is, none of the students from higher socio-economic classes or castes were failures. There were no 'failures' in the private school, LAPS.

*

The primary school in most Indian villages is an institution established by the state following its agenda of development through 'modernisation'— a paradigm that recognises education as the most important vehicle through which people can acquire a 'modern' rationality. The school has also been viewed as an object of reform, from a liberal–humanistic perspective on childhood and learning. More recently, it has been projected as a refuge from child labour, as an arena where children's childhood can be preserved and protected from work. However, we see that in Kasimpur this space of the school, once created, resonates with voices and images, rituals and practices that bear little or no relation to either the modernist or liberal–humanist agenda, and even contradict that rationality. The children in Kasimpur village who enjoy 'childhood' submit to a regimen built on the notion of incompleteness of the child and the need to grow up—by giving up traits such as playfulness and by being more adult-like. The future world of the adult acts on the present in the form of a coercive, evaluative discipline. The fear of entering into the stigmatised world of the illiterate seems to coerce the 'failures' to continue their ritual participation in the processes of schooling, hopeful of postponing entry into this immediate future if not miraculously escaping from it. Explanations such as laziness and *mota dimag* seem to provide these children with new reasons, now attributable to individual characteristics, for being at the bottom of the social pile.

Based on the discussion in this chapter it is possible to understand a common experience of people involved with initiatives that try to reform primary school curricula by introducing play and activities. When grafted onto a framework/theory of childhood and schooling in which play must be given up, they do not thrive. If they survive, it is often in a devalued form—as a way to attract children to school and to be used only in the first six months of Class I as a method meant for children who are not educable. Parents of children in government schools are also suspicious of new, experimental curricula where there are many activities for children which seem to extend the period of childhood in school rather than enabling children to grow out of it. Teachers themselves, unconvinced or unable to appreciate the pedagogic and cognitive worth of alternative curricula from their own theoretical resources, are in no position to convince the parents and community that the intentions are otherwise.

It seems that apart from the idea of IQ, which some teachers referred to as an explanation for the so-called 'backwardness' of the village children, other modern ideas on childhood or education have not penetrated or found a place in the framework of local beliefs. In the next chapter on the relationship of the teacher and the pupil, we again find evidence that schooling seems to be organised largely on the intellectual support of cultural stereotypes and everyday beliefs.

Notes

1. The use of the three terms, 'local', 'indigenous' and 'traditional', is to emphasise that although found within the school, these conceptions and theories are not the universal, pan-Indian, humanistic conceptions on which the educational policy of the Indian state is structured, for example the National Policy on Education, 1986 (Government of India 1986). This chapter shows the extent to which conceptions and theories are drawn from local, folk, popular and traditional motifs and ideas about children and schooling. The roles and relationships of teachers and students are explored in Chapter V. In anthropological literature, a variety of terms, including 'folk' and 'everyday', are also used when speaking about theories and ideas which are not a part of the dominant Western/scientific paradigm. These terms and their connotations are contested and far from unambiguous (see, e.g., Agrawal 1995). Antweiler (1998) presents a useful analysis of the diversity of terms used for 'local' knowledge and the range of connotations—from factual knowledge to complex belief systems—and the methods used to elicit, document and analyse local knowledge. He calls attention to the dynamism and pluralism of local 'knowledges' and their interactions with each other. I have drawn upon this insight in the last chapter of this book in the section 'Whither Schooling'.

2. The analysis presented here is taken from papers presented at the DHIIR Conference: Creating the Future, the Use and Abuse of Indian Role Models, University of Cambridge (Sarangapani 1998) and at the International Conference: Rethinking Childhood, Bondy, France (Sarangapani 2000).

3. 'Balvritti ki anupam mahima' by Dada Dharmadhikari in Kalyan (1953), pp. 65–66. Translations mine.

4. The entire proverb is 'Padhoge likhoge hoge nawab; kheloge kudoge hoge kharab': 'read, write, you will become a nawab, play, jump, you will become worthless/spoilt'. The article quotes only the second part.

5. In an essay exploring conceptions of youthfulness that can be derived from narratives of three divine incarnations popular among Hindus—Rama, Kartikeya and Krishna—Ram Prasad (nd) notes that while for the devout, the divine provides guiding ideals for human life, it may also be that an understanding of divinity consists in distinguishing

its nature from human nature. The author of the article in *Kalyan* seems to have opted for this second understanding of the divine to deal with the radical paradigm presented by Krishna's childhood.

6. One also heard the Hindi proverb '*Laton ke bhoot, baton se nahin mante*', which roughly translates to mean: 'The ones/ghosts who are used to beating/who are beaten, will not/ cannot listen to/be made to agree by the means of words.'

7. The '*bada admi*' ambition was discussed in the Chapter III in the section 'Why is schooling important?'

8. The *pandvani* is a traditional folk style of recounting stories from the Mahabharat from the Chhatisgarh region of Central India. The popular artiste, Shruti Verma, has the unique distinction of being both a woman artist and from a low caste. She began performing on stage at a very young age. A few days before this episode, the government television channel, Doordarshan, had telecast a short feature on her in the prime time slot.

9. The grammatical error is in the original.

10. The moral was first stated in Hindi, and then repeated in English. It suggested an added truth value that the moral acquired, by virtue of being an English proverb.

11. The verse means: 'The half-wakeful sleep of a dog, the intent concentration of a stork, the diligence of a crow, moderation in eating, and good conduct—these are the five qualities of a student.' I thank Kshama Rangarajan for providing the translation of various Sanskrit verses and the research details included in footnotes 14,15 and 16.

12. The stories were typically very simple: the basic theme was—a boy disobeys his elders and fails, then he begins to obey them and succeeds.

13. '*Param tatvopadeshta guru aur jigyasu sishya*' by Dr Mahaprabhulalji Goswami in *Kalyan* 1988, pp. 257–60. Translations mine.

14. The *Sarada Tilaka* is a medieval text. According to Raghava Bhatta, a fifteenth-century scholar who wrote the introduction to the text, the book was written to impart knowledge on various forms of worship to those unable to master the different *tantras*. By the time of the *tantras*, there was emphasis on rote learning, especially in religious studies (Avalon 1982).

15. The article mentions only the names of these four boys; nowhere in the volume are there more details on their lives, etc. In fact, as the following brief accounts of these child protagonists, taken from the *Puranic Encyclopedia* (Mani 1996), show, their role as student/son is quite ambiguous and cannot be easily taken as endorsing the quality of 'obedience to the guru'. Svetaketu, whose story is told in the *Chandogya Upanishad*, was repeatedly chastised by his father and guru for his intellectual arrogance. But he is also highly regarded for his codification of certain sacrificial rules. Prahalada (in *Bhagavata, Seventh Skanda*), the son of the demon king Hiranyakasyapu, disregarded both his father and his preceptor to follow his chosen path to salvation, even when it resulted in his father's death. Nachiketa was pained by his father/guru's hypocritical attitude and admonished him, and was consigned to the world of the dead, *yamaloka*, by his irritated parent. There, he boldly confronted Yama, the god of death, and demanded answers to his questions. This story is told in the *Kathopanishad*. Dhruva (whose story is elaborated in the *Vishnu Purana*), stung by his father's indifference, left home to seek Lord Vishnu.

16. '*Adarsh vidyarthi*' in *Kalyan* (1988) p. 280. The fourth story is not really about ideal students, but glorifies the guru's impartial treatment of Krishna and Sudama. The brief, one-line stories of these student-heroes that follow, are based on information from the

Puranic Encyclopedia (Mani 1996). Aruni, a student of Dhaumya rishi, used his body to stop the flood waters and obtained his guru's blessings (Mahabharata, *Adi Parva*). Upamanyu, in trying to obey his teacher Dhaumya's injunction, lost his eyesight, and following the same irascible teacher's advice, placated the Ashwini gods and regained his vision (Mahabharata, *Adi Parva*). Eklavya excised his thumb when Drona, whom he regarded as his teacher, demanded this as his guru *dakshina* (teaching fee) to ensure that Eklavya would never be able to defeat his favourite student, Arjuna (Mahabharata, *Adi Parva*). Sudama, along with Krishna, was a student of the sage Sandipani, and the two friends were assiduous in serving their teacher (*Bhagavata, Tenth Skanda*).

In this volume, the story of Nachiketa, who dared to question his father and later fearlessly dialogued with Yama, or the story of Satyakama, are not included. The *Balakank* has two sections titled '*Bhakt balak*' (Devoted boys) with accounts by Sitaramji and Sudarshansingh (Kalyan 1953, pp. 540–58) and '*Gurubhakt balak*' (Boys devoted to teacher) by Mubarak Ali and Zahoor Bhaksh (ibid.: pp. 612–17). As the section titles suggest, the main traits highlighted in these stories are those of obedience and devotion to either God (as teacher) or guru. Among these, the stories of Ashtavakra (who, from his mother's womb, questioned his father) and Nachiketa have been included. Though they contain episodes where the young pupils question their guru's authority, they are elaborated beyond to a final acceptance of the same authority in a higher form.

17. This discussion of the guru–*sishya* relationship is taken up again in the next chapter: 'The Teacher and the Taught'.

5

The Teacher and the Taught

Social roles in their orientational function provide epistemologies, basic categorial schemes, preference systems, and methodologies through which the role occupant organises the encountered experiences and provides explanations for them. A mode of analysis usually reserved by the intellectual historian to the social role of the highly accomplished man of knowledge, such as philosophers or scientists, must by extension be applied to the roles enacted by the 'common folk'.

—Holzner 1968: 165

In the preceding chapter we began exploring the nature of social control that the teacher exercises in school. The discussion so far suggests that the school cannot be conceptualised simply as a totalitarian institution coercing unwilling children into accepting its norms. We saw that teachers, children and the community shared beliefs about the nature of childhood and growing up, which seemed to support the centrality of 'discipline' in the process of schooling. In this chapter, we continue to explore the nature of the teacher's authority and the question of how its absolute character is realised: how it becomes a naturalised, taken-for-granted feature of school life.

The first section looks at how the state-provided definitions of membership to the school community and roles, and the basic institutional arrangements of the school, constitute the school into a 'knowledge community'—distinguishing it from the village and providing the basic hierarchical social arrangements of the school. The analysis in the section titled 'teacher–pupil relationship' brings out the dyadic and layered construction of teacher and pupil identities and their interrelationship. As shown in the last chapter, the local, indigenous or traditional character of their frameworks is significant. Pedagogic activity is both regulatory and instructional. We see how the roles of teacher and pupil orient them simultaneously to both these dimensions, i.e., how pedagogic authority is able to perform the function of maintaining moral order through controlling behaviour and also perform an epistemic function—constituting the epistemic identities of the teacher and the taught and ultimately regulating knowledge construction. These themes, of authority and of the moral-cum-epistemic nature of school experience, recur in the chapters that follow.

I
Institutional Arrangements

Schools generally have two primary institutionally defined roles: teacher and student. To be a member of the school community, one must be able to occupy one of these two roles. Both roles are based on the assumption that the occupant of the role has a particular relationship to the specific body of knowledge encoded in the school curriculum. The teacher is the one who 'already knows' and the student is the one who 'comes to know' through being engaged by the teacher in the process of learning. Typically, institutional norms allow only those officially participating in the process of teaching and learning, or pedagogic activity, to be designated 'teacher' and 'student.'

Institutional membership

The KBMS was typical of government primary schools all over the country, including Delhi, in the structure of its institutional roles and role occupancy. Employment norms of the MCD permitted only those who had completed Class XII, had been trained and had qualified in the selection process, to be posted to a school and occupy the role of the teacher.[1] There were 13 such teachers in KBMS. About 400 children between the ages of 5 and 13 years were members of the community as students. They had become members by virtue of being registered and admitted to the school as students.[2] Each student was additionally assigned to a specific section of a class, ranging from nursery to Class V.

The teachers and students continued as members from the time they joined until they left the school. For teachers, this was when they either retired or were transferred to some other school. For students, this was when they graduated out of Class V or left the school earlier, either to stop studying or to join some other school.

In addition, there were a few adults who were not employed as teachers but were treated as members of the community. All MCD officials from the Department of Education, especially the inspector, were ex-officio members, even though they rarely visited the school. These officials were regarded as members of all those schools over which they officially had jurisdiction. Their interest in all matters of the school—from administrative issues to individual students—was regarded as legitimate. Two other adults, the caretaker from the Boys' Home and I, were given access to the community as quasi-members, this membership being granted by the headmaster and other teachers. The headmaster included the caretaker with other teachers. Students were expected to wish him when they saw him. They called him 'Master-*ji*'. He was often given charge of classes when teachers were absent, and his good singing and drawing skills were especially appreciated.

In my case, there was an initial effort to turn me into a quasi-teacher, which I resisted. I was then allowed to define my own role as a researcher within the community. My activities could not be integrated into the existing social arrangements within the school. But, as teachers did not constantly teach and monitor children, there were spaces where I was able to interact with and talk to the children. The overall school routine was thus not disrupted on my account. My presence was legitimate as I had obtained permission from the relevant MCD officials and had the additional recommendation of a senior MCD education official who was well known to the headmaster. In the girls' primary school (GGPS) also, I was able to establish such a quasi-membership. In the private school LAPS, this effort was not completely successful; at one point the principal withdrew permission to study the school. Also, the overall strict control on children's activities and time made it more difficult for me to conduct my activities without disrupting the existing organisation of the community.[3]

Non-members and boundary maintenance

The boundary between the school and the rest of the village community was largely physical—the school had a distinct space allocated to it, separate from the community. In addition, a psychological boundary was also evident. Other adult employees of the school, like the two chaprassis and the sweeper, even though a part of the school, were not considered members of the community. Education psychology generally accords parents and care-givers an important role in the education of the child. The MCD officially recognises this relationship and has tried to institutionalise it in the form of the parent–teacher association (PTA), and by requiring parents to sign report cards and provide explanations for their children's absence from school, etc. They could therefore claim some form of membership in the school community. In practice, however, parents and other older people—siblings, relatives, tuition teachers—concerned with children's learning of school knowledge outside the school, were not treated even as quasi-members.[4] Both teachers and students defined and maintained a strong boundary between the school and village community. Parents' claim to quasi-membership on the grounds of their natural interest in their children's education and the institutionalised forum of the PTA, was de-legitimised through several practices which were organised around the broad rubric of 'What do the villagers know about education?'

First of all, the teachers ensured that the language used in the school and the one used in the community were well differentiated. Within the school, only standard Hindi was to be spoken, in contrast to the village where Haryanvi was spoken. Children who lapsed into Haryanvi in school were ridiculed by the teachers and corrected by their friends. Teachers often spoke of the importance of speaking with the 'right accent'. The use of Haryanvi was described derogatorily as *ganvar* (rustic). Enquiries about their children's education from parents who spoke in Haryanvi received only monosyllabic responses from most teachers. On one occasion, after a parent had left, one of the teachers observed to me: 'They can't speak properly and they want to know if studies are going on well. Even if I tell them, what will they understand? They can't even help their children at home.' Such comments, which emphasised the cultural discontinuity between the home and the school, were common.

On some occasions, when more educated fathers came to speak with the headmaster, to complain that classes were not held or to find out what lessons would be included for the coming examinations, he politely told them that the teachers did their duty in school. The parents had to do their duty at home, send their children to school neatly dressed and make sure they learned their lessons. The educated, well-dressed mothers who came to school usually spoke only to the women teachers. These teachers handled their enquiries very lightly. Once Krishna Kumari remarked to me: 'They are not interested in their children, they come here only for an outing.' Only those parents whose children were favoured by teachers, and who came to enquire after the teacher once in a while, were entertained politely.

Some of the teachers drew further support for de-legitimising parents' interest in children's education by holding them responsible for the dysfunctional PTA. In fact, on one occasion when they did hold a PTA meeting, the teachers spread out durries on the stage and waited, but no parents showed up. I found out later that no notice had been sent to the parents about the meeting. When the teachers loudly commented on the futility of expecting anything from village people, I asked them if the parents knew about the meeting. The young, university-educated male teacher in charge of the PTA told me: 'They know, they are not interested.' The other teachers from the village did not seem concerned about the PTA or its dysfunctionality.

The boundary had an uncomfortable existence because of the awkward status of the teachers in relation to the rest of the community. As pointed out in Chapter IV, in the profile of professions, primary schoolteaching is accorded the lowest status among service professions since it requires only a high school (Class XII) level education and a short training. However, they did have official status within the school and in the classroom they were totally in power. Educated villagers, within their homes, were very critical of the teachers who, they believed, were not doing their job well. But they did not try to assert their opinion in the school.

While the teachers were primarily responsible for defining and maintaining the boundary between the school and the larger community, within the school students ensured that adults and children who were not officially part of the school were aware that they were not members. Unless accompanied by an adult, young children who were clothed differently could not even enter the school without encountering threatening sounds. Children were also conscious of the essential non-membership of adult employees of the school like the chaprassis (peons) and sweepers who, at most, had only a Class V pass certificate. But as it involved adults, maintaining the boundary between the school community and these adults was tricky. They often did so under the cloak of humour.

Social arrangements within the school

The various institutional roles in the school related to each other through an institutional hierarchy of roles. The flow of authority is presented diagrammatically in Figure 5.1.

Within the school: The headmaster exercised authority over all the teachers. Among the teachers, there was no institutional hierarchy. The

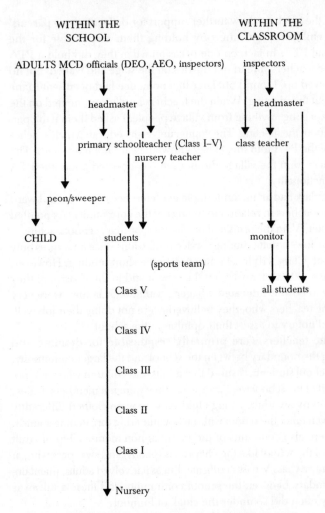

Figure 5.1 Schematic Representation of Authority Structure

teachers circulated among the five classes, I to V, going up with a group of children in one class over five years. There were no occasions or activities where any of them could operate in a manner that made the teachers of higher classes more powerful than the others. Even a senior teacher, drawing a higher salary, could be teaching Class I, while a junior teacher could be in charge of Class V. The nursery class teacher was institutionally ranked lower than the others and drew a lower salary. Also, she was employed as a nursery teacher and would never be given the charge of any higher class at any point in her career. A special feature was that none of the teachers was either formally or informally placed in any direct relation to any teacher other than the headmaster. In this sense, all teachers were equal and below the headmaster. But, as we will see in the next section, several teachers sought to institute hierarchy amongst themselves by broadening their identity beyond the institutional definition of 'teacher'.

The peons and sweepers, though they had adult roles in the school, were still outside the institutional epistemic framework. Their ambiguous status in the power structure of the school will be looked at in the next section under the adult–child dimension of the teacher–student relationship. All the students of the school were the objects of the teachers' authority. The school recognised a slight role differentiation for children who were a part of the school sports team—they had certain privileges and could be called out of class for practice any time by the sports teacher. In the power arrangements among students, those in the higher classes were higher than students in the lower classes. The former could be placed in situations of control over the latter, usually to maintain discipline in the classroom. This was rarely done in the boys' school, fairly common in the girls' school, and never done in the private school.

Within the classroom: The inspector and the headmaster both had special powers within the classroom. As a part of their supervisory duties, they could come in and check what the students were learning. No other teacher in the school could do this with another teacher's class. Within a given class, in addition to the basic authority of the teacher over the taught, there were other arrangements which were not an official part of the institutional plan. Each teacher appointed a monitor who was placed directly under him or her and enjoyed authority over all the other students. Those who had been designated as 'failures' by the teacher also had a slightly differentiated role.

We can already see that within the basic institutional structures and hierarchy in the school, there are some features which reflect a local reinterpretation and elaboration of the institutional definitions by the participants themselves. The MCD recognised a role for parents in the school, but the teachers, who seemed to have a different opinion on the ability of village parents to contribute to the process of schooling, subverted this, effectively excluding the parents and the village from the school community.

II
The Teacher–Pupil Relationship

In the study of the nature of authority in education, the work of Peters (1966) is an important reference point. Peters suggested that the teacher's authority has a legal–rational basis.[5] He drew attention to the nature of the teacher's authority and its relationship to the teacher's knowledge. He proposed a distinction between 'being in authority' and 'being an authority', and suggested that

> (t)he teacher is an authority figure in both the above senses. He is put *in* authority to do a certain job for the community, and to maintain social control in the school while doing it. He must also be *an* authority on some aspect of the community's culture which he is employed to transmit (ibid.: 240, emphasis in the original).

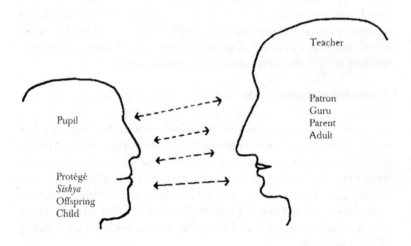

Figure 5.2 Multi-layered Dyadic Teacher–Pupil Relationship

This amounts to a *de jure* authority in virtue of his office, as well as a *de facto* authority held in virtue of his subject (epistemic authority) and the method of teaching.

As was pointed out in the first part of this chapter, the school institution itself accords its teachers formal authority and places teachers 'in' authority with regard to their students. This authority is believed to have a legal–rational basis; it is based on the recognition that the teacher is 'an' authority in matters relating to the school curriculum—both subject matter and pedagogy.[6] In the Kasimpur school I found that the acceptance and operation of the teacher's authority was more complex. This was because the identity or role of teacher was not simply the modern institutional one. The teacher–pupil relationship was multilayered, with the curriculum-referred relationship being merely *one* of these several layers. The identities of teacher and student were elaborated *beyond* the modern institutional context of the school to include other dyadic relationships of adult–child, parent–offspring, guru–*sishya* and patron–protégé.

Adult–child

At the base was the relationship of adult–child. This is a relationship in which teachers and children already existed by virtue of being members of the larger village community, and it was predetermined by this primary membership.[7] In the village community, the child was the inexperienced human—an adult in the making. The world into which the child was growing and about which he/she was learning, was essentially the world as seen by the adult. The adult seemed to be naturally placed ahead of the child in matters relating to knowledge of the adult world, and also in a position to exercise power over the child. This was a part of the 'natural attitude'.[8] After all, the child does have limited experience of human relations and physical situations (therefore 'experiential knowledge') as compared to the adult. The adult has negotiated the world for many more years than the child. He/she is also physically mature, unlike the child.

In Indian families, being older is in and by itself sufficient warrant to expect respect from one who is younger. This is most certainly so within the family, including the extended family, but it also extends outside the family to the entire community. Even if there is a marked social class difference, one who shows respect for an older person, regardless of his caste, class or sex, is regarded favourably. Children were aware of the requirement to acknowledge the basic position of authority of the adult, regardless of whether they were their teachers or not.

'*Badon ka adar karna chahiye*' (elders should be respected) was a value nobody could dispute—it was regarded as obvious. It did not need to be articulated except when there was a situation where it was deliberately flouted. The fact that this was an operative value became established from situations in which the students challenged it. Sundari, the sweeper in the girls' school, often made the girls help her clean the school ground, asking them to collect fallen leaves and papers that were thrown about. The girls, especially the older ones in Classes IV and V, did not like to do this and tried to avoid Sundari in the mornings. However, when she pointedly instructed them, they could not refuse and reluctantly helped her. On one occasion a group gathered around me and complained:

EPISODE 5.1 (GGPS)
Sarita: Do we come here to study or to pick up leaves?
Why don't you ask her that?
They were shocked at the idea: We can hardly say that.

This episode suggests how children, especially girls, were bound by the social norm of obedience to the adult. Even though they were conscious that the authority of the adult sweeper did not follow from her institutional role, and did not have direct institutional sanction, yet there was nothing they could do about it. They could certainly not protest or flout it. If children did challenge this unspoken norm, it was under the cloak of humour which provided them with the medium to be heard by adults, but protected them from the seriousness of consequences that acting in the adult world entailed.

EPISODE 5.2 (BHARDWAJ'S HOME)
I accompanied the children who take tuition from Bhardwaj to his home near the school. Finding that their Guruji was not home yet, they began playing. Mira, Bhardwaj's wife, ordered the children to sit down and begin whatever work he had given them. Even as the children began settling down, Ajay deliberately provoked her. Laughing, he announced that he was going to climb the roof to retrieve the ball that had got stuck there. When Mira advanced, threateningly waving her broom at him, Ajay dodged her and, laughing, proceeded to climb up to the roof and fetch the ball. All the while Mira, not very seriously, threatened to inform Bhardwaj when he returned. Ajay jumped down with his ball and with a great show of industry opened his bag and began his work.

In this episode, Ajay disobeyed an older person, but under the protection of humour, to convey that he did not mean it as an insult. His subsequent industry, too, was aimed at conveying that he did take her orders seriously. It is likely that he took the liberty that he did because she was a woman, and also because he knew she was illiterate and obviously rustic.

EPISODE 5.3 (CLASS V)

Bhardwaj had to leave the school for half-an-hour to attend to some urgent business. He had been doing arithmetic with his class. He left Krishna, one of the school peons, in charge till he returned. Krishna came into the room with a stick in her hand and set about disciplining the class, instructing them not to make any noise and to keep working.
Manoj asked her cheekily: Aunty, check my work!

Under the cloak of humour, Manoj was drawing attention to the fact that Krishna was occupying an institutional place to which she had no legitimate claim, especially as she was illiterate; and that she had no authority in her own right but drew it from the teacher who had given her charge. This is in contrast to occasions when the class monitor was left in charge. He was recognised as having epistemic claims to authority. Overall, the fact that the teacher was an adult and the student was a child automatically placed the former in a position of authority with regard to the latter. The students' obedience was tacitly accepted as a ground rule, an extension of the social norm into the school.

Parent–child

The teacher's authority was further extended and legitimised by adding the non-institutional dimension of the parent–child relationship over and above the basic adult–child relationship. Berne (1963: 198–213) points out that this is one of the basic interactional styles that people adopt to relate to each other. The structure of the Indian family set-up gives parents, especially the father, absolute authority over the child. Both Lannoy (1971) and Kakar (1981) describe the enormous cultural traditions and rituals within which the relationship (especially parent–son) is realised, all of which mark the primacy of the parents' position and ensure that it remains outside the boundaries of enquiry.

The authority of the father is akin to the subtle authority of the stranger. The mother, on the other hand, is a familiar figure. In popular representations, her authority draws from the selflessness of her love for her children and the enormous sacrifices she is capable of making for them.[9] Virtually all the children I spoke to were scared of being in the bad books of, or being found worthy of punishment by, their fathers. But they did not ever suggest that they found the punishments or beatings unfair—even on the few occasions when, after a beating, the child confided in me that he was not the culprit. On the contrary, if they were beaten, it was for their own good, so that they would not fall into bad ways. Parents were believed to do things for the betterment of their children. Doing as their parents wished and making them happy was the first and foremost duty of all good children.

The teachers often drew parallels between themselves and the children's parents, claiming that, like parents, everything they did was because they wished the best for the child: 'The guru is like a parent (ma-bap). All things we say and do, we do for your good' (Headmaster, morning assembly); 'You must always touch the feet of your parents and teachers' (Bhardwaj, morning assembly). The explicit parallels suggested that the teacher's actions, like those of parents, were benevolent, with the children's interests at heart, even when such actions involved disciplining and punishing. They also suggested that, therefore, children must give to their teachers the same respect and unquestioning obedience as they would to their parents.

The women teachers in the school seemed to deliberately eschew the role of mother, preferring to remain distant like fathers.[10] The Class II teacher Sunita especially enforced the distinction. In many government schools women teachers are referred to as 'Aunty'. On occasions when children called her 'Aunty', Sunita objected, telling them she would not indulge them like their mothers. She ordered them to call her 'Madam'. The children could not treat the guru like familiar members of the family, certainly not like their indulgent mothers. The teacher's authority, like that of the father, was to be feared and respected. By casting the teacher–student relationship in the parent–child mould, the teacher's actions became sanctified, and placed beyond the purview of the child.

Guru–*sishya*

Another layer in the teacher–student relationship took the quasi-religious overtones of the Vedic ashrams. Here the teacher is cast as a guru—a religious, spiritual knower/teacher. His authority springs from being closer to God and salvation. The student is cast as his disciple. The idea that the village schoolteacher is like an ancient religious, spiritual teacher was conveyed to the students by references to Sanskrit *slokas*, ancient texts and through folk and mythical stories about gurus and their disciples. One of the most popular verses quoted on several occasions by teachers during assembly was:

Gurur brahma, gurur vishnuh, gurur devo mahesvarah.
Guruh sakshaat parabrahma, tasmai sri gurave namah

The teachers usually also interpreted this verse in Hindi for the benefit of the children, saying that it meant that the teacher is like Brahma and Vishnu, like God.[11]

The guru–*sishya* relationship competes with the mother–child/son relationship for reverence and idealisation in Indian folklore. The tradition of guru–*sishya* can be traced back to Vedic times. The teacher, as sage, was one who renounced society and sought spiritual revelation or *moksha* (liberation). The Upanishads deal with instructions and initiations received from forest hermits by 'sitting at their feet'. Lannoy traces the popularity and cult-like nature of the tradition in present times to the later Bhakti period (Lannoy 1971: 347–72). He suggests that at a time when all interpersonal relations in Indian society were strictly regulated by caste and hierarchy, the guru–*sishya* circle became the only one where human beings could meet, free from formal constraints (ibid.: 347). The teacher was there to help the *sishya* find his sense of wholeness. The relationship, while intensely emotional, was essentially unequal; the only requirement was the complete surrender of the pupil's will to the guru's sacred authority.

According to Lannoy, the Vedic ideal of teacher as sage evolved into the concept of bhakti (ibid.: 347, 362) in the Bhakti period. This is re-echoed in Kakar's analysis of guru–*sishya* (1991: 41–63). He also observes a shift in the dominant image of the guru

> toward the *moksha* (liberation) rather than the *dharma* (virtue) guru, toward the bhakti (devotional) guru rather than the *jnana* (knowledge) guru, or in *tantric* terms toward the *diksha* (initiation) rather than the *siksha* (teaching) guru who taught the scriptures and explained the meaning and purpose of life (ibid.: 42).

Unlike Vedic gurus, the teachers of the Bhakti period were popular figures with large followings. They preached in the common language and drew on familiar, everyday themes in their songs and discourses. Kumar (1991: 71–93) has suggested that the pre-colonial, humble village teacher had inherited the mantle of authority of the Bhakti guru, and this elevated his role and status in the community (ibid.: 88).

In the post-colonial Kasimpur school, the teachers claimed a continuity with the traditional institution of guru–*sishya*. But they drew their symbols not from the Bhakti but the Vedic tradition. Rather than the discourse and traditions of the everyday and familiar in the common language, which was the Bhakti way, these teachers gave importance to Brahminical rituals, texts and the Sanskrit language. The *Kalyan* annual issue on education also ignores the Bhakti inheritance, and one article[12] claims that the Vedic tradition represents the '*Bharatiya* [Indian] tradition of education' (also believed to be dying out under the onslaught of Westernisation) (Kalyan 1988: 47). In KBMS, the aura of the spiritual teacher reflected on the male teachers in a number of ways. The appellation '*guruji*' was the general way of referring to them.[13] They also claimed a continuity with ancient *gurukuls* for the institution of the modern school, and were critical of what they claimed was a general deterioration in present times. Students were exhorted to emulate the purported conduct of their ancient counterparts.

EPISODE 5.4 (MORNING ASSEMBLY)

Surjeet gave the address: In *gurukuls* they study for two minutes, and then they listen to Sanskrit *slokas—tvameva mata cha pita... (he faltered and was helped to complete the* sloka *by the other teachers around.)*[14] They listen very carefully when their guru*ji* is speaking, and they can just memorise.

The teachers also taught the children many religious and quasi-religious things that were not officially part of the curriculum. The morning assembly rituals included the *surya namaskar*, recitation of the *gayatri* mantra and meditation—these were not a part of the secular morning assembly rituals prescribed by the MCD. Nagpal made the children of his class recite the *santi slokas* every morning. The morning assembly addresses often had references to the truths and traditions of the Vedic texts and also occasionally to stories of gods and goddesses.

EPISODE 5.5 (MORNING ASSEMBLY)

Bhardwaj related the story in which gods and goddesses help to catch a thief and punish him for doing wrong. He concluded: ...because what is written in our *ved sastra* is true. It has been written on the basis of people's experiences.

Several teachers, especially Bhardwaj who was a Brahmin, made it a point to demonstrate to the children their extensive knowledge of Sanskrit and of religious traditions. Teachers took a lot of trouble over teaching the children the 'right' way of reciting the *gayatri* mantra and meditating.

EPISODE 5.6 (MORNING ASSEMBLY)
Surjeet: The pronunciation of the *gayatri* mantra should be pure/correct/ faultless (*suddh*). This is a *maha* (great) mantra.
Then all the children began singing the mantra.

With the teacher as a guru, i.e., a spiritual seer, the student became a *sishya*, i.e., a disciple, a seeker of knowledge, truth and salvation. In Chapter IV we saw how the attitudes, traits and actions that tradition attributes to the *sishya* were incorporated into role of the student. The true student would need to revere his guru, with utmost obedience being the most prized value. Obedience, even in situations that challenge ordinary, everyday logic and sense, would bring the sweetest, most desirable fruits of success.

Teacher as patriot/martyr

The government schoolteacher also presented himself as a 'good citizen'— a man who has sacrificed his life and works selflessly for the betterment of society and the nation. The headmaster of the school, two senior retired teachers and an education officer living in the village, all spoke of the importance of their profession in nation-building. They felt they were responsible for instilling good moral values in children. They said they did not need to work for the pay, which, according to them, was in any case far lower than what they could have got. This sense of sacrifice gave especially the older teachers an aura of the patriot and martyr. It also carried a moral authority akin to the authority that Brahmin teachers of the past possessed by virtue of renouncing all claims to property (Lannoy 1971). All the teachers presented their actions as prompted by their laudable desire to educate children to be good citizens.

EPISODE 5.7 (MORNING ASSEMBLY)
Headmaster: Every day we tell you some good things, so as to put good habits into you. So you will become good citizens... So that you may improve your life, we tell you good things.

EPISODE 5.8 (CLASS V)
Krishna Kumari was reprimanding the children for horsing around instead of doing the work she had assigned them: We come here and spend all our time teaching you. Why? Because we want you to succeed.

Several children readily identified teachers along with soldiers, the police and scientists as 'good citizens': 'A teacher is a good citizen. He does things for the nation' (Devendar, Class V). This goodness and self-sacrifice gave the teacher a moral authority over the child. His intentions and actions were to be placed beyond doubt and suspicion. The failure to appreciate this 'enormous' sacrifice would be a sign of ungratefulness. This was especially used against the growing sentiment in the village community, that the government schools were not doing a good job and that the private schools were better.

EPISODE 5.9 (MORNING ASSEMBLY)
Surjeet: We teach you every day. We tell you things so well, but still you don't learn. Where students pay Rs 200, they don't have teachers like here. I went to Maan School. There I met some students and I talked to them. We are much better. Better in Hindi, better in mathematics. And you give 10 paise or 60 paise as fees! Tell me, is that any fees? Here all the teachers are BA, and have BEd. We keep saying learn, learn. You don't....

Private schools, on account of the high fees they charged, could not claim self-sacrifice. The villagers who sent their children to these schools claimed that their profit-making angle was obvious—otherwise why would they run the schools? Still, the proprietors of two of the five private schools in the village also tried to claim moral authority. They claimed that they invested everything they earned back into the school; that they ran their institutions efficiently and were more ethical than the government schools as they gave parents and children the 'goods' for which they came to their schools.

Patron–protégé

While the representations discussed in the preceding paragraphs were true of all teacher–student relationships, the relationship of patron–protégé was more specific to some of the teachers and students. When the teacher regarded himself as culturally more elite than his student, a relationship of benevolent patronage operated. The distancing of the school from the village community by devaluing the village folk as *ganvar* has already been discussed. From the discourse of teachers it seemed that the feeling of superiority could have originated in any one of the several possible differences between the teachers and children; caste, class, knowledge of English and access to the city were some of these. The feeling of cultural superiority was not directed at just the student, but also the student's family/community.

Three of the women teachers of KBMS, Sunita, Asha and Krishna Kumari, seemed to feel superior on account of being middle-class Jats living in nearby large towns. Surjeet, too, was very conscious of being a Jat. He often declared that like all Jat males, he too was tough and had great physical prowess. He and Ajay Gupta, apart from their higher caste, were also conscious of having studied in Delhi University and knowing English. Bhardwaj drew his sense of superiority from being a Brahmin and having access to religious texts.

The attitude of benevolent patronage was exhibited particularly during assembly when there was a large audience, and especially when the students chosen for special mention were from castes that were lower in the traditional caste hierarchy. The teachers rewarded Vipin, who belonged to a migrant Bihari family, when he won the zonal drawing competition. They praised Sandeep, who was from the Chamar caste, for his prowess in sports and his good academic record, observing that 'even though he is SC/ST, he has shown himself worthy' (Pavan Kumar, morning assembly). Surjeet also announced a personal monthly prize of Rs 10 for the child who came to school regularly. In the first month, the prize went to Vipin. In the second month, the children remembered and speculated on who would get the prize, but Surjeet had forgotten about it and no one dared to remind him.

These dyadic representations seem to naturalise the teacher's authority over the student. They deepen the institutional authority of the teacher to a taken-for-granted, subconscious level of the psyche. This is possible because the authority is construed in terms of already established norms in the community and popular, folkloric constructions of the teacher's role. It is clear that there is much in the acceptance of the teachers' authority which is *prior to and independent of* the considerations of the context of school or school knowledge. These representations emphasise the moral, cultural and epistemic superiority of the teacher and attribute a benevolent intention to his or her actions.

*

Nature of the Teacher's Authority

The elaboration of teacher and student identities in terms of dyads ensures that their roles share the same frames of reference and theories, and are essentially intermeshed with each other. Each role exists only in relation to the other. The identity of the student is structured as essentially an inter-personal condition, realised in the teacher–taught duality. The teacher is a 'meek dictator', whose authoritarianism is derived and sustained by beliefs, perceptions and mores inherent in everyday practice and in the folkloric and cultural inheritance of teacher and students. The ideological bases reflect the local culture and idiom. Contrary to the image of children being oppressed by authority and discipline, we find, from the data and discussions in the last chapter and in this one, that they also actively par-ticipate in creating the reality of the school. They cooperate in instituting and interpreting the power–knowledge regime.

The adult–child and parent–child authority patterns—tacit, informal and already established in the community—are carried over to the context of the school. While the former is simply a continuation of the community's norm into the institutional arena of the school, the latter relationship is appropriated formally by the teacher through symbolic constructions that draw on popular cultural representations of the intentions of the teacher. Obedience is expected to follow as a natural consequence. The moral as-pect of this authority is primary but there is also an epistemic dimension inherent in both. In oral and traditional communities, where everyday and experiential matters are important, age is an important determinant of epistemic authority. The traditional social organisation can still be found in Kasimpur, where 'those who are older know more' operates as a tacit norm.

The other representations of the teacher–taught relationship—of guru–*sishya* and patron–protégé—are derived from older pedagogical traditions that are a part of the folklore and shared cultural inheritance of the com-munity. Both these have a strong moral–epistemological character. The guru's authority is both traditional and charismatic, following Weber's typology (Weber 1968: 46). It has the sanctity of tradition and also elements of the exemplary character of the individual; it commands reverence and obedience. It is only suggestive of the potential of developing into 'legal–rational' when related to expertise in subject knowledge.

In addition to the superiority of the guru in the moral realm and his concern with developing the *sishya*'s moral character, the guru's authority as described in popular articles on this subject in *Kalyan*'s annual volume on education is also explicitly epistemic (Kalyan 1988). An article on the guru–*sishya* relationship[15] says: '*Moksha* is the aim/goal of tradition (*sam-pradaya*) and without the guru's guidance it is not possible. This proves the importance of the guru. The *Mundakopanishad* says clearly that learning must be received straight from the guru's mouth' (ibid.: 257). Another article[16] states even more directly the need for learning to be mediated by a guru: 'We need learning to rise above everyday life. Without the teaching of the *acharya* no one has the right to enter into this area of learning. Only learning from the guru can bring any fruits' (ibid.: 47). Knowledge worth knowing and the process of learning are completely controlled by the guru and exist only in relation to him. The identity and character of the learner, too, take shape in relation to the guru.

In the details of the presentation of self and construction of identity, one notices a variation in the authority exercised by individual teachers. Many of them preferentially cultivated certain representations of their role. The Brahmin teacher staked a claim for actual guru-hood by taking every opportunity to demonstrate his knowledge of the Sanskrit language, *slokas* and religious observances. Post-Independence associations of the teacher with patriotism and missionary zeal for nation-building activity accrued especially to the older teachers in school, heightening the charisma they derived from the reputation of selfless activity. Younger teachers projected their performance in areas of cultural value, such as knowledge of science and English. They cultivated a personage of benevolent patronage, and in so doing derived a charismatic authority. Interestingly, the women teachers cultivated an image of strict adherence to the institutional role of teacher and of exercising simple bureaucratic authority (Weber 1968: 66–77). Here rules exist and must be implemented, simply to ensure maximisation of efficiency in teaching and learning. This basis for authority also seemed to be significant in LAPS, the private school. It is possible that the low status of the profession of primary schoolteacher make considerations that arise directly from the institutional context alone insufficient grounds for the establishment of authority. Therefore, the adult (male) members drew on more powerful symbolism to establish authority.

One may expect that where an elaborately legitimised authority is operational, there would be little direct use of power and that the control of the teacher over the child would be invisible and implicit rather than visible and explicit (Bernstein 1977: 116). Yet, within the school, there was a palpable tension and awareness of the teacher's authority. The exercise of authority/power was a routine feature of all teacher–pupil interactions during classroom instruction. Name-calling, verbal threats and corporal punishment were common. Even very small instances of misconduct could receive very harsh punishment. Children were kept in strict control by teachers and teacher-appointed student monitors who 'extended' the teachers' controlling eye.[17]

This could indicate that the teachers perceived a threat to their authority or that it was incompletely defined and not fully accepted by the community. However, in the Kasimpur school there was no indication that this was the case. Neither was there any 'counter-culture' among the children that formed a source of resistance to the teachers' authority[18] and necessitated the use of power. De Castell (1982) has suggested that Peter's legal–rational framework, referred to at the beginning of this chapter, is not sufficient for understanding the teacher's authority in real classroom situations. Drawing on Keddie's (1977) empirical study of classroom practice, she found that the students' acceptance of authority was often irrational. The analysis of teacher authority and students' compliance in the Kasimpur school, presented in this chapter and the previous one, suggests that in the Indian context the conceptual analysis of pedagogic authority cannot be only within the legal–rational–irrational framework, and that it would be useful to include Weber's other basic categories: 'power' and 'persuasion'.

Authority is generally understood as legitimised power. According to Max Weber (1968), authority differs from power in two respects. In authority, people comply with requests made of them voluntarily while in power, compliance is achieved by either the direct use, or the threat, of sanctions. In authority, people willingly obey directives without questioning their wisdom; authority is able to achieve compliance without calling attention to itself or to the nature of its demands. In persuasion, compliance is not automatic but based on judgement. The person voluntarily cooperates not because of threat, as in the case of power, but because he feels that his welfare will be enhanced. Persuasion is different from authority; unlike in authority, the willingness to comply is not because the requests and directives are in accordance with basic values.

This analysis helps us understand authority from the perspective of the actors exercising and experiencing it in a given situation. We are able to move from the phenomenon of social control to understanding the circumstances and limits of the situation in which it is justified and justifiable. There is a value congruence between teachers and students which legitimises social control. But the socialising function that social control is expected to perform and achieve, i.e., its pedagogic function, suggests that compliance is not necessarily automatic but may also be constituted. In the Kasimpur school, the dyadic structure of identities provides legitimacy for the teacher's control, and the '*adarsh vidyarthi*' model ensures that, to a large extent, obedience to the teacher's directives is automatic. But the condition of being 'children-who-are-growing-up' has an inherent duality.

The basic character and needs of a 'child' are believed to be contrary to that of a 'student'—they would rather play than study, they do not remember what is good for them and they are prey to temptations and dishonesty. So their obedience is not complete and persuasion is also necessary to achieve compliance. Children recognise and are also often reminded that eventually they will benefit from it. At the same time, teachers retain and exercise a discretion along with their authority. Chapter VI introduces the *teachering device* and the techniques of surveillance, where discretion or unpredictability built into the pedagogic activity seems to enable it to achieve its aim. Children were tricked or forced into exposing their weaknesses and failures, so that teachers could school them better. The addition of discretion to authority turns it into power.[19]

We begin to recognise in the institution of the school the features of an 'epistemic community' as characterised by Holzner (1968). There is a meshing of similar role orientations, unified by a common epistemology and frame of reference. We see that the relationship of this community with the surrounding society is a matter of concern for all its members; they deliberately differentiate the school from the village community, and also regulate the exchanges between the two. Not only is there a congruence of values in the school community, but there are also power arrangements in the exchanges or interaction processes, simultaneously sustaining the shared perspective once it is established and influencing its acceptance. In the following chapters we will encounter this and other features, such as the high level of power consciousness among members and the regulation of privileges and situations that members can access (see Appendix A). All the representations of the teacher–taught relationship oblige the child to accept the moral and epistemic superiority of the teacher and therefore to concede his authority. The power relationship in which the teacher and students are bound together is an essential aspect of their roles and orientation to each other. The position of authority is a part of the identity of the teacher and the acceptance of authority is a part of the identity of the student. In the next chapter we will see how this layered epistemic authority, especially its tacit dimensions,[20] operate in regulating knowledge.

Notes

1. Private schools in the village did require their teachers to have a Class XII pass certificate, but did not require any sort of teacher training certificate.

2. In India, given late admissions, retention and failure, the spread of primary school entering and leaving ages would be between the ages of 4–5 years and 10–13 years. The MCD's admissions to Class I are strictly determined by the age of the applicant. In admissions to higher classes, the applicant is also assessed for previous knowledge and skills. The private schools in Kasimpur claimed to have stricter admission norms, assessing applicants more rigorously for previous knowledge and skills, even at Class I level. They also relaxed the lower age limit and were more stringent about the upper age limit of the students they admitted.

3. A more detailed account is included in Appendix B.

4. This was so in the girls' school as well as in the private school. The separation of the school community from the village was even more well defined in the private school.

5. This is based on Weber's distinction between traditional, legal–rational and charismatic authority, on the basis of the grounds of their acceptance by those who comply (Johnson 1995: 18).

6. Candidates who have either completed a two-year diploma course of teacher education at the elementary level (i.e., the Junior Basic Training or JBT) after their Class XII, or acquired a BEd degree after an undergraduate degree, are considered eligible to apply for teaching jobs in the MCD-run primary schools.

7. This held true even for teachers who did not belong to the village. The village mores extended the expectations of the relationship to all children and adults.

8. The term 'natural attitude' was used by Alfred Schutz to characterise the attitude with which we approach everyday life:

> The mental stance a person takes in the spontaneous and routine pursuits of his daily affairs, and the basis of his interpretation of the life world as a whole and its various aspects. The life world is the world of the *natural attitude*. In it, things are taken for granted.

This definition is provided in a glossary by the editor, H.R. Wagner in Schutz (1970: 320). Also see Appendix A.

9. In popular stories, it is the mother–son rather than the mother–daughter relationship that forms the prototype.

10. In fact, those male teachers of the school who came from the village took a more 'motherly' interest in the well-being of their students.

11. This verse is better translated as follows:

> Guru is Brahma, the creator/demiurge, Guru is Vishnu, the all-pervading one.
> Guru is Maheswara Deva, the shining one who is the Lord of all, (or, guru is the great divinity Shiva).
> Guru is verily the Transcendent Absolute Reality.
> Salutation to that auspicious Guru.

12. '*Chhatra aur adhyapak*' by Swami Maheswaranandji Saraswati in Kalyan (1988), pp. 47–50. Translations mine.

13. The women teachers were referred to as 'madam-*ji*' or 'aunty-*ji*'. In LAPS, the term used was 'sir-*ji*'. All these appellations implied more 'modern', 'secular' and 'non-traditional' aspects of the relationship, which were distinctly colonial in origin.

14. The full verse is:

> *Tvameva mata cha pita tvameva, tvameva bandhuh cha sakha tvameva.*
> *Tvameva vidya dravinam tvameva, tvameva sarvam mama deva deva.'*

Thou art my mother and my father; thou art my companion and my friend.
Thou art my learning and my wealth; thou art my everything, my God.

15. *'Param tatvopadeshta guru aur jigyasu sishya'* by Dr Sri Mahaprabhulalji Goswami in Kalyan (1988), pp. 257–60. Translations mine.
16. *'Chhatra aur adhyapak'* by Swami Maheswaranandji Saraswati in Kalyan (1988), pp. 47–50. Translations mine.
17. The conduct of classroom control and the role of the monitor are discussed in the next chapter. Also included is an inventory of the kinds of threats and punishments to which students were subjected.
18. It is interesting to contrast this with Western studies of common schools, where such counter-cultures are an important motif of life in the school (see, e.g., Woods 1979; Willis 1976, and other papers included in the section titled 'Pupil Cultures' in Hammersley and Woods 1976).
19. Barry Barnes suggests this as an alternative to the received view of the relationship of power to authority, where to possess authority is to possess more than power, i.e., authority is power plus legitimacy or power plus consent. He proposes that power is more expedient and advantageous than mere authority; it is able to direct a routine with discretion. Power is authority plus discretion (Barnes 1986: 181–82).
20. Polanyi (1958) in his discussion of knowledge transmission also draws attention to the importance of such tacit acceptance of the teacher's authority in apprenticeship situations and in the transmission of personal knowledge. Allen (1987) draws on Polanyi in his critique of R.S. Peter's rationalisation of pedagogic authority.

6

Teaching and Learning:
The Regulation of Knowledge

Krishna Kumar's description 'textbook culture' (1988) evocatively conveys the centrality of the textbook to the Indian school curriculum. Mainstream schooling, both state and private, is structured around the study of pre-scribed textbooks and examinations conducted on their basis. The term 'textbook culture' signifies not only this control on 'products of learning', but also includes the regulating effect of textbooks on what transpires within the classroom between teachers and pupils and on the process of learning itself. The words 'control' and 'regulate' seem to suggest an external top–down imposition or coercion. But as we have seen in the last two chapters, it is also possible to regulate and control from the inside, by becoming a part of the ideational framework from which teachers and children derive and interpret their classroom activities in the form of beliefs about knowledge, knowing what knowledge is worth knowing, and the image of the 'educated man'.

In this chapter I will be looking at the activities in the classroom that simultaneously constitute knowledge and regulate—realising a curriculum where the textbook is central. I will be concerned with understanding what functions as classroom or curricular knowledge, how it is constituted and the processes by which it is taught and learnt. In the Kasimpur Model Boys' School, there were primarily three pedagogic activities: teaching new lessons, answering questions and revision. These could be regarded as three stages through which all lessons were taught and learnt. I have retained these stages as the basic organisation of this chapter. Each of these activities permits us to focus on a particular epistemic-cum-regulatory aspect.

The section 'teaching lessons' looks at what is included as school or curricular knowledge (as opposed to out-of-school or non-curricular knowledge) and how it acquires its character as legitimate and 'ought-to-know' knowledge. It introduces the ideas of the *'teachering device'* and *'framing'*. The section on 'learning lessons' deals with the reconstitution of school knowledge as 'answers-to-questions' and the strict regulation of the form in which legitimate knowledge must be learnt or encoded. The third section, titled 'showing-that-one-knows', deals with revision—the process by which children become epistemic subjects and experience their own identity as 'knowers'. This is followed by a note on 'monitoring' which shows how the teachering device is extended and made more effective by student monitors.

I
Teaching Lessons

The mere fact of transmitting a message within a relation of pedagogic communication implies and imposes a social definition of what merits transmission, the code in which the message is to be transmitted, the person entitled to transmit it or, better, impose its reception, the persons worthy of receiving it and consequently obliged to receive it, which confers on the information transmitted its legitimacy and thereby its full meaning.

—Bourdieu and Passeron 1970: 109

device: An arrangement, a plan, a scheme; A thing designed for a particular function or adapted for a purpose; an invention, a contrivance.

—The New Shorter Oxford English Dictionary 1993

Pedagogic communication

In order to constitute the activity of teaching, all teachers in the Kasimpur school used a device which I call the 'teachering device'. This device was characterised by the manner in which the teacher used his or her voice and eye. In the classroom, teachers did not merely speak to their students, they addressed them. The voice was uniformly loud and devoid of the inflections and emotions which are present in ordinary speech. The words were uttered slowly with a uniform spacing. While speaking, the pitch varied in a standard manner—it remained flat for most of the sentence, rising sharply at the second last word, and after a very brief pause, dropping again to the original pitch at the last word/syllable:

$$\underline{\quad}\,\underline{\quad}\,\underline{\quad}\,\underline{\quad}\,\underline{\quad}\,\underline{\quad}\,\underline{\quad}\,\underline{\quad}\,\diagup\diagdown$$

India-got-her-independence-in-1947.

This gave the impression that the teacher was making important announcements which demanded that the children must pay attention. By indicating the intention with which the teacher's utterances are to be received by students, it also contributed to the meaning of these utterances.[1] From the sentence quoted as an example, what the children were expected to understand was not only that India became independent in 1947, but also that this fact was important, and they ought to know and remember it. Being an 'ought-to-know' was the most significant characteristic of all school knowledge. The act of articulating this knowledge in itself ensured that it carried the mark of being socially selected, approved, legitimate and worthy of being known.[2] Children usually echoed the last word of each sentence, giving the impression that they were listening and following—and conscious of receiving this knowledge.

The eye and look of the teacher, the other feature of the teachering device, was used like a micro-technique of exercising power. When they were not looking into their books to read, the teachers were expressionless, staring unblinkingly, looking through the children. They would move their gaze slowly over the room, from child to child, as if conducting a surveillance. Occasionally and unexpectedly, they would shift their gaze, as if to catch some unsuspecting child who may be off-guard and doing something he was not supposed to do. No one could tell when which child would be subjected to this penetrating gaze. While the voice of the teacher demanded attention for what was being spoken, the teacher's eye ensured that children did not veer from their duty. Ultimately, it seemed that every child would internalise the 'eye of the teacher', a *'Panopticon'*,[3] and regulate himself even in the teacher's absence.

It is hardly surprising that the knowledge which was encoded in the textbooks was the focus of most teaching–learning activity. It constituted the most important component of 'ought-to-know' knowledge.[4] At the time that I began fieldwork in the Kasimpur school, in the month of November, several lessons had already been taught and were being revised; in one case for the seventh time.

A typical lesson, from the Class IV and V science, language or social studies textbooks, was about 3,000 words long. All the teachers followed a similar structure while teachering. The text would be read out, a few sentences or a paragraph at a time. There would be occasional pauses in between for comprehension questions and explanations. When a lesson had been read through completely, the class would proceed to answer the questions that followed. Here, each question would be read out and answered, one by one. The focus of didactic activity was the establishment and endorsement of the right answers. The entire process typically went on for one-and-a-half to two hours, without a break. It usually ended with the injunction: 'Memorise the lesson at home.'

Framing in a textbook culture classroom

It was in the course of such monotonous, routine teaching–learning that knowledge was constituted and regulated. To analyse these classroom negotiations, I will use Bernstein's concept of 'framing' (Bernstein 1971). In the classroom, teachers and pupils participate in varying degrees and through their interactions construct what we call 'curricular knowledge'. The concept of framing focuses on their roles in defining curricular knowledge both in the matter of what is taught, i.e., the selection, and of how, i.e., its organisation and pacing. Bernstein focuses on the relative influence that teachers and pupils exercise in these matters and thereby their control and influence on what becomes constituted as knowledge in the classroom. A strongly framed curriculum is one where the teacher exercises maximum control. The teacher is the primary actor, deciding what will or will not be done, who will do what, etc. Children are not consulted; their opinions or feelings are not sought by the teacher. In contrast, a weakly framed curriculum would have a more democratic and unauthoritarian communication structure. Decisions would be taken more interactively with the children's involvement. The concept of framing thus helps us understand the nature of curricular knowledge in relation to the authority and communication structure of the classroom.

The concept of framing applies not only to pedagogy but also to the degree of insulation between school and out-of-school knowledge. A weak frame suggests that a great deal of out-of-school knowledge enters into the classroom, while a strong frame suggests that the two arenas of experience do not mix. In Bernstein's model, a weak frame can exist only with the support of an unauthoritarian, democratic communication structure.

As is expected of a textbook culture, the classrooms in Kasimpur were centred around authoritarian teachers. While transacting a lesson, all the teachers read out the text, explained and checked for comprehension by asking questions. This may lead us to expect that but for the voice of the teacher, the classrooms would be quiet, that children would hardly be heard. This was indeed the case in the classes of some of the teachers. In others, however, children's voices could be heard a great deal. The four episodes that follow give a flavour of four different classrooms: who spoke and how, what was said and what was responded to.

EPISODE 6.1 (CLASS IV)

Asha was close to completing the lesson 'Kabaddi' [5] *(Class IV, Language). She kept reading the text in a monotonous voice. She paused in between to arch her eyebrows, frown and ask a question. She did not wait for a reply and proceeded to repeat the lines from the text as answer or explanation. The whole class was sitting in absolute silence and following the text with their fingers. Occasionally, they murmured the last word of the sentence that was repeated. Except for Surya Prakash, who was looking up at the roof and out of the window. The failures were quietly doing some written work of their own.*

Asha employed the teachering device in full force. She made no reference to the fact that the children played *kabaddi* every day in the school. The children also gave no indication of their familiarity with the game. Asha's explanations consisted of repeating verbatim whatever had just been read out, only more slowly. It was as if the meaning would become obvious when the words were read out with deliberate emphasis. The asking of questions to check if children were following was also merely a ritual. She did not seem to expect any answers as she did not wait for them; nor did she make any effort to locate children who could answer. Occasionally, Jogi or Satish, the two class monitors, provided the 'right answer' in very soft but audible voices. These were completely ignored. Their occasional wrong answers were also ignored.

Krishna Kumari, the teacher in the episode that follows, also focused entirely on the text and used the same technique of repetition for 'explanation'. When she checked whether the students were following, she asked questions—which consisted of repeating the sentences in the text verbatim, with the tone rising at the end to suggest that it was a question. The children seemed to be familiar with this 'cued-questioning' (Edwards and Mercer 1987: 142) and they obligingly echoed 'yes-*ji*' to each of the pseudo-questions.

EPISODE 6.2 (CLASS V)
The first paragraph of 'Force, Work, Energy' (Class V, Science) was being read out.
Krishna Kumari: Every day we need to work?
Class: Yes *ji.*
We need to make things *gatisheel* (in motion rather than move)—like the cycle or lifting?
Yes *ji.*
What do we need for this?
Energy *ji.*
For difficult work, we need more *bal* (strength rather than force in common parlance).
Yes *ji.*
And for less work, we need less *bal*?
Yes *ji.*
To make difficult work easy, we use machines?
Yes *ji.*
She then read out the definition of machine from the text.

In contrast, when Nagpal and Bhardwaj taught, they included a great deal of information not originating from the textbook. Their classrooms were quite noisy. In the episode that follows, Nagpal was teaching a lesson on different types of soils. He demonstrated the experiment in the book on how to distinguish between different types of soil by mixing some garden soil in water and allowing it to settle. While waiting for the soil to settle, he began telling them about how soil forms. He then drew them back to the experiment and noted the property of clay. Children had their own observations to add to all that he was saying.

EPISODE 6.3 (CLASS IV)
A science lesson on soils was going on. Dinesh suddenly interrupted and began to describe a train accident where two trains collided.
Nagpal did not rebuke him. He ignored him, raised his voice and continued explaining how water gets into cracks in the rocks, forming ice and causing rocks to break as the ice expanded. He then also talked about how rocks fall and break, becoming soil. Nagpal then got back to the experiment he had started with, and made the children repeat: Clay drinks water.
Children: Clay drinks water.
Some children add: ... and it slips; ... yes *ji*, it slips If you walk on it, *ji*, you will slip.

This was ignored. Nagpal pointed to the glass with soil and water and asked: Which are the particles making the water murky?
The whole class shouted back: Clayey soil!
Nagpal then added that the potter, after making his pots, dried them in the shade. Sulaiman shouted: Because they will stick (*satak jaenge*).

Bhardwaj's style of teaching was even more non-textbook based. He often went into long asides, telling children anecdotes, jokes, stories and supplying all kinds of information, sometimes barely connected with the text.

EPISODE 6.4 (CLASS V)

The lesson was 'Manavta ke Pujari' *(Worshippers of Humanity) (Class V, Social Studies). He read out the paragraph on Gandhi.*
Bhardwaj: Have you seen English people?
Ashok and Ajay shouted out: Yes, yes!
Bhardwaj: How do they look?
Ajay: Fair-fair.
Ashok: Very-very fair-fair.
Ajay continued: I saw them in the Red Fort.
Ashok: They wore small underwear till here (*he moved his hands on his thighs*) and were holding a *chidi chakka* (badminton racquet) in one hand and waving and saying bye-bye.
Ajay: I saw them. They took a photo of Joni and me.
Manoj: They used to loot.
Bhardwaj: No, they just took away raw materials from here. *He went on to talk of how we Indians didn't even produce a needle when we became independent.*
Ajay: The man who grew wool and cotton, did the English give him money?
No answer. Bhardwaj began talking about the old days and how much each of what cost. He used the old units of measure.
Manoj: What is *ser, ji?*
This was ignored.
Bhardwaj referred to jaggery.
Manoj: How much is a maund of jaggery?
Sunil: Manoj is asking how much is a maund.
Ajay: Five kilos is a maund. For 5 paise one could get lots and lots of toffees.

Pankaj: They used to be round-round.
Manoj: They were of brass.
Ajay: Why wasn't there a war?
Bhardwaj told them about the Dandi march and opened the book to show them the picute of Gandhi. The bell rang and the class broke for half-break.

The contrast between the two pairs of classrooms—Asha and Krishna Kumari's on the one hand and Nagpal and Bhardwaj's on the other—is marked. In the former, the children were very silent. These teachers were obviously in control, using the teachering device to its full potential, and there is little doubt that the framing was very strong. In the latter, children could be heard making spontaneous, loud observations and contributing information, not all of which was directly relevant. Often their questions and observations were connected with the ongoing lesson, but equally, if they had associations with a word being mentioned, they would almost instantly blurt them out, sometimes softly and sometimes loudly. If one goes only by the presence or absence of classroom talk, one may conclude that in the latter case the framing was weak and children shared control with the teacher; this seems to be a contradiction because both these teachers were also basically authoritarian.

In fact, there is no contradiction because, although there seemed to be an involvement of children in the classroom and the presence of non-school text-based knowledge, *the framing was basically strong.* Even though non-textbook knowledge entered the classroom, the teacher completely controlled what would be treated as knowledge to be received by the students. This becomes apparent only when we examine the details of the transactions.

In Nagpal's class, the children's contributions were never incorporated into the lesson. Only the information that the teacher provided was treated as knowledge to be received by students. The knowledge that children had was simply ignored, suggesting that it was not worth any consideration. In Episode 6.3, one can see how Nagpal never responded to the children's observations. Once, when Dinesh insisted on supplementing every line that Nagpal spoke in class with information of his own, Nagpal slapped him. Later, commenting on this incident, Deepak said: 'Guru*ji* had to slap him. He acts like he knows everything.' Nagpal made it clear that only he could be the source of knowledge in the classroom and attempts by students to enter and shape the pedagogic discourse would not be tolerated. Bhardwaj's use of pedagogic authority merits special attention as it brings out the variety of epistemic techniques with which teachers controlled the boundary of the school curriculum.

Epistemic authority in framing

On the face of it, Bhardwaj's classes seemed to be a 'free-for-all'. Bhardwaj often veered from the text, making associations with words, phrases and ideas, and launching into long asides and tangentially connected stories. While he talked, almost all the children reacted with interest and made verbal contributions of associated or related information, experiences, stories and ideas. Bhardwaj often exhibited his knowledge of Sanskrit and his expertise in religious matters. He liked to quote Sanskrit *slokas* and give religious information. For instance, in the lesson on directions, he moved from the mention of East to where the sun rises every morning, to moonrise, to traditional beliefs regarding the *krishna paksh–sukla paksh* (waxing and waning) of the moon and ended with a verse in Sanskrit connected with these beliefs. Bhardwaj also spoke about a lot of mundane village matters, bringing in local and everyday knowledge of life, rituals, agriculture and gossip. The children were able to make associations with several of the things he said. His classes were often more noisy than others because of the spontaneous talk they generated, as can be seen in Episode 6.4.

Nevertheless, Bhardwaj's classes were not weakly framed. He strictly regulated the non-textbook knowledge that would be additionally considered an ought-to-know. He used the teachering voice—slow and deliberate, in the mode of making announcements. This gave everything he said, whether mundane or esoteric, the character of being 'ought-to-know' knowledge. Only the non-textbook knowledge that he himself spoke of could be considered a part of the lesson and the classroom discourse. The only exception he made was for the class monitor, Vipin. All facts and observations offered by other children 'hung' about the lesson, never becoming a part of it.

Bhardwaj used three techniques to delegitimise information that children provided and to strengthen the frame boundary. All three techniques were based on the teacher as an epistemic authority responsible for the child's intellectual and moral development, rather than only a bureaucratic/institutional authority.[6] In all three, we see the functioning of epistemic authority. The first method was to ignore children's contributions completely. This was the technique most commonly used by all teachers. Ignoring gave the impression that the things children were saying were worthless, or at least unimportant; the knowledge was not worth incorporating into the classroom discourse. It was not that what children were saying was not true or in some way inaccurate. To comment on truth or falsity, on accuracy and inaccuracy, would imply that the statement was worth such a truth consideration and therefore must itself have some value. That would automatically make it a part of the classroom discourse. Ignoring it completely would mean that the statement was simply not worth knowing—not worth even the consideration of whether it was true or false.

The second technique that Bhardwaj used was to dismiss the information provided on the ground that the student was violating the rules of good behaviour and being impertinent. The information thus provided would thereby become illegitmate and be kept outside the frame. In Episode 6.5, Bhardwaj selectively rejected Ashok's contributions about the camel on the ground that he did not respect the rules for communicating in the classroom and that 'he talks too much'.

EPISODE 6.5 (CLASS V)
Bhardwaj: What are the animals of the desert?
Amit, the only one with his hand raised, was asked to answer: Reindeer, dog....
Vipin cut him short: Not those of the ice lands... of the desert, like Arabia.
Silence continued. I interjected: **Guess (andaz lagao)** *from the vegetation. It is dry and sparse. What animals do you think you would find there? Only Vipin had his hand up.*
Bhardwaj asked Vikas to answer. He thought a bit and said: Camel.
Bhardwaj: It stores water.
Vipin, who until then had been standing and teachering *with Bhardwaj, now returned to his place on the mat:* In its hump it stores food.
Ashok: They get milk from the *oont* (camel[m]).
Bhardwaj: Nonsense.
Ashok: Guru*ji*, you said so.
Bhardwaj: I said so? I may have said oontni (camel[f]).
Ashok: Ji, if there are *oont,* then there would also be *oontni.*
Ashok was standing, twisting his handkerchief behind his back. He continued: Its skin is used for making things. *The whole class was very quiet. Still he didn't seem able to stop himself as he continued to make connections and provide more information.*
Bhardwaj (angrily): Is this a class or a playground? (He) talks too much.

Bhardwaj was able to assert his control of the frame boundary through his pedagogic function of regulating the moral order of the community and defining what would count as acceptable behaviour in the classroom as opposed to the playground outside. We see in this episode that Ashok first argued his case: if there are male camels, then obviously there would also be female camels! He then added more information about camels. It seems a contradiction that Ashok continued to talk and supply more information when the reception of the first statement itself was negative. He seemed to be trying to convince Bhardwaj that he knew what he was talking about; that his first statement was not a falsehood but merely a slip of the tongue. This was, most likely, a tactic Ashok was using to gain credibility.[7]

The third technique that Bhardwaj used to challenge and disqualify information that children provided was to 'establish' that it was based on false criteria and therefore could not be considered knowledge. He would further give the information the colouring of lies rather than incorrectness—and the speaker would become a liar with pretensions rather than simply someone who had a misguided belief.[8] This technique was used even if the child's statement was correct, perhaps especially so in such circumstances.

EPISODE 6.6 (CLASS V)
They were reading about Martin Luther King.
Bhardwaj: His only sin was he was black.
Manoj: Discrimination on the basis of colour *ji!*
Bhardwaj (mockingly): You were not born then. How do you know?

EPISODE 6.7 (CLASS V)
They were reading couplets (doha) *from their language book. One had a reference to the pot that is hung above the* linga *in the Shiva temples, from which water drops onto the* linga *below.*
Surinder, Manoj and Ashok raised their hands, nodding agreement and indicating they knew this.
Manoj: Like in Amarnath!
Bhardwaj rudely asked him: Have you been there?
Manoj (defensivly): Yes, when I was very young.
Bhardwaj (making a disbelieving sound): They don't let children there.
Manoj (softly): No *ji. (More softly, so only I sitting in front of him could hear):* It is a very beautiful place.

In both these episodes Bhardwaj questioned the basis on which Manoj was making his observation. His comments 'you were not born then, how do you know?' and 'they don't let children there' suggested that therefore Manoj's statement need not be taken into consideration.

While establishing that the answer was faulty, Bhardwaj sometimes used his authority to simply distort the truth and attribute blatantly absurd responses to the student. Bhardwaj used this technique in Episode 6.8 to create reasons to reprimand Ashok.

EPISODE 6.8 (CLASS V)

Balbir (the Boys' Home caretaker) was drawing pictures on the blackboard for the children to copy. Bhardwaj caught Ashok and Pankaj talking softly with each other.
Why were you talking?
Ashok: I wasn't talking to him. He was talking to me.
Bhardwaj: What about?
Ashok: He was saying national flag.
Bhardwaj: Here Balbir sir is drawing, ask him if you don't know. In the last exam what did you draw for the flag? What colours did you fill?
Ashok was silent.
Bhardwaj asked the class: What are the colours of the flag?
Several hands went up. Amit was selected to answer: Saffron, white, green.
Bhardwaj: And you know what he filled? Saffron, red and blue!!
Ashok: No *ji*, I did it right.
Bhardwaj ignored him and continued: And in the centre you didn't put a circle.
Ashok, more softly: No, I did.
Bhardwaj: If you did, how did it get erased? Talks too much. When *Bhai saab* is here, why can't you ask him? Ask him if you don't understand something in drawing.

From these episodes we can see that controlling the boundary was not simply a matter of exercising bureaucratic or institutional authority. Nor was it a matter of the teacher just asserting, 'because *I* say so'. Even when Asha and Krishna Kumari ignored the children, the form of control they exercised had an epistemic dimension. Certainly, in the case of Nagpal and Bhardwaj, the control involved a more elaborate exercise of epistemic authority *embedded* in the regulating hierarchical order within which teacher and students related to each other. The fact that children could be heard saying so much in their classrooms, although framing was strong, is worthy of some comment. Both these teachers lived in Kasimpur village and were familiar figures outside the school, meeting and interacting with the children's families. In contrast, the two women teachers came from towns further away and perceived themselves as more urbane and socially superior to the children. Consequently, contrary to the myth that children are happier with women teachers, the children were more free with the two male teachers from their village.

There was only one student in the school who enjoyed a weak frame and was able to intervene and alter classroom discourse. This was Vipin, one of the Class V monitors. In his negotiations of frame boundary with the teacher presented in the following section, we can see the epistemic and cognitive significance of weak framing.

Negotiating boundary control

Vipin had a special place in Bhardwaj's class. Like all monitors, he *teachered* when the teacher was absent.[9] In addition, Vipin enjoyed another unique privilege. He was the only monitor who teachered even when the teacher was present, and even when a new lesson was being taught. Vipin had the privilege of a weak frame. The non-textbook knowledge that he brought was given a legitimate place in class and incorporated into the lessons.

Vipin brought counter-factuals to bear on statements that Bhardwaj made, occasionally challenging Bhardwaj's own formulations of knowledge and forcing him to accommodate. Unlike the observations of Manoj or Ashok described earlier, Vipin's interjections were not ignored; instead, Bhardwaj responded to them. Even if Vipin was wrong, Bhardwaj did not abuse him but proved to him that he was wrong.

EPISODE 6.9 (CLASS V)
Bhardwaj asked the class to tell him the characteristics of living things.
Several children answered: Living things move.
Bhardwaj accepted this and was about to move on when Vipin interjected: Guru*ji*, what about the needle of the watch?
Bhardwaj put this question back to the class.
The children answered: Non-living.
Bhardwaj and Vipin: Then how come it moves?

There was no answer. Then Bhardwaj explained: Movement is not enough—the hands of the clock do not move on their own. Living things can move on their own.

EPISODE 6.10 (CLASS V)

Bhardwaj: Are animals and birds the same? What is the difference between a bird and an animal?
Sunil answered: Animals have four legs and birds have two.
Bhardwaj rejected this: No, some animals have two legs. A kangaroo has two legs. Have you seen a kangaroo? (*There was a weak 'yes' from the children.*) It stands on two legs, the other two are hands.
Joni answered next: Birds fly, animals don't fly.
Bhardwaj: Han ji. This is the real thing. Birds fly, animals don't fly.
Vipin: But what about the bat?
Bhardwaj: It flies, it is a bird.
Vipin: But it has four legs.
Bhardwaj: But birds also have legs.
Vipin: But it has four legs, birds have two.
Bhardwaj: But it flies, it is a bird.
Vipin: It is in the Class II book, it is not a bird nor an animal.

In these episodes we see that Vipin was directly contributing to the knowledge being constructed. His observations on the movement of the hands of a clock and the ability of the bat to fly had consequences for the concepts of 'living' and 'bird' that were being formulated. He was making observations with epistemological consequences and not simply making associations. By taking cognisance of these observations and incorporating them into the pedagogic discourse, Bhardwaj allowed Vipin an active role in the construction of curricular knowledge. Vipin could contradict what the teacher said and, at the end of a debate, even refuse to give up a belief in the absence of adequate proof to the contrary. All student monitors shared the privilege of being allowed to 'teacher' in the teacher's absence. But the weak frame for Vipin was a significant additional privilege in the otherwise teacher-centred epistemic community. This could have been because of Vipin's charisma. He had won several zonal-level awards in drawing competitions and was admired for this achievement by all the teachers in the school. I will not comment further on *why* Vipin was different. These episodes have been included here in order to show that, even in a classroom with strong framing, there can be some individual pupils who are allowed the privilege of negotiating the frame boundary.

The episodes also illustrate the epistemic and cognitive richness of a weak frame.

II
Learning Lessons

New lessons were taught with strong framing. In other words, both the knowledge that could be included and the pedagogic options of how it would be organised and paced were controlled and regulated by the teacher. In this section we will see how both the manner in which this knowledge would be learnt and ultimately also the student's identity as a learner were regulated.

After a lesson had been 'taught', the focus of the teacher's attention was to ensure that this knowledge would also be 'learnt' by the children. While in educational and everyday discourse, the term 'learning' implies the development of some abilities, there is no general agreement either on the concept of learning itself or on the abilities it includes: understanding and comprehension, making connections with other things, applying and solving problems, formulating and doing things, etc. In the Kasimpur school the process of learning involved establishing what would be considered the 'right answer to a question' and then ensuring that it was memorised in exactly the same form. Through this process these statements acquired the quality of being 'commonable' knowledge, i.e., being common (in the sense of being shared), public and objective (Welbourne 1993: 6).

Although ultimately there was a great degree of agreement on what would count as 'the right answers' among the children and teachers, this was not established by brute diktat. Children were not expected to remain silent, waiting to be told the answer to a question. Teachers did not simply dictate answers. But an agreement was arrived at through a negotiation wherein the teacher could actively establish what would be considered as 'correct'. Thereafter, in revision sessions and eventually in the examinations, these answers would function tyrannically as the only possible answers to given questions.

Establishing the 'right answers'

Monitoring learning was even more time-consuming and intensive than teaching new lessons, as 'right answers' had to meet very stringent criteria.

The criterion of matching or being based on the textbook, both for content and language, was the one quoted by teachers most often.

EPISODE 6.11 (CLASS V)
Krishna Kumari: Why is it difficult to walk on a *chikni* (smooth) floor?
Pankaj: Because the shoes will slip.
Krishna Kumari: No, your answer must be based on what we have learnt in the book.

The guidebook also functioned as a reference but it was not openly endorsed by the teacher. More rarely, something that the teacher had in mind could function as the right answer to the question asked. Children had to learn that their own observations, understanding and articulations would not be acceptable. They had to learn to conform and restrict themselves to the book in content, style and language. The following discussion is based primarily on episodes taken from the classes of one of the teachers, Krishna Kumari, of Class V.

EPISODE 6.12 (CLASS V)
Krishna Kumari asked a question which was not given in the textbook. If you push the table, will it be set into motion (*gati*)?
The children chorussed: No.
Why?
Because it does not have wheels...
No, that is not the answer.

As can be seen from Episode 6.12, the teacher did not ask questions in order to explore what the students were thinking; in the Socratic dialogue, for example, the question would have such a pedagogic function. The children's 'wrong answers' were of no interest. Even after almost five years of schooling, children had not yet ceased to think and respond to questions with their spontaneous intelligence. The question served simply as a stimulus to bring out these answers. The teacher then selected and reinforced one of them as the appropriate response or the 'right answer'. In the course of this, she communicated to them that it was unacceptable to bring in relevant, everyday experience or to use their own language to express themselves. Their spontaneous tendencies were thus checked. As in the case of framing, one of the most common techniques was to ignore all wrong answers. The teacher waited for a particular answer, indirectly suggesting that others were not right.

EPISODE 6.13 (CLASS V)
Krishna Kumari: How are newspapers distributed from the printing office?
Aeroplane.
Motorcycle.
Train.
She ignored all these and asked them to look at the last sentence of the book which said that motors standing outside the newspaper office take the papers to their destination. She asked the question once again.
The answers were the same as before.
She made an exasperated sound. Can the train come to the office to collect the paper? Tell me properly.
The children now repeated the words in the textbook.
Krishna Kumari: OK, sit down.

Episode 6.14 illustrates a slightly more elaborate negotiation where other possible, but non-textbook-based, answers had to be negated. When Krishna Kumari asked the question: 'What are the ways of getting news?', she wanted the children to think only in the restricted cognitive frame of the textbook. Harish, who first answered the question, did not do so. She did not say he was wrong (he was right), but she implied this when she accepted only what Abdul said, repeating and reinforcing it.

EPISODE 6.14 (CLASS V)
A combined Class V, with Krishna Kumari in charge.
The lesson 'Samachar Patr' *(Newspaper) was being read out. After the first paragraph, she asked:* What are the ways of getting news?
Harish answered: Radio, telephone, TV...
She did not indicate that Harish was right. Instead, she interrupted and said: All that you have said is expensive. Can you tell me a cheap way of getting news?
Harish added: ...Telegram.
She then asked Abdul.
He softly said: Akhbaar (newspaper in Urdu).
She just nodded and said: Samachar Patr (newspaper in Hindi). *She asked:* How many of you have TVs?
Though only five children did not have television sets at home, she still said: Look, that means it is expensive.[10]

Very short answers, even if they were right, were not acceptable: 'So small? Say more.' Yet, when children brought in tangentially relevant and interesting facts or extended reasoning and actions to consequences, they were asked to restrict themselves.

EPISODE 6.15 (CLASS V)

The children were answering questions from 'Force, Work, Energy'.
Krishna Kumari read out the question: What are the uses of friction?
Pankaj came up with the first example: If there wasn't any friction, we would not be able to write on the blackboard. If there wasn't any friction, tyres would slip on the road... and-if-car-tyres-are-slipping-it-would-be-difficult-to-stop-it.
Krishna Kumari announced stiffly: Restrict answers to the questions.

In this episode, Pankaj added a sentence of his own—about the danger of tyres slipping on a frictionless road. He was asked to restrict his answers. Originality or deviation in language or expression were not acceptable either. The language used to express the answer also had to be the same as the language used in the book.

EPISODE 6.16 (CLASS V)

She asked: Name five things which when force is applied on them make motion *(bal lagaane se gati karti hai)*.
Five hands went up. She asked Pravin to answer.
Pravin: Rail *gadi*, cycle ... *and then went blank.*
She indicated Pavan-2.
Pavan-2: Rail *gadi*, cycle, ... *(hesitated, then)*... bus, scooter... *She asked the next child.*
Pavan-1 recited: Cycle *bal lagaane se chalti hai* (a cycle moves when a force is applied).
She corrected him, saying: You must say *'gati karti hai'* (makes motion). We are talking in science.

Once the right answer was established, it then functioned as *the only* acceptable answer. Even the word order could not be changed. Children seemed to agree that ultimately there should be no deviations from these standard answers. There seemed to be a congruence on the belief that ought-to-know knowledge must be learnt in the form of 'right answers'. They strictly regulated each other during revision classes, suggesting a high degree of agreement in this matter:

EPISODE 6.17 (CLASS IV)

Sominder was asked to answer the question: From where to where does India extend?

He replied: From Arunachal Pradesh to Jammu Kashmir.

Ashish and several other children pointed out that this was incorrect. The answer should have been, 'Jammu Kashmir to Arunachal Pradesh'. Nagpal, the teacher who was conducting the revision, did not object.

Even essays had 'right answers'—the one that conformed to the essay given in the guidebooks.[11] Children memorised the essays given and reproduced them in their tests and examinations. They were quite certain that they could not add any information of their own to the text. The pressure of having to repeat exactly the same words as the official answer was so great that sometimes the words would tumble out in a senseless, absurd order. When this happened, their attention was not directed to the meaninglessness of what they were saying. Instead, they were exhorted to memorise better and directed to the book again for the 'correct' answer.

EPISODE 6.18 (CLASS V)

The next question was about Bal Gangadhar Tilak. Krishna Kumari asked them to tell her what he said. Some versions of the answers children gave were: Bharat mera adhikar hai, mein isko lekar jaoonga (India is my right and I will take it).

Swatantrata mera janam hai ... (Independence is my birth ...).

She gave up, making an exasperated sound. She read out the correct answer from the book and asked them to repeat it over and over again: Swaraj mera janam sidh adhikar hai aur mein isko lekar rahoonga (Independence is my birthright and I shall have/take it).

Answers based on everyday experience, especially if they did not match the official textbook knowledge, were implicated with a sense of being incorrect. Children also repeatedly exposed themselves to situations where the teacher had to intervene to define the 'right answer' and establish what children 'ought-to-know'. It seemed that if it wasn't for the teacher's epistemic authority, children would not be able to distinguish between 'correct' and 'incorrect' knowledge. Without the teacher telling them, they would not know what could not be considered acceptable knowledge and language in the school setting. But for the constant surveillance of the teacher, they would not know what they ought-to-know.

Pedagogic communication of non-textbook knowledge: The recitation device

It seemed that to all questions that are asked in pedagogic communication there had to be a *right* answer, against which all answers were judged. Even non-textbook questions—and questions about ordinary things and everyday experiences—were handled by teachers as though there was *one* right answer. Of course, as teachers exercised their pedagogic authority also as epistemic authority, it was they who ultimately decided what would be treated as *the* right answer. Accordingly, they imbued any other answer with a sense of incorrectness or inappropriateness.

EPISODE 6.19 (CLASS V)
I am tired, *Krishna Kumari announced. She continued, reminding the class of the headmaster's morning lecture on making a good resolution and asked all the children to make resolutions.*
Pavan-1: Not-to-tell-lies.
You can't take such a big oath. *(Then to the class)* Each one of you has to, so think of something.
Pavan tried again: The-work-I-am-to-do-I-will-definitely-do.
You already have been doing that till now, just left it off one or two times. That will continue...
She turned her attention to Krishna Maan.
Krishna Maan: I haven't yet thought of anything.
When will you think? Does that mean that the HM's speech was a waste?
Krishna Maan: No *ji.*
She turned her attention to the farthest line in which several of the 'weaker' children were sitting. All of them stood up one after another and said nothing.
She announced: The whole line is useless.
Vikki: I-will-read-good-books-like-patriotic-books.
When will you read? Before meals or after meals?
Vikki was quiet, not knowing how to respond.
Krishna Kumari continued: Things won't add up *(Baat nahin banegi).*
You will have to take time in the morning. Then things will add up.
She made Vikki repeat the resolution.
He said: I-will-read-good-books-in-the-morning-or...
She cut him short. Don't put in an 'or'. Say for sure when you will do it.
She asked Pankaj. He too said he would read good books.
Before or after school work?

Pankaj: Before.
Even if school work gets left out?
She then announced generally: Without reason I will not talk. I will talk
only after work. Who will take this oath?
Hands began to go up.
She observed: The hands are going up slowly. This should not happen.

The child's moral development was a legitimate concern of the teacher
but it was an area where the textbook did not define the questions and
answers. The children had been asked to take their own oaths, yet Krishna
Kumari could find fault with what they were saying, evaluating their
answers against some invisible standards she had in her mind. The manner
in which some of the children responded is important to note here. When
Pavan responded he altered his tone, making it flat, and spoke the words
in a staccato, evenly-spaced fashion. This made it seem as though he was
reciting them from memory, without comprehending what they meant.
As in the case of teachering this effect was achieved with the use of the
voice. I call this the 'recitation device'. Children used this as a technique
to give their own original, non-textbook-based answers an air of legitimacy.
By using a flat tone and speaking the words in a monotonous, rhythmic
fashion, they conveyed the feeling that they were giving a standard, right
answer that had been learnt from some other (valid) source. The impression was that what they were saying was being retrieved from memory—
received knowledge—and not the result of any independent thinking
process. We see Pavan using this device again on another occasion:

EPISODE 6.20 (CLASS V)
Krishna Kumari began a vague, desultory discussion on eating fruits. She
asked *them vague questions like:* How many fruits do you eat? Do you
eat on holidays? On school days? Why 'no'?
*Ramesh, who was sitting near me, answered in a very low voice. His answer
was based on what he did.*
Pavan stood up and answered in a loud, recitation voice: I-eat-fruits-every-
day.

The topic that was being discussed was strictly non-curricular, though
it did have something to do with 'values' that children were supposed to
imbibe. By being brought into pedagogic communication, it was transformed and acquired a new status. Just as teachers used the teachering
device to turn non-textbook knowledge into ought-to-knows, children used

a parallel 'recitation device' to give non-textbook knowledge the form of remembered, or learnt, 'correct' knowledge.

The right question

Not only were there right answers to questions, there also seemed to be 'right' questions—questions for which such right answers could be expected. These were questions from the textbook. Children did not expect to be asked to answer other questions. As illustrated in Episode 6.21, if such questions were asked, children reacted to them with nonchalance or surprise, unable to formulate a sensible answer or perhaps too frightened to try.

> EPISODE 6.21 (CLASS V)
> *Krishna Kumari was teaching the lesson on force and motion:* What will happen if you push a cycle?
> *The children were nonplussed. Even Pavan, who had memorised all the textbook answers, was unable to say anything.*
> *Finally, she herself said:* If you push the cycle it will fall. *Then she asked:* Where do you need to apply force to make the cycle move?
> *Again, there was no answer.*

Children sometimes pointed out that the question being asked was somehow wrong or invalid, since it was not the question in the book. They would even 'correct' the question, or direct the teacher to where the correct question was to be found—the textbook or the guidebook, as in Episode 6.22. The class had read a lesson about development, with names of dams that have been built on various rivers.

> EPISODE 6.22 (CLASS IV)
> *Nagpal asked them to answer the question:* On which rivers are the various dams built?
> *There was no answer. He asked Ashish to read out the answer from the guidebook.*
> *Deepak:* It isn't written in the guidebook. We only have to tell the names of the dams, not which rivers they are built on.
> *Nagpal did not insist that they answer this question.*

When such questions were asked by me, they simply brushed them aside, showing no inclination or interest to answer and pointing out that they were invalid questions.

EPISODE 6.23 (CLASS V)
The Class V children requested me to ask them questions from a lesson.
What is the story about?
Amit: Can't tell, one can't remember (*Yaad nahin rehta*).
What happens in this story?
He started giving me very detailed sentences which, it turned out, he was repeating verbatim from the book.
I interrupted: **No, tell me the important things (vishesh baat).**
Amit: Vishesh baat ... And went on to give me more detailed sentences, all taken from the book.
I then asked a few questions about the incidents in the story.
Sunil-2: The questions you are asking are not questions. Ask questions from the textbook or guidebook.

III
'Showing that One Knows'

Revision

Teachers felt that in order to be considered a good teacher, they should repeatedly revise lessons, so that children would be able to perform in examinations with ease. In Class III, at the time I began my fieldwork, not only had all the lessons been taught, but they had already completed one round of revision and were beginning the second. Later that academic year in March, Pavan Kumar, their class teacher, spoke to me of his plans for the new academic session, when they would be in Class IV. The new session would begin on 1 April (1993). He would work '*ḍhadadhad*'[12] to finish the entire course by 15 May. Then he would spend the rest of the session (from July 1993 till March 1994) revising the lessons three times over. 'By then children will be able to do (the examinations) without even reading.'

In Chapter IV we saw that developing a '*pehchaan*' and signalling it was an important part of becoming educated. During the revision of a lesson, all questions in the textbook at the end of the lesson would be asked in turn and students would have to 'show that they know': they had to demonstrate that they had learnt what they were supposed to. These were opportunities to perform—as rehearsals for the examination. The only difference was that for revision, children were tested on only their knowledge of a few lessons at a time, while for an examination their knowledge of several lessons was tested. Hoskin (1979) points out that in the form of revision, examinations become a constant pressure in education practice, of keeping students 'up to the mark' and testing performance. For teachers, these were not sessions to teach something new, but to monitor students' knowledge and their identities as knowers, i.e., those who knew the answers.

Revision sessions were greatly enjoyed by those who knew the answers to the questions being asked. When a question was asked to which several children knew the answer, there was always a lot of excitement, with each child being eager to be the one chosen to answer. Children would begin to repeatedly chorus: 'Aunty-*ji*/Guruji, *hum batayen?*' (may I tell?), until someone was chosen to speak.

EPISODE 6.24 (CLASS V)
Bhardwaj asked which lesson should be revised. Ajay shouted out a lesson number immediately.
Sunil told me: He (Ajay) asked for that exercise because he has learnt everything by heart.
Ajay heard this but did not deny it. He said: He's jealous.

EPISODE 6.25 (CLASS IV)
In Nagpal's class, Ashish was asking questions in social studies from the guidebook, and childen were shouting out answers. There was a lot of enthusiasm.
Nagpal intervened: You will not shout out the answers. You will raise your hands and answer, because otherwise you shout out the answers even before the question is complete.
Naresh told me excitedly: I know all the answers.

The children exuded a triumphant exhilaration when they could show their teacher and the rest of the class that they knew. They would usually preen self-consciously and throw glances at those who did not seem to know. Others who also knew the answer would often join in and chorus eagerly. There was worth attached to attainment and a keen awareness of this. This was especially so in mathematics. Often one heard children say to each other: 'Look, I got it right and you got it wrong' (Neeraj, Class IV), or 'Look, you got it wrong. I told you and you got it right' (Raiz, Class V).

The revision sessions were a source of great tension and terror for those who either did not know or were not sure of the right answers. It was not a simple matter of not knowing the answer. The child was made to feel guilty on two counts: of laziness in not applying himself to memorise the answer and, worse, of trying to hide and cheat the teacher. This meant that simply exhorting the child to memorise or ensuring that the child memorised the answer would not be enough. The child would have to also be punished and disciplined so that he would get rid of these morally bad traits of laziness and lying. Punishments could be extremely severe for such moral slips.

Types of revision sessions

The teacher-led revision sessions were of primarily two kinds. While the first involved simple threats and punishments, the second was a more elaborate form of interrogation. Occasionally, the appointed class monitor also was given this responsibility. The sessions led by the class monitors were occasions for them to teacher using the teachering device, and showed how the eye of the teacher was made more penetrating.

Threat and punishment: In the simple kind of revision, a question would be asked; if the child was unable to give the right answer or was simply unable to answer, he would be threatened with punishment or be punished. It seemed that this was a matter of not having learnt the lesson well, not concentrating or being careless and lazy.

EPISODE 6.26 (CLASS IV)
Asha came up, looked into Navin's book, pulled him up by his ear, twisted it, slapped his face and said: You want to go out?
He stared back at her, open-mouthed.
She walked around and asked the others to show her their books. She looked into one and said: Now if you make a mistake, I'll hit you four times *(char-char bar)* with a stick. Concentrate and work!

Verbal chastisement was common, but so were punishments that involved actual or threatened physical discomfort of some kind. Generally, children were not allowed to sit if they got an answer wrong, or else they had their ears twisted or cheeks pinched. Sometimes they were asked to stand on one leg and raise one or both hands in the air. Sometimes they were slapped hard across the face. Occasionally, they were beaten with a stick.

Verbal chastisement involved name-calling and threats of physical discomfort. In addition, actual or threatened excommunication was also used as a punishment. Being made to stand outside the class or being sent home from school signified a temporary withdrawal of membership in the community.

There was no hierarchy of punishments that operated for major and minor lapses. All lapses were treated as equally major, and the particular form of punishment meted out seemed to depend on the individual teacher and on the mood of that teacher. Barnes (1986) has noted that the arbitrary exercise of power is more absolute and inspires more fear than a regular, logical exercise of power.

Nagpal was the least likely to beat children. Bhardwaj did not beat children with a stick in my presence, but children confided to me that he did otherwise. On some occasions, I did see a stick on his table and children crying bitterly but quietly and nursing bruises after what had obviously been a whipping. Asha and Krishna Kumari did not use the stick very often but were quite free with pinching cheeks, twisting ears, beating and punching children very hard, even in my presence. Often, when a child came up to Asha with some work to be corrected, her first move, even before beginning to read, was to grab the child's ear and proceed to twist and pull it with every error she spotted. Children were also made to sit in the '*murga*' (rooster) pose—their arms were arched under their knees and their ears held with their hands. Sometimes they would be made to do their corrections sitting like that—holding an ear with one hand and writing with the other.

EPISODE 6.27 (CLASS V)
Krishna Kumari called all those who had got the answer wrong up to her table. She picked each notebook up by turn.
To Om Prakash: Can't even add (*punched him*).
To Sachin: Written wrong figures (*slapped him hard on the face*).
To Virendar: Can't add (*twisted his arm*).
To Anil: Why didn't you write the figures? (*beat him*).
To Raj Kumar: Class V and can't write the figures (*screwed his ear and slapped his cheek*).
To Pramod: Can't add (*slapped him*).
Then to all the six: Now you look. *She copied out the numbers on the blackboard and explained. She essentially just repeated the algorithm. She sent the boys back to rework the problems and get their books rechecked. Anil and Om Prakash got their answers wrong again even after the 'explanation'. She ordered them to sit 'murga' and work out the problem sitting like that. She began dictating the next problem, warning them:*

Do it carefully. If you don't, you will be beaten with a stick. And sit in straight lines. No one will look into anyone else's work.

Interrogation: While all the teachers conducted this kind of 'simple' revision sessions, two of them, Asha and Krishna Kumari, preferred the interrogation type of revision session. While in the first case, some children who did not know the answers could escape detection and punishment, the interrogation type of revision made it very difficult for them to dodge the teacher's eye. The teachers were not interested in simply identifying those who did not know, but in *exposing* them. The technique emphasised the students' lack of knowledge and their lower epistemic status. It also served to show them that they could not hide this ignorance from the teach-ers, who used these occasions to remind the students of their need for strict pedagogic authority and an authoritarian teacher. Episode 6.28 illustrates the basic interrogation technique that was used. The teachering device was used in its full form—controlled voice, expressionless face and surveillant eye. The aim was to trap those children who did not know the right answers. Krishna Kumari would ask several children to answer the same question and reserve all comment, whether communicated verbally or through facial expression, until the end.

EPISODE 6.28 (CLASS V)
Krishna Kumari began the true–false exercise: Friction is always a disadvantage.
She first asked Pankaj to answer: True.
Next: False.
Next: True.
Next: False.
She kept all the children standing and continued asking them, one after another, until 15 children had answered true or false. She did not give them even the slightest indication of whether they were right or wrong.
She then announced: All those who said false sit down.
The relief of these children was obvious. She asked Vikki, one of the seven who were still standing, in an ironical, triumphant tone: So you thought the answer was true? Why?
Vikki's eyes were wet with tension and fear.

Krishna Kumari herself did not seem interested in the answer. She surveyed her 'catch' before moving on to the next question. A variation of this technique consisted of playing on children's psychology and deliberately misleading them. In the middle of the interrogation, which proceeded column-wise, she would ask the class monitor to answer and then return to the original sequence. Typically, all the children who answered after the monitor echoed his response.

EPISODE 6.29 (CLASS V)
Krishna Kumari took up the next true–false questions: A force can change the direction of another force.
She asked Navin: True.
She asked Parveen: False.
Parveen was the class monitor. All the children who were asked after him also said false.
Krishna Kumari: All of you have become sheep. Can't a force change the direction of a force? Then why don't any of you think and give the answer?

Sometimes, she would deliberately 'caution' them; this usually ended with the children changing their answer to the opposite of what they were going to say. It always pleased her when they fell into her trap and answered incorrectly, because that helped to prove her point that they were ignorant and had tried to cheat her.

EPISODE 6.30 (CLASS V)
Her next question was: By applying grease friction can be lowered.
One after the other children answered: Yes, yes, yes, yes.
Krishna Kumari: Caution, you know what happened in the last two cases.
The children continued to answered: yes, yes, no, no.
Caution, be careful when you answer. Think, answer carefully (dhyan se).
Then she said: All those who said yes, sit down. All those who said no remain standing. *She caught one of the boys by his ear, shook it and said: It's no? It's no? Hain? Hain?*

Another technique was to question specifically to establish that a particular child did not know something. The question would be posed in the manner of a policeman interrogating a prisoner. The expectation seemed to be that the student would either get the answer wrong or keep quiet. A long silence would ensue and one would literally see the pressure build up on the child. If he did get the answer right, then instead of acknowledging it or making any comment, she would extend the questioning. This conveyed the feeling that the first answer was somehow incomplete. Also, in general, questioning was extended in the hope of reaching a point where the student would not know the right answer. In Episodes 6.31 and 6.32 we see how, when the child did answer correctly, the question itself was extended into another, giving him another opportunity to answer incorrectly.

EPISODE 6.31 (CLASS V)
Krishna Kumari: When I pick up a cup and let it go, it falls. Why?
Raj Kumar answered after a long pause: Gurutva bal (gravitational force).
She did not indicate to him that he was right. Keeping her face expressionless and giving him a hard look, she instructed: Write it.
He went up to the blackboard and took about two minutes to slowly write it. He managed to get it right.
She did not tell him he was right. Just indicated to him with a nod that he might sit.

EPISODE 6.32 (CLASS IV)
Asha: Which year did we get independence?
Jogi softly said: 1947.
Asha: And date? And month?

Some children, when they were not absolutely sure of the answer, took refuge in silence. This was not tolerated by their teachers who subjected them to sharp, unkind remarks. 'This Bhoop Singh and Raj Kumar are useless; they don't even make us laugh' (Krishna Kumari, Class V). On occasion, Nagpal and Asha would address their questions to the 'failures'. The entire class would roar with laughter at their attempts to answer. They were not reprimanded. The only purpose of asking them to speak seemed to be to provide entertainment. Since the teachers did not seem to expect the failures to answer, they did not punish them. The failures, too, seemed to know that they would not be beaten and so did not mind speaking.

The 'quiz question'

It seems that all questions asked in pedagogic settings were not real questions. For usually it was the teacher who asked questions. Teachers quizzed children on their general knowledge and sometimes the children quizzed each other. This quizzing was also pedagogic and not a simple relation of communication. During this quizzing, questions would be asked and answers given. But unlike questions in ordinary communication—where the questioner wants the answer to something he doesn't know or isn't sure about—in the quiz question, the questioner knows the answer. The tone used to ask the question also conveyed a challenge.

EPISODE 6.33 (CLASS V)
The mathematics class was about to end. Suddenly, Vipin jumped up to take charge. He stood up and announced: OK. Who knows the area of India? *He had the class's attention, but no one knew the answer. A whole minute passed. I asked Vipin the same question.*
He replied: About 15 lakh sq km.
Sunil confirmed this. (Apparently, Sunil in his capacity as the other monitor was not required to answer the question when Vipin first posed it.)

When children asked each other questions, they asked about things that they knew so that they could 'show-that-they-know'. Episode 6.33 illustrates this expectation.

EPISODE 6.34 (CLASS V)
Vikas asked the teacher: What is cobalt?
Vipin intervened and asked Vikas himself: Do you know?
Vikas: No.

Sometimes, when the question was real and the questioner did not himself know the answer, the others would get irritated and ask: 'If you don't know, then how can you expect us to know?' When children asked each other quiz questions, the intention was not to find the answer, but to show that one knew something and to find out if the other person knew it as well. Knowing such items of information seemed to establish a transient hierarchy of status among children. Children liked to ask quiz questions that they were sure the other person would not be able to answer. Such questions were put in a challenging, taunting manner. It seemed like they wanted to show that they had some knowledge that the other child did not. They would often not even provide the answer but preen, as though they were now superior and privileged in some way. In Episode 6.35 Subash seemed to have acquired this status, which was then taken over by Vipin.

EPISODE 6.35 (CLASS V)
Subhash: In which direction does the moon rise?
Ajay: Moon rise?
Subhash: West. *Then he continued:* In which direction does the sun set?
Vipin came up, challenging them in a shrill voice: Do you know? Do you
know? *(pata hai?)* Where does the sun set? *He looked around with
satisfaction, happy that no one knew what to make of this question. He
continued:* Do you know, where does it set?

Given a setting where general knowledge is regarded as cultural
capital,[13] the ones who possessed it could feel superior to those who did
not. Surjeet and Gupta, teachers of Class I, often projected themselves as
possessing a great deal of this capital and considered themselves to be far
superior to the '*ganvar*' village children. Episode 6.36 is taken from
Bhardwaj's class.

EPISODE 6.36 (CLASS V)
*Surjeet and Gupta, both Class I teachers, came in. They ignored Bhardwaj
sitting in the front, leave alone wishing him or inquiring what he was doing.
They just announced to the children:* Han children, we are going to ask
you some general knowledge questions. Who knows the name of our
country?
Navin: Bharat.
They asked four other children who said: Don't know.
Ajay: No *ji*, India.
*All the while, Surjeet and Gupta looked very pleased and simply did not
acknowledge any answers. They paused pointedly at each child who did not
know. Then Gupta asked the class:* How many forms are there of water?
Ajay said: One, like we say the water which is the source of all waters
is the pure water of the Ganga.
*Gupta looked very pleased with what he was hearing and tried to catch my
eye and signal. He said to me in English:* What stupidity you are hearing;
unscientific answers.
He continued: And if you keep water in the fridge it becomes?
Some children shouted: Cold.
Vikas said softly: Ice. *(But this was not heard.)*
Surjeet repeated: Cold... cold... *He came around to hit those who had said
cold.*
Bhardwaj tried to dissuade him, saying: You ask in a very negative way.
Gupta: Which is the longest river in the world?

Sunil: Ganga.
Sumit: Brahmaputra.
Gupta: No, that is in India, not in the world.

Surjeet and Gupta also claimed that there was a hierarchy of general knowledge information. They created situations to 'prove' to the children that their general knowledge was very basic and that it was a shame that they did not know even these simple things.

EPISODE 6.37 (MORNING ASSEMBLY)

Surjeet: I will ask five questions of general knowledge. Which is the tallest peak in the world and in which country is it situated?
Deepak (Class III): Mt Everest in Nepal.
What is the capital of our country?
About 30 children raised their hands and answered: Delhi.
Bhardwaj corrected them and said: It's New Delhi, but if you say Delhi also it is okay.
Where is the Qutab Minar?
One child said: Mehrauli. *Another said:* Delhi.
All these things you should know. In which city is the Taj Mahal?
(*About 50 hands went up.*)
Who built it?
(*About 50 hands went up.*)
In which city is the Charminar?
(*Not a single hand went up.*)
The longest river?
Someone answered: Ganga.
All these questions were of ordinary knowledge (common knowledge). They were of Class II level. Now stand to attention and sing the National Anthem.

Having the opportunity to say something and to show-that-one-knows something within the pedagogic setting gave the children a lot of excitement. Sometimes, they would tell me what to ask them, so that they would have something to say. One day, Bir Singh eagerly told me: 'Ask about Holi, very nice-nice things... Ask about Ram*ji*—I know.' Bhardwaj often spoke of very mundane matters in pedagogic communication style, giving them an air of 'ought-to-know'. Also, he asked questions about very obvious and trivial matters in a quizzing mode. Such questions did not seem to bore the children. In fact, they responded with a great deal of enthusiasm, eager to be the one chosen to answer.

EPISODE 6.38 (CLASS V)
Bhardwaj: What is the *pehchaan* of the peacock?... Some special recognisable feature *(vishesh pehchaan)*?
Vipin: It has a long tail.
Bhardwaj ignored this.
Ajay answered next: Feathers *(pankh)*.
Bhardwaj: Han ji, feathers. We also call this *'chanda'*. They are coloured. Have any of you seen the peacock spread out its tail and dance?
Many of them answered excitedly: Yes, we have seen it on TV.
Bhardwaj: This is a gift of nature. Who wears a feather here? *(indicating forehead with left hand).*
Eveyone shouted out: Krishna *ji.*
He carried on: What is the peacock of the country?
Many hands went up: Hum batayen...
Ajay answered out of turn: National bird.
Bhardwaj: And the koel, what colour is it?
Several children shouted, waving their hands in the air: Black.
And how does the koel sing?
The whole class began calling like koels: Coo! Coo!.... *Bhardwaj selected Sunil-2 and told him to 'coo' and show the whole class.*

Since it was not really the questions or answers that were important but the opportunity to show off one's knowledge, children used questions simply as a device to create such opportunities. They would ask questions and quickly, without giving the other person an opportunity to respond, would also give the answer. The others didn't protest; they usually joined in, asking their own questions and providing the answers themselves. Episode 6.39 illustrates this.

EPISODE 6.39 (CLASS V)
Subhash pulled at Joni's shirt: Karan, whose son was he? *(And he answered, without giving anyone a chance.)* The sun's. He wears a sun on his forehead.
Joni: You tell me, why did Dronacharya ask him for his thumb? *(He also answered without waiting.)* Because then he wouldn't be able

to hold an arrow. They hold like this between finger and thumb. (*He showed everyone how.*)

Note on Monitoring

Teachers monitored *how* knowledge should be acquired, effectively controlling both the process of learning/knowing and the identity of the child as a knower. The teachering device was extended and made more effective through the institution of monitoring by students. Episode 6.40 presents the typical monitoring process which came into action when the teacher left the classroom:

EPISODE 6.40 (CLASS V)
Bhardwaj had left the class. Sunil and Vipin immediately stood up.
Vipin shouted: Vikas Jain, read.
Vikas started reading.
Vipin meanwhile straightened up, and began taking a round of the class. Sumit was lounging near the blackboard, following the reading with his finger. Vipin noticed that Sumit had his drawing book open and was completing some picture. He grabbed the book and scratched out the drawing. Sumit protested and tried to grab it back. Vipin gave him two kicks, and made a threatening sound. Follow the lesson! *he barked.*
When about a page had been read, Sunil ordered: Stop! Pradeep.
Pradeep jumped up to read, but Vipin intervened with a counter-order. Stop-stop. Big-Sunil *(referring to the second monitor),* read.
Sunil started reading. A few sentences later, he adopted an exaggerated accent. The class found this quite droll. They exchanged grins surreptitiously and a few started tittering....
Vipin ordered Sunil to stop and took up the reading himself. A few children in the class hummed along.

Vipin and Sunil were the monitors of Bhardwaj's section of Class V. They had been appointed by the teacher. An unstated rule that operated in the school was that the students who stood first and second in the examination would be made monitors. They were the 'best' students of the class. Sumit privately disagreed with Sunil being a monitor: 'His brother Amit is a better student, but Guru*ji* made Sunil the monitor because he is older.'

In every class two children were appointed by the teacher to be monitors. These students wielded a great deal of authority in the classroom

and functioned as quasi-teachers, monitoring the conduct, actions and
learning of other students. When the teacher was absent or taking a break,
the monitors teachered in his place. Their main functions were to maintain
discipline and conduct revisions. They did the former by acting as the
teacher's surveillant eye, looking into small acts of students that would
otherwise escape the teacher. If they caught anyone disobeying orders,
they took action against them. This meant threats, beating or reporting to
the teacher. In the Episode 6.41, Vipin closely monitored his fellow class-
mates to ensure that they followed Bhardwaj's instructions to the last—he
made certain that everyone wrote in his notebook and copied from the
blackboard, not from their textbooks.

EPISODE 6.41 (CLASS V)
*Bhardwaj asked them to close their mathematics books and take out their
language books. The children said that they wanted to do word-meanings.
Bhardwaj agreed and started writing words and their meanings from the
glossary at the end of the book on the blackboard. Everyone began copying
them down. He read out each word as he wrote it and in his sing-song way,
also read out the meaning.*
*I noticed Navin had his textbook open and was copying from there. Bhardwaj
asked Shankar why he wasn't writing.*
Shankar: Sirji, I have already done it.
Vipin loudly announced in a threatening voice: You have to do it again.
Then he turned around and saw Sumit, writing on a slate: Sumit, write in your
copy. *He then said to Navin:* Who has got the book open? Close the book.
*In the first column, Pankaj also had his textbook open. Ankur signalled to
him to close the book.*
Vipin came up to Sumit who was still writing on his slate: Mr. Sumit! Copy!
Sumit: Look, I have done it all, already.
Vipin: Why have you written everything? Write again, otherwise I will
tear off the page.

Getting everyone to do their work and checking what they had done
or how well they knew their 'ought-to-knows'—all provided the monitor
with opportunities to exercise his authority to discipline and punish. In
the absence of the teacher, the monitors exercised complete authority in
all knowledge learning matters, defining the nature of work that the other

students were to engage in. They also maintained silence in the class when the teacher was absent or away.

EPISODE 6.42 (COMBINED CLASS V)

Krishna Kumari left the room. Sunil went up to the front. He and Sumit, along with Parveen and Rajkumar from the other section, noted down the names of the boys who they claimed were talking. From time to time they would announce: We have written down so-and-so's name *or* We are going to write down so-and-so's name.

Sumit went around with his rubber chappal (footwear) in his hand and beat the boys. Later, when Krishna Kumari returned, he gave her the list of names.

Sometimes they dictated problems to be solved or conducted revision classes, checking how well answers had been memorised. In classes where the teachers themselves were less involved in teaching, like Bhardwaj's class, the monitors exercised absolute authority. (This was also true in both sections of Class I, one of Class II and most of the classes in the girls' school.) They were often called on to teach, even while the teacher was in the class. The tasks *they* set had to be done. They had the authority to decide the kind of action to be taken if students were disobedient or had not got their answers right. Sometimes they left the matter to the teacher, but they also beat and abused the other children themselves.

Apart from situations where they were called on to regulate knowledge— as, for instance, while conducting a revision class—monitors also con- structed situations where they could legitimise their power by exercising it as a consequence of epistemic authority. In Episode 6.43, Vipin suc- ceeded in fooling Ajay into giving the wrong answer. Since he knew more than Ajay, he could play tricks on him. In such situations, monitors were able to consolidate their own position as the knowledgeable ones and that of the other students as being ignorant and stupid—deserving to be punished.

EPISODE 6.43 (CLASS V)

Vipin was conducting a revision lesson in Bhardwaj's presence. He asked a true–false question.
Vipin: Ajay?
Ajay: True.

Vipin: False.
He asked Ajay again, who now said: False.
Vipin smirked and turned to Bhardwaj: Look, I said false, so he is also saying false, when actually it is true.

The monitors helped extend the eye of the teacher, making it more penetrating and omnipresent. They assisted the teacher in making the teachering device more effective and in drawing all children into the hierarchical network of the classroom's epistemic community. Teachers not only tightly regulated the frame boundary, they also used questions to control and monitor both the nature of knowledge children were expected to learn and their status as knowers. The pedagogic practices ensured that all children were aware of this. They were also aware of themselves and each other in terms of who-knows-more and who-knows-less. Opportunities to answer questions were used and created so that they could show that-they-know and renegotiate their social location in the classroom.

*

This chapter began with an introduction to pedagogic communication and the role of the features and form of the discourse itself in producing a regulative grammar, creating order and identity, and defining what merits transmission and how it is to be received. With this background, field data were presented and analysed to highlight both features and consequences of the pedagogic device, in particular its epistemic function, i.e., the regulation of knowledge.

The first feature of the teacher–student pedagogic interaction was identified as the teachering device used by teachers. It was behaviourally recognisable in the control of voice and facial expression through which teachers presented themselves as dispassionate and keen observers of students. Knowledge presented and transmitted through the teachering device had the status of 'ought-to-know'. Teachers used it to elevate ordinary and mundane knowledge into privileged classroom knowledge just as the textbook converted ordinary knowledge to privileged knowledge by presenting it in printed form. The teachering device, especially the teacher's eye, was extended throughout the classroom through student monitoring, drawing every person into the power network. The identification of the monitor, and indeed all students, with the teacher could be compared with the tendency of the colonised/oppressed to identify with the coloniser/oppressor, noted by both Memmi (1967) and Freire (1974).

In the headmaster's room

Asha checks Neeraj's work

Playing *gitta* in the classroom

Annual examination time in Class V

Hasan and Irshad, failures in Class IV

The Girls' Primary School

The Little Angel's Public School

Eating hot *jalebis* at the Shani Bazaar

The most important function of teachering activity was defining and maintaining the 'frame' of the school curriculum. The frame was detectable not so much in the presence or absence of everyday knowledge in the classroom, but more in whose and what knowledge became legitimised by entering into the classroom discourse. The parallel aspect of distribution of control clearly shows that the boundary strength was strictly maintained and regulated by the teacher. The phrase 'textbook culture' refers to this strong framing of the curriculum and the conception of knowledge as received rather than constructed, which it supports and from which it is derived. In addition to framing knowledge, the epistemic functions of peda-gogic discourse were also visible in the regulation and shaping of 'right answers' and the conduct of revision and examinations.

The technique for maintaining a strong boundary was not through the exercise of raw power, but through the exercise of a pedagogic authority which has both instructional and regulating functions. The discussion in Chapter V on the teacher's authority drew attention to the fact that it is moral-cum-epistemic and also multilayered. In this chapter, we see that in the process of teaching and learning, teachers not only draw on their authority over the student in both epistemic and moral matters, but simul-taneously also legitimise the need for this authority. With both knowledge and the process of learning being construed as a moral-cum-cognitive development, we also see that the teacher often realises his epistemic authority through the moral dimension. Epistemic authority is defined and operationalised through a broader pedagogic authority, and epistemic authority also legitimises the need for pedagogic authority. At the same time, we notice that the teachers also exercise power, disguised as authority, through the use of discretion.

'Knowing' was equated with the recall of 'right answers'. These were answers that matched exactly the ones that were given by the teacher, taken from the book or guidebook. In the course of pedagogic communi-cation, students had to show that they could recall and repeat the right answer. They adopted a *recitation* voice, parallel to the *teachering* voice, through which they conveyed that what they were saying was learnt or remembered rather than self-concocted. They used this device while responding to any question the teacher asked in the pedagogic mode, so that even their own knowledge or understanding acquired a recall form. Quizzing was also a popular activity wherein children created oppor-tunities to reveal their *pehchaan*, by showing each other that they knew things that were regarded as valuable. Children did not even mind questions that involved very mundane knowledge because it gave them opportunities to show-that-they-know.

   The child's status as knower was completely in the control of the teacher and monitored from task to task. The teacher ensured that knowledge was not to be independently extrapolated beyond the context in which it had been acquired and certified by the teacher. The child was never permitted to function as an independent knower, the one notable exception being Vipin, who was allowed to shape and influence discourse and thereby participate in the construction of knowledge.

   The definition of what counted as important knowledge for children emphasised memorisation as the primary process of learning. In the next chapter we will see its influence on the learning culture—on understanding and the concept of intelligence.

Notes

1. Searle in his theory of speech acts takes a Gricean approach and points out that every sentence carries not only a proposition-indicating element, but also a '...function-indicating device (which) shows how a proposition is to be taken, or, to put it another way, the illocutionary force the utterance is to have' (1971: 43).

2. Bourdieu and Passeron (1970) draw attention to the role of language in instituting what is recognised as pedagogic communication. They make a distinction between *parole*, the language of the working class, and *langue*, the language of the transmitter. In addition to the distinctiveness of the vocabulary, they also note that the transmitter's speech, which they call 'magisterial language', is characterised by a distinctive intonation and rhetorical form. In the Kasimpur school, this magisterial language has the effect of giving the knowledge transmitted its special character as 'ought-to-know' and received knowledge, which has epistemic consequences.

3. Following Bentham, Foucault describes *Panopticism* as an architectural feature of prisons and a technique of surveillance used to achieve total control on individuals being observed. 'Each individual, in his place, is securely confined to a cell from which he is seen from the front by the supervisor; but the side walls prevent him from coming in contact with his companions. He is seen but he does not see' (Foucault 1979: 200). The inability to know when one is observed contributes to the anxiety of being continuously observed. In the classroom, teachers achieved this effect by suddenly and unpredictably shifting their glance. Foucault also notes that the Panopticon can be used in pedagogy:

   ...among school children, it (the Panopticon) makes it possible to observe performances (without there being any imitation or copying), to map attitudes, to assess characters, to draw up rigorous classifications and, in relation to normal development, to distinguish 'laziness and stubbornness' from 'incurable imbecility' (ibid.: 203).

These adidtional dimensions of the Panopticon were also observed in the Kasimpur school and are discussed later in this chapter.

4. Although the textbooks were the main source of 'ought-to-know' knowledge, they were not the only source. The teachers used the teachering device to give non-textbook and mundane knowledge the status of being 'ought-to-knows'; this is discussed later in this section under 'epistemic authority and framing'.

5. *Kabaddi* is a popular outdoor game, common throughout north India. It requires two teams and no equipment.

6. See the discussion in Chapter V on the character of the teacher's authority.

7. Children used this form of elaboration as an epistemic warrant. This is discussed in more detail in the next chapter.

8. In traditional Indian theories of knowledge, the 'trustworthiness' of the speaker is an important criterion in assessing the truth of an utterance. Lying is a great sin because it destroys the security of speech (Datta 1972: 336). Bhardwaj was playing on this and the additional moral dimension of truth-telling vs. lying. Dewey has also noted that in social interactions, 'the opposite of truth is not error, but the willful misleading of others' (1985a: 14–15). Knowledge from testimony is again the subject of discussion in the next chapter, in the section 'inference and testimony'.

9. See note on monitoring (this chapter) for a discussion of how the teachering device is extended through monitoring.

10. I later found that, apart from Abdul, whose father received an Urdu daily, no one else received any newspaper at home.

11. Though the guidebooks were as much a source of knowledge as the teacher, the latter had established epistemic authority over the former. Almost all children owned copies of the guidebook for their class; yet the popular perception regarding guidebooks was that they are not as good as teachers 'because sometimes they may also make mistakes'.

12. Onomatopoeic word: conveys the sense of rapid movement.

13. See Chapter III on acquiring general knowledge (*jankari*) as an aim of education and as a constituent of cultural capital.

7

On Memorisation and Learning

Having situated the child in the village, the school and the classroom, in this chapter and the next two, we will attempt to engage with the psychological space of the mind. The subject of this short chapter is *yaad karna* or memorisation—the most important activity of learning in Indian classrooms. First, field data is used to explore children's understanding of the process of memorisation and its relationship to learning, understanding and intelligence. Then, a digression is made into the role of memorisation in traditional Indian education, in order to place the present-day phenomenon in its larger cultural context. The discussion is then broadened to comment on present-day reform efforts to dislodge the central place of memorisation in school learning.

'*Yaad karna*' is the Hindi verb for memorising and also for remembering or recalling. *Yaad karna* was the most important activity of the epistemic community. It was the technique by which the students acquired knowledge—by which they learnt. In Hindi, the term '*seekhna*' means 'to learn'. But this was almost never used in school to talk about acquiring knowledge. The term '*padhna*' was sometimes used to describe the activity of reading a lesson. But the term *yaad karna* deliberately referred to the process of acquiring the ought-to-know knowledge. When children were told by teachers or parents: '*padhai karo!*' i.e., when they were exhorted to study, the implication was that they should memorise. Teachers were often heard saying in class: 'Now we have completed the lesson, all of you must memorise the answers at home. Tomorrow, I will ask you in class' or '*Kaun kaun yaad karke aye hain?*' (Who are those who have memorised and come?). If a child could not answer a question, the teacher would suggest: '*Yaad karke batao'* (Recall and tell me). Children would often ask their teacher: 'Guru*ji yaad karvaiye'* (Guru*ji*, make us memorise).

A great deal of time, almost half of each working day, was spent on what may be described as rote memorisation of question–answers, problem–solutions, even entire essays, poems and multiplication tables (*pahade*). These were taken either from the textbook or from the guidebooks or the answers the teachers had made the students copy in their books. Children memorised answers either independently or in pairs— repeating the answers to each other. Teachers or monitors would check if answers had been properly memorised. This was regarded as the way to learn, to acquire knowledge.

In Episode 7.1, children were speaking on how they prepare for examinations. All preparation consisted of memorising answers either from the guidebook or from the book. Even when Amit stated that he could find answers from the book—which indicated that he understood the text and was using his understanding to locate the right answer—this did not mean that he could use his own words to express the answer. Only the exact words from the book would do.

EPISODE 7.1 (IN THE SCHOOLGROUND)
*(To Amit, Shankar and Kuldip of Class V): **How did you prepare?***
Shankar: From the guide—I memorised the problems.
*(To Amit): **And Amit, you also memorised?***
Amit: (I memorised) from the book, not the guide.
*(To Amit): **And you don't look at the guide?***
Amit: Only if I don't know.
Kuldip: Didi, I memorised from the guide.

The ability to memorise long answers was highly valued by the students. They often boasted to each other that they could memorise even the entire text and that they weren't afraid of the length of the answers. This was a way of measuring themselves against others. Their projected self-image—the manner in which they wanted to be regarded by other students—was as good students who could memorise any text, undaunted by its length.

EPISODE 7.2 (CLASS IV)
Neeraj announced: I like socials (social studies). It's easy. Give me an answer of any length, I can memorise it.
Jogi: Small or big, I can memorise them easily.

Children tried to memorise even the entire textbook. They felt this was a foolproof way of preparing for the examinations.

EPISODE 7.3 (CLASS V)
And lessons don't just sit in the head?
Anil, Vikki and Ramesh: They do sit.
Which lesson has sat in your head?
Vikki: The second.
Ramesh: Practice is necessary. ˙
They opened the page. Vikki and Ramesh began competing, with Anil occasionally joining in. They were reeling off the lesson verbatim.

EPISODE 7.4 (CLASS IV)
Asha had asked them all to revise science.
What will she ask?
Bir Singh: Don't know. We are supposed to memorise lessons 1 to 5. She can ask from anywhere.

The technique: memorisation vs '*ratna*'

In order to memorise a particular text, children repeated the text over and over again till they could repeat it verbatim, without any help. They identified this as the technique for memorisation: 'Aunty says learn something, so we go back and repeat it over and over again. Then it gets memorised' (Shobhraj, Class IV). But teachers made a distinction between what they called '*yaad karna*' versus '*ratna*'. '*Ratna*' is a Hindi verb meaning rote memorising or 'learning by heart'. In Indian English this is also called 'by-hearting'.

EPISODE 7.5 (MORNING ASSEMBLY)
Surjeet: ... In many students there is one weakness. Of '*ratta-fication*' (rote learning). Students rote learn. Like, Akbar was a great king, Akbar was a great king ... they repeat, and that is how they memorise/ remember.

Surjeet's morning assembly speech implied that there was a qualitative difference between rote and memorisation (*ratna* and *yaad karna*), suggesting that the latter had some relationship with understanding. However, it was also cloaked with other dimensions, and was still more importantly linked to the issue of memory, i.e., *of remembering the answer* and not particularly of understanding. *Ratna* was considered bad, not because it didn't involve understanding but because it meant forgetting. But why does one forget in the one case and not in the other? What is it that makes them different, if not understanding?

EPISODE 7.6 (LAPS)
Smita: No, there is no difference.
Shalu and Vandana insisted there was a difference but refused to say what they thought it was.

All the children knew there were two different learning activities—memorising and rote learning. All of them described their activity as '*yaad karna*' and were offended by the suggestion that it may be '*ratna*'.

EPISODE 7.7 (CLASS IV)
What is ratna?
Satish: To repeat over and over again.
Deepak: We don't rote learn, we memorise.
So to memorise you don't repeat over and over again?
Satish: We do.
Deepak: No *ji*, I can remember in just one go.
Satish challenged this with a disparaging sound, mockingly repeating his words. And the two got into a scuffle.
Can't you memorise by rote learning?
No *ji.*

Children, even if they claimed that they could remember with just one reading, actually did repeat over and over again. That was the technique of 'doing *yaad*'. It was only when faced with the possibility of this activity being identified with rote learning that they made claims to the contrary. They used two bases of comparing the processes. One was *method*, on which ground they concluded that the two activities were the same. The other was the *result*. The argument was that rote learning leads to forgetting and memorising to remembering. The technique was the same; the result would determine whether the technique that had been used should be called rote or memorisation. Episodes 7.8, 7.9 and 7.10 bring out these two contrasting features for comparing and evaluating these processes.

EPISODE 7.8 (CLASS V)

*I entered the classroom. Navin, Pavan, Parveen and Krishan were around.
They had their guidebooks open and were learning synonyms by repeating
the word pairs over and over again.*
Are you memorising or rote learning?
Memorising.
But isn't **'ratna'** *repeating over and over again?*
Krishan: By rote learning, we forget. Not by memorising.
Pavan: There is no difference between memorising and by-hearting *ji.*
Kamal: I don't know the meaning.
Parveen: By rote learning, we forget in a day but by understanding we
don't forget. By memorising, we won't forget in our whole life.

EPISODE 7.9 (CLASS IV)

Do you memorise or rote learn?
Memorise.
Why?
Aunty also tells us to memorise.
If we rote learn, we forget.
How do you memorise?
We repeat four-five times.
And for rote learning?
Repeat-repeat-repeat.

EPISODE 7.10 (CLASS V)

So what is the difference?
Ramesh: Not much difference, if you keep rote learning, you forget. If
you just have it in memory (*yaad rakha*), you don't forget.
Amit: Memorising well is rote learning.

These were attempts to construct the basis of the difference, but none
had anything to do with understanding. The two parameters considered
were of technique and result.

Memorisation as learning

But why memorise? When asked to learn, children responded by memorising. Whether it was to 'increase knowledge' or to 'prepare for examinations', the method was memorisation. Vikas (Class V) explained: 'We
have exams from the 19th. That's why we keep repeating the questions

again and again. So that we can memorise them. Then we can do the ones they ask in the exam... They ask from among these.'

EPISODE 7.11 (LAPS)
Vineet: If our knowledge increases, we can become *'bada admi'*.
Harish: If we increase our knowledge, we can get a better job.
And how do you get knowledge?
By memorising.

Memorisation was essential to be able to succeed in examinations—to be able to answer the questions asked without consulting either books or others for the answer. Memorisation helped one become *independent* of the teacher and the text. One would know the facts and answers that one ought to know. When asked, one would be able to answer independently, as the knowledge required would now be in one's own brain. One would not have to be told or have to refer to books and other sources: 'After memorising, it (the answer) goes to the brain' (Vipin, Class V); 'We repeat over and over again till it sits in our heads' (Shobhraj, Class IV).

EPISODE 7.12 (CLASS V)
Sunil: By memorisation, we 'seat' it in the brain *(dimag mein bithate hain)*. I did the problem from my brain, not by copying.
OK, so you have to memorise in science, not in mathematics?
No, in mathematics also.
How?
Because by memorising you put the answer in the brain.

EPISODE 7.13 (CLASS V)
We had been discussing whether one needed guidebooks to do problems.
Vikki: I do them (i.e., the problems) from the book and I don't have to look for the answers.
So how do you do them?
From the brain *(dimag se)*.
How do you do it from the brain?
By thinking *(sochkar)*.
What is to think? (**Sochna kya hai?**)
Remembering/recollecting *(yaad karna)*.

It is interesting that memorisation was not regarded simply as a way of coping with school knowledge and passing examinations. It was regarded as a way of gaining knowledge and developing the ability to think on one's own, from one's brain. The activity of recalling does not involve, at least obviously, either another individual or the book. As we know little about how the brain works, cognitive activity is usually spoken of metaphorically. The language of vision is often used, as in 'I *see* what you mean', 'insight', etc. The children in Kasimpur used a vocabulary drawn from physical movement. When asked what they did when they memorised they said: 'We make it sit it in the brain' (*dimag mein bithate hain*). When asked why they could not remember, they said: '*mota dimag hai*' (the brain is fat/ thick and, by implication, moves sluggishly). The language graphically created the feeling that knowledge is a physical object that can be moved from one place to another—from the book to the brain, from where it can be later moved onto an examination answer-book, or spoken during a conversation or interview.

Memorisation seems to be regarded as a way of putting knowledge in the brain, from where it can be retrieved. Thinking is recalling. The learner is now independent of the book and the teacher and able to solve problems and answer questions on his/her own. With the focus on the ability to answer questions independently, both memorisation and learning by developing a cognitive understanding sound dangerously akin to each other.[1]

Memorising and understanding

EPISODE 7.14 (CLASS V)
Pavan: Understanding (*samajhna*) is when you can't do it and someone tells you. *Yaad karna* is when you can do it from your own head/brain (*dimag*).
In math do you memorise or do you understand problems?
He thought for a bit, then replied: Memorise.
*What is **samajhna** (to understand)?*
When someone explains.
*And **samjhaana** (to explain)?*
Samajhna (understanding) is when somebody explains.

Typically, it was when a student was unable to memorise some answer, and in that sense unable to learn something, that the teacher offered to explain (*samjhaana*). Therefore understanding (*samajhna*), which in Hindi shares the same root as explaining (*samjhaana*), is the result of explaining.[2]

This was seen as something that only the less capable students needed.[3] Children seemed to regard memorising as better than understanding or knowing the explanation. 'Explanation', as conducted by the teachers, seemed to be intended to enable less capable students to memorise.

EPISODE 7.15 (CLASS IV)

Asha was checking if students knew their answers verbatim. If they didn't, she commented sarcastically: Can't get it? Can't understand it? Repeat over and over again, and you will understand.

Learning by understanding had a lower status than learning by memorisation. It seems that one of the reasons for this was that understanding, or comprehension, is 'easier' than memorising verbatim. The fact that memorisation was difficult seemed to give it value. Those who were able to memorise were regarded as better students.[4] All the children had no doubt about the centrality of memorising (*yaad karna*)—whether from the guidebook or from the book—for the examination.

EPISODE 7.16 (CLASS IV)

Contrasting the two, Shobraj said: Aunty says learn something, so we go back and repeat it over and over again, then it gets memorised.
And understanding?
She gives us something, we look at it carefully/with concentration, then we understand it .... Memorising is difficult (*he emphasised this*), we have to repeat it a few, about eight or nine times. (*Pause.*) For exams we have to memorise, there is very little understanding involved.

EPISODE 7.17 (CLASS IV)

Naresh and Bhim were sharing with me general knowledge facts about the metro rail in Calcutta.
Do you understand these things?
There is nothing to understand. Only to remember.

In LAPS, children averred, 'Hindi is for understanding, English is for memorising'. This may have been because, primarily, all the answers memorised were in English. One possibility was that children would find it easier to remember answers that they also understood. But this did not seem to be the case. It was only the length of the answer that determined what was easy or difficult to memorise.

EPISODE 7.18 (LAPS)
What is easier to memorise?
Science, not socials (social studies). The answers are too long.
Both science and GK (general knowledge). The answers are very, very
short.

The ability to write answers on one's own was regarded as having a
distinctly lower status than writing standard answers that had been
memorised. Deviating from the authorised versions was seen as either
taking liberties, being cunning or being too lazy to take on the tough
activity of memorising. Krishan, when he told me of writing his own
answers, had the embarrassed air of having confided a guilty secret.

EPISODE 7.19 (CLASS V)
Krishan: I memorise less. I make answers on my own.
Why?
The answers are too long. So I make them short.

Kamal and Devendar were sitting with us when Krishan said this. I
wondered if they were impressed by Krishan's ability. When asked if they
also made up their own answers, they replied defensively, self-righteously
and very emphatically: 'We memorise!' They seemed to feel that by
writing answers on his own, Krishan was taking an easy way out. They
were certain that they would not stoop to making up short answers on
their own. They didn't need to, as they could memorise.

EPISODE 7.20 (CLASS V)
I asked Kamal: **Do you memorise or write on your own?**
I memorise.
Why not write on your own?
If you read carefully, with concentration, you can memorise.

EPISODE 7.21 (CLASS IV)
Do you ever write answers on your own?
Deepak: Yes, we do.
Dinesh: We don't do it from our guides.
Then how?
Deepak: First our G*uruji* writes the answer on the board, then we
memorise it. He says write without looking, quickly, and we write.

Never from your own mind (**man**)*?*
Both (shocked): No!

EPISODE 7.22 (CLASS V)
Krishna Kumari was asking the entire class questions from the end of the lesson: Who are the king's own messengers?
While she was conducting the question–answer session, Krishan softly told me: Listen now, I will tell you my own answer. *And he whispered his answer to me, which seemed correct.*
When did you start making your own answers? From Class I?
No. In Class V. The answers were very big. That's when I started. Till then I used to memorise. In Class IV, the answers were not very long. I could memorise. Even now I do, when the answers are not too long.
How do you know it is right?
One doesn't have a way of knowing (*pata nahin chalta*). Aunty tells us.

Episode 7.22 shows that, even for Krishan, writing on one's own was too risky to use all the time. In general he did memorise; he wrote an answer on his own only when the prescribed one was too long. Interestingly, even when he did this, it had to be ratified by the teacher. Sumit tried to discredit Vipin in my eyes, telling me: 'He is very *chaalu* (sly). He doesn't memorise, he makes up his own answers.' Vipin's own answers, intelligent guesses, were tolerated by his class teacher, but they were not regarded as good. The ability that counted was remembering.

EPISODE 7.23 (CLASS V)
Bhardwaj asked the class: Which part of Africa is Zaire situated in?
Vipin was the only one with an answer: Somewhere in the middle.
Bhardwaj: You are guessing aren't you? You don't remember, isn't it?
Vipin nodded assent.

Memory and intelligence (*buddhi*)

An outcome of treating knowledge and knowing as essentially memorising of facts was that capability, or intelligence, was now assessed in terms of ability to retain facts in the mind and recall them. This section on '*buddhi*' is based mainly on a conversation with Devendar of Class V, which is reported in Episode 7.24.

EPISODE 7.24 (CLASS V)

Why can't you tell?
Devendar: I have less intelligence (*buddhi*).
Why?
I am still small. I will go to the big school, then my intelligence will grow.
Does intelligence ever stop growing?
Yes.
When?
When you leave studies.
Like (for example)?
When you join a job.
So a scientist doesn't need intelligence?
No, he does. He has to think.
Doctor?
Yes.
For housework?
No. Sweepers don't have brains ... An officer has ... not a bus driver ... not those who work in the fields ... not a clerk.
So why does the officer need intelligence?
Because he reads big-big files. If he forgets something, then he can read and memorise it again.
(Pavan joined us.)
Devendar: The one who makes pictures, he doesn't have *buddhi.*
Why do you say so?
Devendar: He doesn't read.
Pavan objected. (His chacha *was an artist, and being called* 'anpadh' *or without* 'buddhi' *was stigmatising.)* Of course he does read while making pictures.
For shopkeeping do you need brains?
Devendar: Yes!! He will become educated (*padha-likha*) and then keep shop, so then he can think and do things for his own convenience.
How?
Like for accounts, you have to read.
And the one who sells vegetables, does he need **buddhi?**
Yes, to recognise weights, like 2 kg, 100 g ... Otherwise how will he know?
Do they teach all these things in school?
Yes. We have learnt.
In previous times they didn't have schools. How did they keep shop?
Devendar: Don't know.

Pavan: Yes, *ji.* They were uneducated mostly.
So didn't they have buddhi*? Didn't they get jobs?*
Devendar: They had *buddhi.* If you do something with dedication (*lagan*), then you can get *buddhi.* Headmaster said you can even become a HM or the president.
Pavan did not believe this: How can an *anpadh* become a president?
Devendar: This Bhoop Singh and Amit, they have less *gyan* (knowledge). They have less *buddhi.* They don't go home and study.
Do soldiers (sipahi *and* fauji) *have* buddhi?
Devendar: Yes!! You need *buddhi* to fight enemies.
Pavan: Bruce Lee had *buddhi.*
Devendar: For transfer and for promotions they have to give interviews. They are ranked first, second...
Do wrestlers have buddhi?
Devendar: Yes , they have *buddhi.* They study.
Who has more buddhi, *the wrestler or the scientist?*
The wrestler.
And who has more strength?
The wrestler.

Buddhi, or intelligence, seemed to be primarily connected to schooling and studies. While aspects of general problem-solving and thinking were mentioned, the focus was on *buddhi* as a consequence of schooling. It included more than just the ability to read and reckon that was learnt in school, e.g., the amount of knowledge and facts that were learnt as a part of the school curriculum. In the class, the best students—the ones who did best in studies—were regarded as having the most *buddhi;* those who did poorly were considered to have the least. Children seemed to think that *buddhi* was related to the extent of schooling. Children in lower classes had less *buddhi* and children in higher classes had more *buddhi,* because it grows. It also stops growing when one leaves school.

The assessment of whether *buddhi* was required in a given profession or not was based on whether it required abilities and knowledge that were imparted in school. So, while scientists and accountants needed *buddhi,* painters and sweepers did not. It is interesting that Devendar mentioned that '*lagan*' (dedication) also helped to increase *buddhi.* It is the same value that teachers wanted their '*sishyas*' to practise.

Memorisation consists of the labour-intensive activity of repeating and thus involves a lot of hard work. It follows that the more *hard work* one does, the better one can retain facts in the memory and recall them. *Buddhi,* unlike intelligence, does not seem to be a genetically inherited capacity. It is something that can be acquired and increased by working hard to memorise.

By this logic, even the failures were not 'stupid'. They were lazy. They were shirkers. They didn't work hard—that is why they didn't remember and that is why they failed. It was in this sense that the failures were seen as 'bad' and worthless (*nikamme*). And it was partly on this basis that the teacher acquired the right to be extra hard on them; laziness, unlike stupidity, is transmutable and therefore need not be tolerated. The responsibility for not learning is that of the students. They don't learn because they don't try hard enough, not because they cannot. Laziness, unlike stupidity, can be corrected with disciplinarian methods, harsh treatment and ridicule.

Nine of the 12 failures in Asha's section of Class IV had begun to pick up the techniques of reading and writing, but three had not mastered anything. Bakri was in a class of his own, obviously mentally handicapped. The other two were Irshad and Hasan. One reason given for their failure, not but by the teacher by the failures themselves and their mothers, was *kamjor dimag* (weak brain) or *mota dimag* (thick brain). This suggested a lower ability to retain things that are to be put in the head by memorisation, a lower capacity to memorise. This was regarded as something that nothing could be done about. Either one has been born with it or it is the result of some accident.

Memorisation in traditional Indian education

It is a widely held belief that, in India, the traditional system of learning was essentially memory based. To this day, Brahminical learning is based on memorising *slokas*, verses and entire texts. (The term '*kanthastha*' literally means 'situated in the throat'.) Learning Sanskrit in school requires memorising various grammatical forms of innumerable verbs and nouns. Radha Kumud Mookerji, in his study of ancient Indian education (1989), writes that the cultivation of memory was certainly accorded a most important place and the powers of verbal memory were developed to an extent quite unimaginable today.

In the traditional knowledge system of Vedas and Shastras, memorisation was a key aspect of learning. Exact recall was valued and much emphasis placed on complex patterns to be used as exercises to develop and support exact recall. This is not to say that questioning, argument, explanation, etc., were not permitted; but these followed after a text was committed to memory. In the modern schema theory of memory, cognitive processes such as questioning, explanation and making connections are believed to assist in 'deep encoding' and regarded as ways of improving memory.[5] In the traditional Indian system of learning, which was oral, they do not seem to have had any such role. Instead, mnemonic devices were used. These were based on syllabic patterns and voice modulations, etc.— *samhita, pada-paatha, krama-paatha* and several *vikriti-paathas* based on permutations of syllabic sounds, accents, postures and hand movements. These ensured that sacred texts were preserved to a high degree of accuracy over hundreds of years. The system lent itself to the teacher's control over knowledge, as he alone could decide whether or not to teach a particular student something which he knew. But even then, there was a clear recognition among scholars such as Panini that rote memorisation was not enough. Mookerji (1989: 329) quotes Yaska [*Nirukta* i, 18]:

> The person who is able only to recite the Veda but does not understand its meaning is like a post or a mere load-bearer; but he who understands its meaning will attain to all good here and hereafter, being purged of sins by knowledge. For the words that are simply memorised and not understood will merely sound when uttered and not enlighten, just as wood, be it ever so dry, will not blaze if it is put into what is not fire.

Especially after the creation of Upanishadic literature, learning by questioning, observation and illustrating the text with stories and parables also developed. Nevertheless, memorisation remained central.

Saraswati (1972), also writing about traditional systems of learning, distinguishes between three kinds of knowledge systems traditionally prevalent in India: *para vidya, apara vidya* and *laukic vidya.* The first two are Shastric, i.e., to do with systematised knowledge contained in texts such as the Vedas, the Upanishads and the Dharmasutras, etc. *Para vidya,* or knowledge through which the ultimate reality is known, was accessible only to those pupils who had a talent for *tapas,* a rigorous system of self-discipline for self-realisation. For the other students, the method of learning was aimed at transmitting already revealed Shastric knowledge, codified in the form of hymns. The methods used to learn this *apara vidya* were the techniques of memorisation which have been mentioned earlier. Although of the oral tradition, this Shastric knowledge has a *textual* base—it is codified and systematised. Along with the Vedas and Sutras, knowledge of medicine and architecture which has been systematised may also be included in this.

This Shastric tradition is different from another oral tradition which is represented by what Saraswati calls knowledge of the people or *laukic vidya*, meaning, 'of the people' (1972: 153). This includes knowledge of various arts and crafts, which has not been systematised and is essentially experiential, such as the craft of the potter or the basket maker. The modes of learning are essentially oral–observational. The knowledge is descriptive and it can be learnt only through demonstration and emulation. Shastric knowledge on the other hand, is prescriptive; it is transmitted through text and various other linguistic devices which do permit interpretation and innovation. But, in any case, it is essentially transmitted by word of mouth and preserved through memorisation.

We can recognise that although *laukic vidya* is important, it is knowledge embedded in common and everyday life. *Shastric vidya* is learning that 'brings on *vinaya* (development of inborn power or modesty), which, in turn, enhances the worth of man' according to the *Hitopadesa* (Saraswati 1972: 153) and which 'brings on enlightenment and leads to the formation of character' according to the *Raghuvamsam* (ibid.: 154); this is the learning that is sought after. This *apara vidya*, or knowledge which is worthy of being known, is akin to 'cultural capital'. (*Para vidya* is perhaps too esoteric and the chances of acquiring it also quite remote.)

Memorisation vs learning

It is easy for one to be dismissive of learning based on memorisation and to declare that there is really no learning going on here—only rote. In fact, in the popular 'progressive', 'child-centred' approach to education and learning, memorisation is the least important aspect. It is even felt that memorisation is contrary to learning and comes in the way of 'real/true' learning and understanding. There is a feeling that only when one does not understand, does one resort to memorisation; memorisation is thus taken as an indication of non-comprehension. The extent of memorisation in the classrooms and in all teaching and learning implies that basically, children do not understand. The argument is that the texts are far removed from children's lives and too full of information, which is why children have to memorise.

It may be partly true that the textbooks used in the Kasimpur school did contain information that was far removed from children's lives. But memorisation was not believed to be simply a way of handling irrelevant information included in the curriculum. As the data show, children believed that in order to learn it is necessary to memorise. This is also supported by the traditional system of learning, where memorisation plays a critical role in the acquisition of *apara vidya*. As in the case of the identities of teacher and pupil and their interrelationship, in the method of learning, too, we seem to find that the understanding prevailing in the school draws on traditional cultural inheritance. School/textbook-based knowledge is comparable to *apara vidya*. In contrast, everyday knowledge and out-of-school knowledge is comparable to *laukic vidya*. This, as we saw in Chapter VI, was kept outside the strong frame of the curriculum. Traditional/home occupations such as farming and cooking, based on non-school knowledge, also had the stigma of being 'manual' and therefore jobs meant for the illiterate. When asked how these were learnt, the general opinion of children was that there is nothing to learn in these, they just go into the head. They were even surprised that there could be something to do with learning in these areas of activity.[6] After all they had never experienced making any special effort to commit these to memory!

In Indian education, two different theories of knowledge and learning seem to be simultaneously in operation. On the one hand is the traditional Indian system in which memorisation is central to learning. The purpose of learning is to put knowledge in memory. Knowledge is already known and is 'out there'. This system also makes a clear distinction between Shastric and *laukic* knowledge; in the present context, this may be seen as the distinction between school and out-of-school knowledge, and between what is worth knowing and what is not. This theory is linked to the oral tradition and to the preservation and transmission of knowledge. On the other hand is the theory of learning which places understanding at the centre. Memory is treated as simply a by-product of learning. This theory has emerged from a literate tradition and is oriented to the production of new knowledge by building on what is already known. What is already known, therefore, has no special sanctity; its preservation does not depend on memory. The orientation is towards finding out new things, verifying their validity, etc. Furthermore, it makes no distinction between Shastric and *laukic* knowledge, not just as sociologically relevant, but also cognitively relevant categories. In the first system, each student must be a receptacle and receive known knowledge; in the second system, each student himself or herself is expected to actively create and re-create knowledge.[7]

The first system is fraught with the widely prevalent problem of emphasising only memory. By not attending to any of the other activities such as observation, dialogue, questions and discussions of 'wrong' answers, students remain 'load-bearers' with little interest in engaging with meaning (though not necessarily lacking in the ability to do so). The latter system has a more subtle problem. To begin with, it does not squarely deal with the place of memory and memorisation in learning. Moreover, this system does not address the problem of the cognitive load that must be borne if each one of us is to create all the knowledge we need, without dipping into society's storehouse. Our common sense tells us that in a number of situations, even the most ardent votaries of the progressive/cognitive theory of learning do take a lot of knowledge simply on trust, and do rely on memory of things read and heard. Many who insist that multiplication tables must not be memorised are also confronted by children's difficulties in solving problems which they could easily do if only they remembered their tables.

There is no doubt that the former system is mistaken in emphasising memory to the point where knowledge itself becomes like a physical object and a burden to be borne. At the same time, many curriculum reform programmes not only ignore, but actually demonise memorisation. This may contribute to why the idea of learning for understanding has not been able to take root in the school system. When asked to innovate or create their own learning activities, teachers often come up with 'activity-based' memorisation and 'joyful' memorisation such as rhymes and songs to remember the tables or the names of the six great Mughal emperors. Traditional learning theory cannot be simply dismissed from the schooling system and supplanted with a theory that does not adequately address how 'school knowledge' must be learnt. School knowledge is more akin to Shastric than to *laukic* knowledge. This difference is not only of sociological significance; as we saw in Chapter VI, school knowledge is considered 'worthy of being known' and being remembered. The difference also has a cognitive significance; memory, certainly of the community or society, but also of the individual, is central. Moreover, the fact that, even though it may have arisen from experience, it is now formulated and systematised in a linguistic and textual form is also significant. Unlike knowledge which is formulated out of experience, this is available as a social artifact. There is need for concern that this knowledge does not become the burden of non-learning that every child carries: the ubiquitous heavy bag on the stooped back of schoolgoing children that R.K. Narayan expressed his concern for in the Rajya Sabha, and the Yashpal Committee was set up to address (Government of India 1993). In the next two chapters on children's epistemology, this received, propositional knowledge will be one of the main concerns.

Notes

1. Revision in mathematics was similar to teaching: problems were dictated, and were then solved. Many students preferred revising mathematics units to units in other subjects. There was visible relief whenever mathematics revision was announced. What was surprising, however, was that some 'good' students did not attempt solving problems afresh. They actually tried to recall how they had done it the first time. Even among those who did solve problems afresh, the certainty about the result was not from a confidence in their own understanding. It was because it matched what they had done the first time.

2. *Samjhaana* is the causative of *samajhna* (to understand), therefore acquiring its meaning: to make (someone) understand.

3. Experiments in learning science seemed to have a similar dubious quality and negative connotation. This is discussed in Chapter IX: Children's Epistemology–2.

4. Though this did not seem to exactly imply higher capabilities, it indicated that they worked hard; hard work, diligence and obedience were the marks of a good student. The main weakness of these children, according to Surjeet, was that they did not listen to the teacher with attention:

   > If you listen carefully/with attention (*dhyan se*), then you understand and you always remember. Here some magician comes, you look at him with such attention, and you remember everything. And what we tell you in the class, you don't listen with attention. That is your weakness and you must get rid of this weakness (during assembly).

5. See, for example, Anderson (1995) for a discussion of modern theories of learning and memory.

6. We will return to this dichotomy in everyday and school knowledge from the perspective of how it is learnt in Chapter IX.

7. John Dewey, in his essay *The Problem of Truth* (1985a), drew attention to two fundamentally different ways in which societies relate to their 'corpus of knowledge'. He used the metaphors of 'looking backward' and 'looking forward' to characterise two different epistemic stances. According to Dewey, these standards do not in themselves constitute a differential concern for truth. The difference is more a matter of how truths function in society:

   > Truth is not a colorless, intellectual matter in either case; it is the principles by which men direct their lives. The difference is that one standard looks backward and the other forward. One assumes a society bent on preserving and enforcing a truth it already has, the other projects a society that makes its own progressive change, change even of its own ideals and standards, an integral part of its conception of itself (ibid.: 30).

8

Children's Epistemology 1:
Children as Knowers

The search for truth, the appraisal of beliefs, and the distinctions we draw among knowledge, rational (or probable) belief, and mere belief determine the actions we perform and thus the lives we live.

—Butchvarov 1970: 43

Epistemology is the branch of philosophy that is concerned with questions regarding the origin of knowledge, its production, its relationship to experience and reason, and the relationship between knowledge and certainty. Our interest is in 'naturalised epistemology',[1] or the study of actual knowledge formation by the children of the Kasimpur school, and not the construction of a philosophical 'theory of knowledge'. In Chapter VII, we began this with an investigation into memorisation. We saw that children's understanding of memorisation as a way of learning and its relationship to understanding were shaped by the pedagogic context of the school and an understanding of school knowledge as received knowledge. In the present chapter and the next one, there is a selective focus—the theory and analysis presented here relate to the epistemological issues arising out of and bearing upon 'received knowledge' and the social context of knowledge construction. When placed in perspective, given the child's rich and varied experience and construction of the world, and the almost indistinguishable divide between fact and fantasy in children's lives, the scope of the terms 'knowledge' and 'knowing' in this chapter may often seem 'narrow'[2] and restricted. In the children's conversations that I have reported in these two chapters, I have included many apparently 'extra-neous' comments and asides, which often encompassed the bizarre and the magical. This is not only to retain the character of children's discourse but also to remind ourselves of the limits of our own analytical framework. A more comprehensive account of children's epistemology which can weave together the varieties of knowledge and knowing is in order. The present enquiry is an attempt to deepen our understanding in the domain of knowing school knowledge.

Following the resurgence of interest in Vygotsky, theorising and research in cognitive development and education are increasingly sensitive to the need for a nuanced understanding of the physical, the social, the individual and their interrelationships.[3] The physical world varies not only according to geographic location, but also according to different socio-economic and cultural locations. The world as shaped by others in turn shapes, enhances and limits our own actions and choices. The world carries the memory of previous cognitions and reality constructions which impact and shape the nature of experience in the present. The world also contains symbolic 'artefacts' of previous cognitions—sentences, propositions, state-ments—which are acclaimed as Knowledge or 'Truths'. Sensitive to their role in the child's life, Dewey described these as 'learning'. His use of the noun–verb colloquialism was probably deliberate, to signify their ubiquity and their object-like status in everyday life. '... [L]earning is the sum total of all what is known, as that which is handed down by learned men. It is something external, an accumulation of cognitions, as one might store material commodities in a warehouse' (Dewey 1916: 334–35). These truths exist in society, and we come to know them through social processes and interactions with older members of society—forms of education both direct and indirect.

This knowledge corpus is significant both within the everyday world of the school and outside it, in everyday life. In Chapters VI and VII we saw that virtually all learning activity in the school was directed at acquiring this knowledge. Given its importance in children's life, both within and outside the school, 'verbal testimony', i.e., knowledge encoded and avail-able in propositional form, in texts or in the utterances of others, will domin-ate this chapter and the following one. The chapter begins with some theoretical considerations which will help us analyse 'verbal testimony' as a source of knowledge. Beginning with the classical philosophical for-mulation of the analysis of the term 'to know', I will try to clarify the dif-ference between 'knowing' and 'understanding' propositions. This will sharpen questions that can be asked about children's knowledge construction and also shed more light on the analysis and interpretation of field data. A short note is included on methodology, as the study of epistemic issues required the use of focused/critical interviews within the broad anthropological framework. The remaining sections of this chapter and the next are devoted to expositing and interpreting field data. The section which follows, titled 'speaking from knowledge', examines the speech acts in which children make knowledge assertions. The next, 'epistemic activity: finding out and verifying', looks at the sources of knowledge and certainty. Issues relating to the nature of school science and the relationship of school knowledge to everyday knowledge/reality are taken up in the next chapter.

I
The Knowledge Corpus

A knowledge claim is a symbolic mapping of some aspect of reality as experienced by some observer who makes the assertion. For example, our observer, a young girl called Ammu, makes a knowledge claim: 'It will rain this evening.' The standard epistemological definition of knowledge is 'true belief based on sufficient evidence.'[4] Taking the example, the verb 'to know' is analysed as follows:[5]

'Ammu knows that it will rain this evening' implies:

(1)   It is true that it will rain this evening.
(2)   Ammu believes that it is true.
(3)   Ammu has *sufficient* reason to believe that it is true.

For this, Ammu must know what counts as necessary and sufficient evidence. She must know, for instance, that the presence of clouds is necessary but not sufficient for rain.[6] Like belief, knowledge is dispositional and may influence and inform action. Very likely, in anticipation of the rain, she will not water the plants in the garden, and if she steps out, she will take an umbrella with her. This is essentially an account of first-person epistemic judgements—Ammu formed a valid judgement on the basis of evidence.

It is in the very nature of the symbolic medium, the word, that it can become disengaged from the utterer, the observer, and acquire an ossified existence of its own, as an utterance or as a written proposition, a symbolic artifact. Such disembodied[7] propositions form what has come to be regarded as a 'corpus of knowledge', facts or information, in society. It is in this sense that Einstein's pronouncement '$E = mc^2$' or 'Siraj-ud-daula was defeated in the Battle of Plassey' are regarded as knowledge. They are the constituents of books and libraries—Karl Popper's third world. In philosophical discourse, this source of knowledge has been called '*sabda*' in the Indian tradition or 'verbal testimony' in the Western tradition. As more propositions are generated, society's 'storehouse of knowledge' increases.

School knowledge, to a large extent, is a *selection* of such propositions from society's storehouse. This is knowledge believed to be necessary knowledge for the child, and put into textbooks. Several issues arise out of selection—such as the consequences of being a selection, which, as we saw in the last chapter, gave school knowledge its particular characteristic of being 'ought-to-know'.[8] The present concern is to clarify the implications of treating verbal testimony, i.e., propositions from society's storehouse, as 'knowledge' and the problems of applying the verb 'to know' to such third person (i.e., not first-person or even second-person) epistemic judgements.

'Understanding' and 'knowing'

In educational discourse we are accustomed to being concerned more about learners' understanding than about their knowing. We would find it interesting and relevant to ask the question: does Ammu *understand* the proposition '$E = mc^2$'? We rarely ask: does Ammu know why the statement is true? Or, how will she find out if it is true? The term 'understanding' seems integral to the process of learning. 'Knowing', on the other hand, seems to relate to the products or outcomes of learning episodes. Yet philosophers like Frege point out the insufficiency of the psychological formulation.

According to Frege (1993), a proposition can have a cognitive value for a person only when she has reflected on the truth conditions for the belief. Consider the problem of applying the verb 'to know' to a statement that a reader, in our case young Ammu, has read in a book. For the present discussion, let the proposition be Einstein's equation '$E = mc^2$'. Let us apply the earlier analysis of the verb 'to know' to see what might constitute a third-person epistemic judgement. When Ammu says '$E = mc^2$', we cannot automatically assume that Ammu *knows* it. This is regardless of whether indeed E is equal to mc^2 or not. Accompanying conditions must also be satisfied: Ammu must believe in the proposition, and we must know what the roots of her certainty are and whether they are valid. In other words, we must ask: does Ammu know why the statement is true?

The mental state described by understanding is not concerned with issues of truth or validity of knowledge claims. While listening to an epic poem or fairy-tale, we are fully engaged with sense-making, i.e., with understanding. Yet the concern is not with the establishment of truth, but of truth-likeness or verisimilitude (Bruner 1985: 97). A theory of meaning cannot in itself explicate or characterise the relationship of knowing.[9] At the same time, it is necessary that one understands in order to be able to assess truth; it is a necessary requirement for knowing. Pointing out that this requirement is not simple, Welbourne provides an important analysis of 'understanding' which he recognises to be a 'many layered, many faceted notion' (1993: 21). One layer is that of '*lexical understanding*', which has to do with the linguistic meanings of words. In general, a dictionary will help overcome problems of error or lack of understanding of this nature. A second layer is what he calls '*referential understanding*'. On hearing (or reading) a proposition, the hearer must 'latch' on to the reference in order for the proposition to convey knowledge. For instance, if Ammu tells me: 'Pilloo is on the tree,' I must know what or who 'Pilloo' refers to in order to understand fully what she is saying.[10] An important point here is that failure to understand in this case cannot be cured by taking recourse to a dictionary.[11] It is interesting and important to note that even if I do not know who Pilloo is, I may still pick up some attenuated knowledge that 'something is on the tree'. Also, if Ammu and I share more knowledge about Pilloo, then this sentence may carry more significance. If both of us know that Pilloo has missed school today on the excuse that she was not feeling well, then Ammu's observation could have more influence on what we do next.

Another type of understanding is '*speech act understanding*'.[12] For a satisfactory transmission of knowledge, the hearer/reader must correctly apprehend the nature of the speech act. When I hear Ammu say: 'Pilloo is on the tree', I must correctly apprehend that speech act. I must apprehend that Ammu knows that what she is saying is true, and that she intends that I should believe what she says, i.e., that Ammu is 'speaking from knowledge'. If, for instance, Ammu is lying or guessing, then I would have failed in understanding the speech act. Welbourne adds that these are not 'senses' of the word understanding, but *layers*: 'When you understand what someone says to you, or better, perhaps, understand him when he says something to you, each layer is liable to be implicated and understanding does not occur independently at each level' (1993: 21).[13] In general, the ability to act appropriately on knowledge is determined by the extent of understanding.

The relationship of the child to knowledge propositions, including those which form a part of the textbook (and curriculum), involves acts of 'knowing' rather than simply acts of 'understanding'. The layers of understanding described by Welbourne are necessary—not substitutes—for epistemic activity. This means that when Ammu says: 'The earth is round,' we can say that she knows it only when all of the following are satisfied:[14] there must be lexical understanding—the meaning of the words earth, round, etc. There must be referential understanding—what 'earth' refers to. In addition, her speech act must be one of 'speaking from knowledge', whereby she is able to communicate that she intends to convey knowledge and is not playing a game, e.g., where 'earth' is a code name substituting for some unknown object. She must also be able to identify and assess what will count as relevant supporting evidence for this statement. We would hope that other *epistemic activity* would arise as a part of the activity of knowing this statement. The changing view of an approaching ship is often provided as 'proof'. Ammu must be able to reason whether the observation supports the view that the earth is round. She must also realise that the fact that the horizon looks like a circle when viewed from the second-floor terrace of her home is not evidence of the sphericity of the earth. This knowledge would relate to life and activity—she would not worry that when her father flies off to Peru from India, he may fall off, although she may still wonder how people living in Australia are able to stand (as knowledge of gravity is additionally involved in this). We would be happy if she wonders why, if the earth is round, it looks and feels quite flat.

It is in this sense that 'knowledge' is fertile and significant—cognitively in the epistemic activity it requires, generates and engenders, and also pragmatically as our construction of reality determines and influences how we act in and on the world. 'It is the world of inquiry and action rather than casual social talk that is the true home of the concept of knowledge', (Butchvarov 1970: 43).

Verbal testimony as a source of knowledge

Words plus trust generates knowledge directly.

—Matilal 1990: 62

Can verbal testimony be considered a source of knowledge? Can we verify the truth claims of testimony by means other than inference or perception?

If not, how can it be considered an independent source of knowledge? These were the kinds of questions to which philosophers of *advaita* and *nyaya* schools of Indian philosophy addressed themselves in their effort to give scriptural knowledge a firm epistemological ground.[15] They argued that *sabda*, or testimony, can convey knowledge independently, provided the utterer is *trustworthy*. We must be sure that he is not lying, nor is he misguided in his belief, in which case we would be justified in believing him. It was for this reason that *sabda* was also referred to as *apta vakya*— the word of a trustworthy person.[16] They also pointed out that while many truths which we learn through testimony can also be acquired via perception or inference, that does not displace its claim to being a source of knowledge. This is also true of other sources of knowledge, e.g., seeing smoke rising from behind a screen we may infer, correctly, that there must be a fire there. The same knowledge could have been acquired by simply going to the other side and looking. Satprakashananda (1974) adds that especially in everyday life, testimony as a source of knowledge is important. Furthermore, like inferential knowledge, *sabda prama* or knowledge from words is mediate.

Welbourne (1993) approaches the concept of knowledge from the language games in which it dominates, rather than through truth–conditional analysis. The linguistic-cum-psychological mechanism he presents, by which knowledge is conveyed from one person to another, has as its first element the notion of 'speaking from knowledge'. In the most complete sense of this speech act, the speaker knows that what he is saying is true and, in addition, he *intends* that this utterance be accepted as warranted and therefore expressing knowledge. Someone who knows and 'speaks from knowledge' also speaks with authority—the authority of the knower. This carries with it the right to pronounce on facts and to be believed. In the narrow sense, 'speaking from knowledge' refers to a speech act where there is a transmission of knowledge, regardless of whether the speaker actually possesses the knowledge which, in thus speaking, he purports to have. For example, if our young subject Ammu announces that 'the earth is round', her speech act would be one of 'speaking from knowledge', in the complete sense if she makes this claim after having gone through and evaluated the evidence. But if she is simply repeating what her teacher told her, it would be an act of 'speaking from knowledge' in the narrow sense. 'Telling' is one form of 'speaking from knowledge'.

In his speech act theory of knowledge transmission, Welbourne echoes the considerations mentioned earlier—the requirements of understanding, of belief in the speaker and his or her trustworthiness. At the same time,

Hiriyanna (1993) cautions that *sabda* should not be contradicted by reason or inference—it may be above reason, but not against it.[17] It is only too easy for authority to be misused and for verbal testimony to be a source of prejudice and misinformation. It is for this reason that, until recently, Western epistemology disregarded it as a valid source of knowledge. Education psychology, drawing upon this dominant tradition, has a more complete account of cognitive development and knowledge formation through activities like observation, induction and inference. But a framework that is based upon only these methods of knowledge construction and leaves out verbal testimony, is not equipped to help us understand the more pervasive knowledge-related activities in the child's life either in or outside the school. Such frameworks can only function as bases for critique, not for description or understanding. In the discussion in this first section, I have presumed a familiarity with these other ways of knowing, and only redressed the neglect of knowing through words. I have tried to prepare the ground for a phenomenology of children's talk and epistemic activity, so that we begin to notice its features and understand its significance. From this, and in conjunction with other epistemic practices that children engage in, we will evolve a critical response to verbal testimony and other sources of knowledge in the lives of schoolchildren.

Box 8.1 A Note on Methodology

To assess epistemic matters related to school and everyday knowledge, focused interviews were used. These were conducted in the latter half of the fieldwork, in keeping with the overall anthropological approach. They were conducted not only with children individually, but also in pairs and in small groups of children. Apart from a few children each time, the composition of the rest of the group was generally not fixed and children would join and leave as they wished. From their school science and social science textbooks and from general matters, several factual statements were constructed. For example: 'The earth is flat', 'Kasimpur is situated in the Gangetic plain', 'The whale is the biggest fish'. Several such statements were listed on a sheet of paper. They would read each statement out in order. Then I would ask them to tell me if it was true or false (*sahi ya galat*) and also ask them to tell me how they knew. If they said they didn't know if it was true or false, I would ask them: 'How will you find out?' These interviews were generally easy to conduct. Most of the children quickly gathered that it was all right to say, 'I don't know', especially as they had further opportunity to think about how they would find out. The children also seemed to enjoy answering these questions and figuring out the answer in each instance.

> Apart from these interviews, I also had extensive conversations with children outside the school, while accompanying them back home or in the fields around the village where they played. In their homes, they did not have much opportunity to speak to me as there were other, older people around who assumed primacy. I also talked to three of the children on a half-day outing when we took a walking trip to the railway line about 7 km away.
>
> **Source:** Extracted from Appendix B on fieldwork.

II
Speaking from Knowledge

To speak from knowledge in the most complete sense is to say something which you know to be the case and to say it intending that your utterance be received as grounded on and thus expressing knowledge.

—Welbourne 1993: 19

The very purpose of speaking is to convey information. Lying is rightly condemned as a great sin—it serves to destroy, through abuse, the security of speech, which is one of the greatest factors that have made human society possible.

—Datta 1972: 336

It is worth noting the point made by Datta (1972) that, while verifying *sabda*, it is the authenticity of the speaker, not the validity of the knowledge itself, which is ascertained or established. The *nyaya* philosophers spoke of the speaker's qualities—such as competence, trustworthiness or reliability (Matilal 1990: 70). Welbourne points out that a successful transmission of knowledge requires that the listener *believe* the speaker (1993: 24). But we also know that misplaced trust can result in error—false beliefs can also be transmitted through words. The authenticity of the speaker is often the only guarantee of the knowledge claim in verbal testimony. These concerns were evident in the acts of 'speaking from knowledge', that children engaged in.

There seemed to be two slightly different kinds of acts of 'speaking from knowledge', depending on whether children simply wanted an occasion to speak or wanted to be heard. In casual talk, where the focus was on taking opportunities *to speak*, a 'primitive credulity' seemed to be operating. There were other occasions where there was an additional effort made *to be heard,* and they had to ensure that their statements would be received with the appropriate 'propositional attitude'—of belief.

Primitive credulity

Both in and outside their homes, children in the village interacted with the physical world around them in the course of everyday life, e.g., learning to cycle, digging up plants, cutting grass or extracting sugar. They knew a great deal about what grows when, and could identify plants and trees. The games they invented often involved features of the physical world in which they lived, which they had cognised. For instance, trying to balance themselves on round pipes or throwing berries onto sloping asbestos roofs so as to make them roll down as fast as possible, both involved skills to deal with specific features of the physical world. Their verbal exchanges on the occasions that we walked through fields together, or spent time outside the classroom playing, were filled with propositional knowledge about the world, articulated in excited exclamations:

> *While throwing banyan fruits onto the sloping asbestos roof of their classroom:*
> 'Look, if you throw it like this, it comes down faster!'
> *While walking in a line through wheat and mustard fields around the village:* 'This will be ready to harvest in two days.'

In most of these conversations, the children were not talking to each other but *at* each other.[18] They rarely took issue with what the other said, but seemed to be concentrating on finding a voice for themselves. They looked for or created opportunities by which they could also contribute to the conversation and say their own thing. It seemed they were taking opportunities to practise engaging in the speech act of 'speaking from knowledge'. Often, the children's conversations would diverge into sub-conversations, where small groups pursued related, but separate, conversations. Occasionally, one of these groups could be intent on reasoning out an issue. But in most groups, these conversations were exchanges of associations, where statements involving the magical and the bizarre often featured. It seems that, in everyday life, knowledge is exchanged not only with the purpose of forming beliefs and acting on the world, but also as conversation or social interaction.

EPISODE 8.1 (CLASS V)
We had been debating whether the ability to fly is a defining feature for the class 'bird'. Someone suggested that snakes fly.
Manoj: The flying snake is always very angry; it flies and hits you here (*he mimed striking the temple*).
Another: No, here (*mimed striking the back of the head*).
Manoj: Yes, here or here.
Sunil: They say if the shadow of the flying snake falls on you, you will die.
Joni: No, you know they burn snakes, if the smoke touches one, one will die.

Though such statements could have triggered off discussion, speculation and debate, this did not usually happen. It seemed that these statements were accepted with an attitude of belief. For verbal testimony to function as knowledge and to be able to transmit knowledge, belief in the speaker is essential. This is the most distinctive feature of verbal testimony. Dewey made an important observation that in everyday life, the natural attitude is to hear and receive knowledge propositions *with an attitude of belief—* he called this a 'primitive credulity' (1985b:197). Matilal (1990: 65–66) also noted that according to the *nyaya* philosophers, in ordinary circumstances when we hear a statement, we do not postpone belief till we have understood and evaluated the truth of the statement; the natural attitude is one of belief.[19]

In general, among friends at least, there was little tendency to doubt or take issue with the other's word. (In any case, very little articulation of curiosity or reasoning involving observations of the everyday physical world was heard.) On a few occasions, when there was articulation of focused reasoning, the situation was one of disagreement and argument.

EPISODE 8.2 (NEAR BHARDWAJ'S HOUSE)
Babloo, Surinder and Joni were playing cricket in the small ground behind Bhardwaj's house. Babloo was bowling. Joni struck the ball and was caught out by Babloo.
Joni: No that ball wasn't bowled correctly. Spin is not allowed.
Babloo: Give Surinder the bat.
Joni: It was spin. Only a spin ball can fly like that. A plain ball can't do that. It was spin. I'm not out.

In this episode, when challenged by Babloo, Joni offered his observation on the path of the ball after it had been struck as the evidence on the basis of which he concluded the ball had been spun. It was only when the interlocutors felt that a situation demanded proof, that any justification was provided. Such occasions, where either a knowledge claim was challenged and supporting evidence had to be provided, or the claim was made along with the supporting evidence in anticipation of challenge, will be taken up again in the section on 'social interaction as epistemic activity'.

Creating propositional attitudes[20]

'Being heard' was more difficult than 'finding a voice'. It meant that children had to be apprehended by the listener as 'speaking from knowledge'. Being doubted or making a mistake could be disastrous. Dewey noted that in the everyday world, where truth has a social function, 'truth' and 'truthfulness' are confounded. 'The opposite of truth is not error, but lying, the wilful misleading of others' (Dewey 1985a: 15). In this situation, to be suspected of error, i.e., to be doubted, reflected on the moral character of the speaker—it carried the danger of being called a liar and not simply being misinformed. In Chapter IV it was suggested that generally in the village, children were believed to be lower in the traditional epistemic hierarchy, and were also perceived as playful and non-serious. Perhaps on account of this, when they wanted to be heard, they felt the need to deliberately signal their trustworthiness, or create circumstances where their statements would be believed by creating the appropriate propositional attitude of belief in their audience.

Attributing knowledge claim to established authority: One technique the children often used to persuade the listener to hear them with belief, was to attribute the knowledge claim to some acknowledged sources of knowledge, or established, accepted epistemic authorities: e.g., 'My mother says ...' or 'My older brother says...'. Such phrases seemed to enhance the truth correlate of the statement, as the knowledge claim itself was attributed to an older member of society, and was particularly effective in a community where age was an important determinant of epistemic status in relation to experiential knowledge. Children referred back to these sources constantly in the course of their own conversations, prefixing their statements with tags:

You know, my mother says...
You know, it is written in a book...
You know, my aunty read in a book...

My uncle says...
Everybody says...
They say...
On TV they showed...
In a book it is given...
In olden times...

or ending with assertions:

...It IS like this.
...Till now everybody has/has not done this.

For example:

'My aunt says, a man has predicted that the whole world will be destroyed in the twenty-fifth century. It is written in a book' (*Devendar, Class V*).

While exchanging information with each other, 'On TV they showed...' was a very common prefix. This sort of exchange was able to create an attitude of belief towards the utterance in two ways: the first was that television shows things which can be seen and therefore believed.[21] The second was that since many of them watched television, they could cross-confirm what the other had seen, and also contribute more information. Some children also swore by their parents to vouch for things they were saying.

In fact, instances where children directly claimed to know something, on the grounds that they *themselves* had seen or noticed it, or had found out in some way, were very few. The claims they made to each other, and the matters they discussed, were mostly things that they had been told or read in a book and things that they had been shown on television. Occasionally, when children made some independent observation, the caution and care they exercised was very evident, as if they were communicating some secret to me. They seemed to want to ensure that they would not be laughed at, be called liars, or have their observations challenged in any way.

EPISODE 8.3 (CLASS IV)
We had been discussing the validity of various knowledge claims. The bell rang and the group around me returned to their class (IV). Ankur stayed

back. He pulled out a ruler from his pocket and told me with the air of sharing a secret: 'You know, this is magic. If you look like this, it becomes bigger.' *He held the transparent ruler over my notebook and showed me its magnifying effect.*

Establishing claim for personal expertise: Establishing claim for personal expertise was yet another technique of creating the attitude of belief in what was said. When asked how they knew if something was right, rather than present direct evidence or attribute the knowledge to some socially accepted source, they simply added more information that they knew about the subject in question. These were not warrants at all. They were simply additional facts and associations. By demonstrating superior knowledge, or increased quantity of knowledge, they seemed to be trying to convince the listener that they knew what they were talking about, that they were speaking from knowledge and therefore should be believed. In Chapter VI, Episode 6.5, we saw that when confronted with the doubting teacher, Ashok used this strategy to strengthen his claim to speaking from knowledge. This was especially true in the case of things that excited them, like the '*hvel machhli*' (whale), about which they had a lot of things to say.

Playing with propositional attitude—rhymes and riddles: Traditionally, propositions uttered in a rhyming format have the ability to evoke the attitude of belief, i.e., to persuade the listener to believe in them. Aphorisms and folk truisms have been preserved in oral memory in the form of rhyme. That they are easily memorisable seems to suggest that they must also be memorable; it seems to enhance their status as truths worth knowing and remembering. This ability of rhyme to evoke the attitude of belief in the listener seems to be the basis of a form of linguistic play that was popular among the children—the riddle.

EPISODE 8.4 (CLASS IV)
Child-1 held up four fingers and asked: How many?
Child-2 was already suspicious, because the answer 'four' was too obvious.
Child-1: It is five. Look, '*aanch-kaanch-poorey-paanch*' (*aanch-kaanch*-all-five). (*As he said the words, he pointed to one finger at a time, as if counting.*)

Mimicking the counting sequence, the child says 'five' on the fourth finger. The use of the initial rhyme '*aanch-kaanch*' lulls the listener, making him forget that this cannot apply as a counting method as the first few words are not counting words, and tricking him into a situation where he seems to have accepted the veracity/validity of a patently absurd knowledge claim. The same kind of game is played holding up four fingers, but 'counting' only till three, using the rhyme: '*een-been-tota-teen*' (*een-been-tota*-three).

Another popular riddle was to hold up the thumb and ask: 'Who is this?' The answer is: 'Your *tau* (uncle)'. Here the trick is to say the rhyme as if counting all five fingers, starting with the little finger—'*au-bau-mein-tera-tau*' (*au-bau*-I am-your-uncle)—ending on the thumb at the word 'uncle'.

III
Epistemic Activity: Finding Out and Verifying

The statement of an authority makes me aware of something, enables me to know something which I shouldn't otherwise have known. It is a source of knowledge.

–J.L. Austin, cited in Welbourne 1993: 86

The proposition which asserts or assumes its own truth is either a sheer prejudice, a congealed dogmatism; or else it is not an intellectual or logical proposition at all, but simply a linguistic memorandum to serve as a direct stimulus of further action.

–Dewey 1985a: 37

Didactic sources of knowledge were very important in children's lives but, as Episode 8.5 illustrates, they were aware of other ways of finding out and verifying knowledge. Here, when asked, they provided a number of different ways of verifying a claim and even distinguished between the ways, depending on the subject matter.

EPISODE 8.5 (CLASS IV)
We'll do an experiment.
Why do we do experiments?
To find out if it is true.
Why do we need to find out if it is true?
And if they ask in the exam?
How else can you find out if something is true?
By reading in a book.
By asking someone.

By thinking by oneself. Like I told you about growing two plants...
In mathematics we can find out if it is right by addition, subtraction,
multiplication, division.
In socials we are told. Like about Gandhi.

EPISODE 8.6 (CLASS V)
And how do we prove things in **samajik** *(social studies)?*
Vipin: From information we can prove.

Not only asking, reading and listening, but children also knew of doing,
experimenting, thinking and reasoning as ways for finding out and
verifying truth.

Authorities as source of knowledge: Being told and asking

Being told:

EPISODE 8.7 (CLASS IV)
Fertiliser is good for plants. (Statement from the true-or-false list.)
Yes, it is true.
How do you know?
Just like that. Everyone says, so I also thought so.
When people say, it must be true. Our guru*ji* also says.

Several things that children claimed to know, they attributed to having
been told by authorities or having read (or seen) in authoritative sources.
Statements made by the teachers or found in textbooks and guidebooks
had an obvious didactic quality. In addition, the testimonies of their tuition
teachers, older siblings and other relatives, and information gathered from
the television also had this mark of the knower's authority.

EPISODE 8.8 (CLASS V)
*They were all looking in the map for the equator. None of them knew where
to look. They just looked everywhere for it.*
Subhash: First all the continents were joined.
Ashok poked fun: How do you know?
Subhash: From TV.
Ashok: Then how did they get separated?
Subhash had no answer.

When asked how they knew, for example, that the earth was round, or that plants take in carbon dioxide and give out oxygen, or that Archimedes was a Greek scientist, the children referred back to books, guidebooks or teachers as the source of their knowledge: 'It is there in the guide'; 'It is in the book, and our guru*ji* also keeps telling us'.

The fact that they had read these things in books or had been told so by their teachers seemed, for them, sufficient reason to believe in their truth. The word of the teacher and the printed word of the book[22] seemed to be received with a primitive credulity. And the two confirmed each other. When asked about it, the children said as much.

EPISODE 8.9 (CLASS VI)

Vipin: Guru*ji* tells us. That is how we know.
Pavan: It is in the book, and aunty has told us.
How does she know?
She has read a lot. Someone may have told her.
Vipin: In books things are mostly right, and guru*ji* tells us during assembly.

EPISODE 8.10 (CLASS IV)

How do you know that it's all true, the things you read in science?
Neeraj: Aunty tells us all the time, so we know.

EPISODE 8.11 (CLASS V)

(I read out a statement from my true-or-false list): **While breathing, plants take in carbon dioxide and breathe out oxygen.**
Vipin: This is true.
How do you know?
This is often written in the science book, and mostly they do write correct things.

When pressed further about the source of the teacher's knowledge, the general opinion was that either the teacher in turn had been told, or that she had read it in books. Regarding knowledge in books, children believed that either people had found out and written it, or that they had been told, and in turn had filled up books. In either case they were not curious about the ultimate source of knowledge that they learnt, i.e., what may have preceded transmission through the oral and written word.

EPISODE 8.12 (CLASS V)
Joni: Scientists have written, in books.
How did they find out?
Scientists must have done *khoj* (research).

EPISODE 8.13 (CLASS IV)
The people who write books, how do they know all these things?
Neeraj: They used to study in school. Then they write in books. They take blank (*khali-khali*) notebooks, and write in them.
But how do they know all this?
Dinesh: Don't know.
Bir Singh: It just comes out of their heads.
Neeraj: They know good things (*achchhi-achchhi baten*).

Asking: For children the most important method of coming to know—gaining knowledge and verifying the truth of statements—was by asking. When asked something they were not sure about, they often said: 'We will ask and tell you'; 'I will ask my brother/sister/uncle/father and tell you'; 'I will ask guru*ji*/aunty and tell you'.

EPISODE 8.14 (CLASS IV)
Don't know.
How will you find out?
Sulaiman: We will ask people bigger than us. Guru*ji*, parents... By sitting at home we can't find out. We can take the train and go and ask. We can also find out a little by telephone.

Asking was not an indiscriminate activity. Children knew whom to ask for what kind of knowledge. They were also aware of the issues of expertise, competence and trustworthiness in knowledge gained from verbal testimony. First of all, the person who could tell them what they wanted to know would have to be older than themselves, as Sulaiman clearly pointed out: 'people bigger than us'. Others, too, indicated this requirement indirectly: 'I'll ask my brother. Not Joni. I'll ask my older brother' (Ajay, Class V).

EPISODE 8.15 (CLASS V)
Rajesh: My sister studies in Class IX... X. She will know.
Rajiv: I never ask anyone. I am the oldest at home. He may ask...

Most commonly, the people they said they would ask were their parents, older brothers/sisters and teachers. Children were specifically aware that they needed to ask people who had been through more years of schooling than themselves. More schooled adults would know more; they would have read more, heard more and been told more. It has been noted earlier in Chapters IV and V that, in the traditional village society, epistemic status increases with age. The epistemic consequences of being schooled did not derive simply from transferring this feature of traditional society into school. The school produced the logic of its epistemic hierarchy through its own structure of grade levels and examinations. Obviously, as one pro-gressed from grade to grade, age also increased. But particularly in this village, which had many illiterate adults, those who had never been mem-bers of school communities had lower status, regardless of their age.

For children, the teacher was the first 'expert/authority'. But in addition, the children did recognise several other experts who could be consulted for knowledge in specific areas. For example, responding to the question of finding out what fuel is used in aeroplanes, they said: 'We'll ask in a pump station.'

EPISODE 8.16 (CLASS V)
If you water a plant with salt water, it will grow better. (*Statement from the true-or-false list.*)
Rajesh: Till now it has never happened.
Rajiv: No *mali* (gardener) ever says this.
Several children: We'll ask a *mali* and tell you.

EPISODE 8.17 (Class V)
There are six holes in our head. (*Statement from the true-or false list.*)
Sunil: I saw in a book... there are no holes.
Vipin counts: Eyes, nose, mouth, ears... six... I don't know.
Subhash: I'll ask a doctor.

Authority arising from expertise in knowledge areas has occasionally been the subject of philosophical investigation. Writing on cognitive author-ity, Wilson (1983) distinguishes between (administrative) authority and expertise, claiming that expertise or cognitive authority is based on the ability to influence thinking rather than behaviour, and that this requires both competence and trustworthiness. It has already been discussed in Chapters V and VI that epistemic and pedagogic authority are confounded in pedagogic practice. In children's lives and behaviour, such a distinction between authority and expertise on the lines that Wilson suggests, cannot be established.

Problem of proper names: Knowledge claims that involved proper names seemed likely to create the propositional attitude of belief. The true-or-false list of statements also contained the following two, and children were asked to comment on them:

Archimedes was a Greek scientist.
The Angel fish is the smallest fish in the world.

They were unlikely to have any knowledge of either of these—they would not be able to 'latch on to the reference' and it was unlikely that they would have come across these on television or in books. None of the children asked who Archimedes or the Angel fish were. Only one child, in response to the first statement, said: 'Who knows/who can tell?' Surprisingly, several children said they felt these statements were true—the statements 'seemed right' (*sahi lagta hai*). The use of the proper name seemed to suggest that something which has a name must necessarily exist, and the quality attributed to it was assumed to be true.[23]

Privileged epistemic positions

As mentioned earlier, children rarely volunteered knowledge from their personal experience on their own; when they did so, it was with caution. Yet it seems they were aware of personal experience as a source of know-ledge—and seemed to have also experienced its quality of being a privileged epistemic position. The feeling of certainty that accompanies what one has seen 'with one's own eyes' often makes the usual epistemic require-ments of evidence and scepticism irrelevant. It is in this sense that personal experience places one in a 'privileged epistemic position'. In response to some statements which I asked them to verify for truth, they responded with great excitement: 'It's true, I have seen!' This knowledge gained from personal experience was significant for them. Perhaps what was more exciting was the opportunity to bring it into display in a social context and accord it legitimacy as knowledge in the public domain: 'This I can't say. We had fields, so I know about that' (Ankur, Class V).

It also seems that, for children, the experiences of their near relatives, especially immediate family and their uncles (*chachas* and *mamas*), with whom children are traditionally more bonded, was virtually like their own experience. They often stated things that their uncles and others had seen on their travels as if it were their own experience, and with the same confidence. This seemed to provide them with enough ground to make knowledge claims. Such statements carried a quality of the certainty and immediacy of personal experience and not merely the testimony of trustworthy others.

EPISODE 8.18 (CLASS V)
Ajay: My uncle has been there.
Manoj: I have been to Nagpur.
Ajay tried to clinch the argument, saying: Whoever is born earlier sees more things. I was born earlier.

EPISODE 8.19 (CLASS VI)
They started talking about fishermen and the size of the fish they catch.
Ashok: I have seen it in Bombay. My uncle (*chacha*) had gone to Bombay. He keeps telling us.
Sunil: My father says if you cut with a blade, you can get tetanus. A blade can kill a whale.
They started exchanging long stories about the terrible cuts they have had.
Manoj: My father went to MP. There he saw a cave full of jewels.

Rakesh Sharma was the first Indian to travel into outer space on a Soviet spacecraft in the 1980s. His trip was described in the Class III science textbook. This seemed to provide children with a sense of personal acquaintance with facts about space. They were very excited that he had been in space. For them, the fact that he had seen that the earth was round from there seemed to be persuasive evidence of its truth. (They also believed that he had visited the moon.)

Autonomy and authority: Inference vs. testimony

The authority of the knower is integral to acts of speaking from knowledge, i.e., verbal testimony. But as we saw in Chapter V, in the section on teacher–pupil relationship, epistemic authority is not easily distinguishable from institutional and personal authority. Nothing inherent in testimony can prevent claims from being exaggeration, misinformation, prejudice and error (whether intentional, i.e., lying, or unintentional, i.e., misbelief). It was for this reason that post-Enlightenment philosophers evolved an epistemology with the ideal of 'standing on one's own epistemic feet', i.e., autonomous judgement. They gave an important role to proof and the activities of reasoning, experimenting or, as Dewey did, to thinking (reflectively). As we have seen, although children often asked or were told by authorities the things they wanted to find out or verify, they were also aware of these other autonomous methods. The section on school science in the next chapter presents data which show that some children could even visualise control experiments. What is especially interesting is that this understanding of experiments did not really free children from the yoke of the teacher's authority. When confronted with situations where they had to assess the validity of these claims in relation to each other, they found elegant arguments to accommodate both, without giving either greater epistemic primacy.

EPISODE 8.20 (CLASS IV)
Plants take in oxygen and give out carbon dioxide. Is this true or false?
Bhim and Naresh thought for a bit and said: Yes.
How do you know that this is true?
We take in oxygen and give out carbon dioxide, just the same way.
How do you know this?
Guru*ji* told us.
No experiment?
Don't have an experiment for each thing. But there are very few things for which there is no experiment.

EPISODE 8.21 (CLASS IV)
I gave them the three pots experiment: There are three pots A, B and C. Water is poured into all of them. In pot A the water seeps through, in pot B the water runs off, in pot C the water stays on top. A has loam, B has sand and C has clay. Is this true or no?
Deepak: Yes.
*And if guru*ji* says: 'clay, loam, sand' who will you believe?*
Deepak: The experiment, because guru*ji* tells us this to see if we have trust in ourselves or not.

Deepak carefully balanced the authority of experiments and the teacher's authority. Even when he acknowledged the irrefutability of a fact established by an experiment, he made sure that it did not diminish the teacher's authority. Of special interest are the few occasions on which the relationship of institutional authority to knowledge and knowing was called in question.

EPISODE 8.22 (CLASS V)
Joni (to me): Why are you asking me? Don't you know?
Some things I know and some things I don't.
Yes. That's so. This morning Virendar was telling us who is Drona-charya's father, then the HM said he didn't know till now. So it is not necessary to know.
So how do you come to know?
You have to practise. Azharuddin did a lot of practice, but still he missed the catch.[24]

For Joni, this official admission that teachers, especially the headmaster, may not know everything brought a very important realisation. It seemed to open up what was earlier not permissible to even think. For most children, however, this was not a possibility. In Episode 8.23, Dinesh and Deepak, who could clearly articulate the importance of doing experiments in science, were careful about the possibility of acquiring knowledge from experiments that was not mediated by the teacher. Autonomy had to be guided and ratified by authority.

EPISODE 8.23 (CLASS IV)
Why do we do experiments in science?
Dinesh: To find out for ourselves.
Deepak: To see if it is true or not.
Dinesh: We don't say we won't believe guru*ji* or the book.
Deepak: He shows us experiments. There isn't that much in the book. He tells us all.
Why?
Deepak: To increase our knowledge.
Why is knowledge necessary?
Deepak: We listen and we can know.
Dinesh: Sometimes we also make and find out.
Deepak: Or how it is used, we can find out. Like bricks are used to build a palace. Because of *gyan* (knowledge). A brick is made from *gyan*. We get most from *gyan*. They give it all in the science book.
Dinesh: What guru*ji* tells us, we believe completely. He tells us and makes us understand in the right way.

By referring their autonomous judgement to authority for guidance and ratification, the overall hierarchy was not threatened. Earlier, in Chapter VII on memorisation, Krishan, who wrote his own answers, also felt they needed to be ratified by his teacher (Episode 7.22). Episode 8.24 is the only one I encountered where the authority of the teacher was actually questioned by a student, though care was exercised to do so out of the teacher's hearing. Not surprisingly, the student in question was Vipin.

EPISODE 8.24 (CLASS V)
All new plants are grown from seeds only. (*Statement from the true-or-false list.*)
Ajay and Vipin: No!
Manoj and Sunil: Yes!
Ajay challenged them: Take a bet.
Sunil: Laga le, laga le (take a bet if you like). I will ask guru*ji*.
Vipin: Banana and bamboo, they don't grow from seeds.
Bhardwaj (teacher) came up and said: Yes. They all do grow from a seeds.
Vipin: What about banana?
Bhardwaj: It's true it can grow from root. But first it grows from a seed.
Sunil and Manoj started teasing Ajay.
Vipin quietly fetched his science textbook, opened it to the appropriate page and said: Look, they need not grow only from seeds.
But what about what your guruji said?
Vipin: Don't bother about that. What does it matter if he says it? *(kehne se kya hota hai?)*

On the whole, the social context of hierarchy did not permit cognitive conflict to directly translate into social conflict. Conversely, as the following section will bring out, in the peer group, social conflict seemed to engender cognitive conflict.

Social interaction as epistemic activity

Social interaction as epistemic activity is brought out in the following group of episodes. These episode are taken from a trip I made with three of the schoolboys. Ajay and Ranpal were native Kasimpurians while Vipin was from the Eastern state of Bihar. Ajay and Vipin studied in Class V, while Ranpal was in Class IV. Vipin, as the star pupil of the school and the monitor of his class, enjoyed a special epistemic status.[25] Ranpal and Ajay lived near each other and were part of the same play group. From the very beginning of the trip, they clearly communicated their disapproval of Vipin accompanying us. We walked 14 km along a road bordered by fields and farms, past the nearby irrigation canal and up to the railway line.

During the trip, there were several exchanges between Vipin and Ajay involving knowledge claims and debate, some of which are reported in the episodes that follow. The two of them seemed to take every opportunity to show that they knew a lot. They seemed to be keenly evaluating each other's statements and looking for ways to challenge them. The exchanges began as we passed the school of the twin village Garhi, situated near the village limits.

EPISODE 8.25 (TRIP TO THE RAILWAY LINE)
Ajay: This school has a very big ground.
. *Ranpal:* It is from here to there, where the *tanki* (tank) is.
Ajay: It must be three times the size of our school's. No?
Vipin (in a loud, conclusive tone of making a judgement): No, it's not very wide. It must be one-and-a-half times I think. *(Then in a tone suggesting challenge)* What Ajay?

In this episode, Vipin, while contradicting Ajay's claim, added the basis for his own conclusion of the area of the ground. When we reached the railway line, we saw that there was a station nearby and a manned crossing. We stopped to look at the criss-crossing tracks. We noticed that some of the tracks were worn out and shiny. Ajay pointed out that there were also gaps between the tracks and plates below the gaps.

EPISODE 8.26 (TRIP TO THE RAILWAY LINE)
Why are the gaps there?
Ajay: That's why the plates are there... We can follow the tracks back home.
Vipin (challenging tone): Have you ever been back home that way?
Ajay: No, but from our house we can see the rail. These tracks aren't set OK, because their surface is not evenly shiny. One side is more shiny than the other.

When Vipin challenged the basis on which Ajay was claiming one could follow the track home, Ajay provided a warrant for the assertion. In the next statement, on why the tracks are shiny, he provided the evidence along with the statement, apparently in anticipation of an objection. In the episode that followed, Vipin gave his own explanation for why some tracks are shiny while others are not. Here it was Ajay's turn to object and challenge Vipin's warrants.

EPISODE 8.27 (TRIP TO THE RAILWAY LINE)

We looked at the other side and noticed a number of people working on the track. Vipin and Ranpal also noticed that there were lines in between the main lines (cross-lines to enable trains to change tracks). Both of them made the observation and puzzled over it.

Vipin pointed out that the second set of tracks were not used and that trains moved only on the first set. He repeatedly pointed this out: See, these (set 1) tracks are shiny and those (set 2) are not.

Ajay seemed to disagree, making disbelieving noises, although it was not clear whether he was challenging the observation itself. Of his own accord, he decided to consult a railway linesman nearby who was hammering nails. I will ask this man. He will know... Uncle, do trains go on this? *(He pointed to set 2.) The man explained:* This (set 2) is used if there is an emergency. If a train becomes faulty, it has to change its line to the other one.

Ajay (triumphant tone, to Vipin): Look, I told you.

The workman's explanation did not contradict Vipin's inference. In fact his information supported Vipin's reasoning that if the lines were in regular use, they would show signs of wear and tear and shine. But for Ajay, the fact that the train may run on the lines, even if only in case of emergency, seemed to contradict Vipin's general claim that the lines were not used. He seemed satisfied that by asking someone who knew, he had been able to get the correct answer while Vipin was just guessing. As in Episode 8.2 reported earlier, when Joni disagreed with Babloo in the cricket game, the demand for and presentation of evidence seemed to be necessitated by their lack of trust in each other and their need to show it.

Ajay's later interactions also suggested the belief that *asking* those who know is a surer source of knowledge than inference. In the ongoing contest with Vipin, he seemed emboldened by this superior access to knowledge. After this, he repeatedly queried men along the tracks who were engaged with some repair work: 'Uncle, what are you doing?' 'Uncle, what is this?' Ajay repeated their answers, transmitting his newly-gained knowledge to us. His general air of satisfaction suggested the authority of a man who speaks from knowledge—which carries the right to pronounce on facts and to be believed. It also suggested that Vipin's conjectures were inferior. Vipin tried to establish his own claim to speaking from knowledge, as an expert. He exhibited his greater familiarity and experience with trains and train travel, as he often travelled between Delhi and Bihar.

EPISODE 8.28 (TRIP TO THE RAILWAY LINE)

We began walking towards the station. Vipin wanted to know which train I took when I went home, and did it go through UP? When did it leave and from which platform? He told me about the two trains he could take to go home—their names and times of departure, and the platforms from which they left.

We walked ahead and sat on a bench. Vipin continued to demonstrate his superior knowledge of trains: Each driver has a duty of eight-eight hours.

Ajay: Ho! Why? That can't be. They are paid to work 24 hours.

Vipin continued, tangentially responding to this with the warrant: One driver can't drive non-stop. They have four drivers. At a station, after eight hours duty, he gets off and another one gets on.

Ajay challenged Vipin: Is that necessary!?... Four-four people driving! Have you seen that?

Vipin: In the engine there are four steering wheels.

Ajay: As if! We'll stop the next train and look in.

Ajay had never been in a train, and may have felt the need to compensate for this lack of experience and personal acquaintance. We proceeded to the station and entered. Ajay now ignored Vipin and went up to the station-master.

EPISODE 8.29 (TRIP TO THE RAILWAY LINE)

The first room had a ticketing counter. There Vipin noted the time table of the trains coming and going. He noted that the next one was at 1.30 p.m. Meanwhile, Ajay and Ranpal had peeped through the window and seen the station-master's paraphernalia. Ajay asked: Uncleji, what is all this?

We went into the station-master's room. The station-master explained how the red and green signals were controlled. He added that one needed to pass an exam and then train for the job.

Ajay had earlier been telling me that the people at the gate knew when they had to close the gate because they got a phone call. He now asked the station-master: Do you telephone from here to the signal office to tell them a train is coming?

The station-master said yes.

Ajay was triumphant: See *didi,* I told you.

Ajay spontaneously referred his earlier statement to the station-master for verification and was very pleased that he was right. It seemed to serve the purpose of demonstrating to Vipin and me that he too knew things about trains. Shortly afterwards, we left the office and began walking back. Earlier, we had flattened out a 10 paise coin by leaving it on the tracks and letting a passing train run over it. Ajay and Vipin now said they wanted to flatten out some more coins they had. I wondered when the next train would be.

EPISODE 8.30 (TRIP TO THE RAILWAY LINE)
Vipin: The next train is at 1.30. I saw it on the timetable.
Ajay: Is that necessary? There can be a train any time.
Vipin: The timetable says so.
Ajay: So what. There could be a train any time.
Vipin: This is a small station, a very small station. In any train you pass a station every 10 minutes.
Just then an express train puffed through the station but did not stop. Ajay was triumphant. He checked my watch and announced: It's 12:15! *Vipin's prediction, based on his access to the knowledge encoded in the timetable, seemed to be wrong.*
We left the railway crossing and headed back. As we walked away, we heard the sound of another passing train. Ranpal remarked: A train passes every 15 minutes. It was 12:15 then. Now it is 12:30.

Vipin's deduction was based on the information provided in the timetable displayed—which, of course, was about the trains that stopped at the station and did not include the trains that went through. But he did not defend his conclusion and for Ajay, this seemed to prove that one can really trust only what one sees, or what one is told by those who know (who have seen themselves).

Vipin and Ajay both reasoned, but in different ways. While Ajay made his own observations and conjectures, he was inclined to refer to older people around (experts) for affirmation and to find out. Vipin, on the other hand, was willing to accept certain givens and to conjecture and reason on that basis. Dewey points out that both these are equally valid ways of producing knowledge, but that there is a difference in the two epistemic stances (1985a).[26] Ajay and Vipin represent two models of the knower. Ajay 'looks backward' to knowledge that already exists in society for confirmation. Vipin 'looks forward'. While both are reasoning, Ajay's stance is one of receiving knowledge, while Vipin's is one of producing knowledge. Ajay seems inclined to treat the occurrence of events as arbitrary and relies on asking to find out and being told, i.e., receives knowledge from those who know. Although he does recognise hypothesising as a way of producing knowledge, yet, for him, this is often simply guesswork and prone to error. Asking those who know is a far more sure way of knowing things than Vipin's reasoning. It is interesting and important that *outside the school,* Vipin's special epistemic status did not hold; his knowledge claims did not receive the same reception as they did within the classroom.

Cognitive vs social: Errors and lies

Asking for or presenting supporting evidence seemed to suggest an atmosphere of distrust and almost automatically infused a competitive edge into the dialogue, as other participants were invited to consider the basis of the claim and acknowledge that it was warranted. In calling *sabda* (verbal testimony) *'apta vakya'* the *advaitins* emphasised the aspect of trustworthiness of the speaker. Consequently, it is an untrustworthy man who speaks untruths. Dewey had noted: 'We forget—I mean philosophers forget—that truth in this aspect is first of all truthfulness, a social virtue, meeting a demand growing out of intercourse, not a logical, much less an epistemological relationship' (1985a: 14).

To children it seemed that if a knowledge claim was found to be false, they were in danger of being called liars. Therefore, the status of interpersonal relations was of importance in deciding whether to challenge a knowledge claim or not. With a friend, if a knowledge claim was to be challenged at all, it would be done through humour, so that the friend did not become a liar. With one's 'enemies', all knowledge claims were to be challenged and disbelieved—because as an enemy, he was likely to lie. The glee at finding that one's enemy had made a mistake also seemed to derive from the satisfaction of 'proving' that he was indeed a liar and not worthy of respect. Assessing truth value seemed to have more a social than a cognitive purpose.[27] It was only in cases where the character of the speaker was suspect that primitive credulity was suspended and statements were reviewed for their truth content.

This suggests that, contrary to what Piagetian scholars like Doise and Mugny (1984) claim, the relationship between cognitive and social conflict is not a simple, direct one where cognitive conflict translates into the latter, and the resolution of the two is simultaneous. In the case of authority and the hierarchical organisation of the community, what we see is the metacognitive awareness of self and others as knowers. This is accompanied by the social need to coordinate perspectives, without cognitive conflict translating into social conflict. This is a feature that Piagetian theorising on the role of social conflict does not reflect when it suggests that there is an easy transfer of the one into the other. The authority structure of the social setting, and the interpersonal relations of the interlocutors, do have a decisive role in what is and is not expressed.

The influence of 'English medium' on epistemic self-identity

Among the various statements presented to children for evaluating truth, there was a small selection of claims about which children could not possibly have had any knowledge. These included the statements on Archimedes and the Angel fish mentioned earlier. They also included statements such as: 'When you mix an acid with a base, you get a salt and water.' To my surprise, there were some children who claimed that these statements were true. All the children of Class IV in LAPS answered with a quick 'madam-yes!' to every question asked. I stopped and asked them how they knew; they were tongue-tied and looked embarrassed. After a minute, one ventured to say: 'Madam you asked and we told you.' She seemed to be suggesting that I was being unfair in asking them how they knew after they had shown me that they did know.[28]

Children seemed to feel that education in an English-medium school, as it was reputed to be better, should give them the knowledge they ought-to-know to answer questions, including the ones that I was asking. By answering, they had shown me that they did know. This hypothesis was strengthened by the fact that the same tendency was noted among children in the government school; and here they themselves stated that it was on account of their earlier stint in an English-medium school: 'I knew when I was in English school' (Jogi, Class IV); 'I used to know when I was in English medium school' (Sudhir, Class IV). Jogi, especially, claimed to know a lot because he had earlier studied in an English-medium school.

EPISODE 8.31 (CLASS IV)
Jogi: He (Bir Singh) can't read, he can't study that much.
So who else (apart from you) in your class can (study)?
Jogi: Satish. When I joined school, Satish couldn't do anything. He was a very bad student. Now he comes first or I come first. I came from English-medium school in the third. That was Sheela madam's class. She gave me a paper. Everything was correct.

The next episode is from an interview with Jogi and Satish where they were asked the true-or-false questions. Satish, though he was also considered a good student, didn't feel compelled to know all answers. Jogi, on the other hand, seemed to feel that he ought to know the answers to all the questions I asked.

EPISODE 8.32 (CLASS IV)
Aeroplanes are run on fuel which is a mixture of petrol and diesel.
Satish: Don't know.
Jogi (very cockily): They don't fill petrol. It runs on a machine. When I studied in English school, it used to run.
Satish: Doesn't it run on petrol?
How will you find out?
Satish: I'll ask my brother.
Jogi: I will ask my *chacha,* or *tau* or *papa.*
Malaria is spread by foul, bad air.
Satish: It's true. Our madam told us in the third (class).
Jogi: In the English school our madam told us in the second (class).
Crores of years ago, the Earth, Sun and all the planets were in the form of one big swirling, hot ball.
Jogi: Yes it's true.
Satish: Eh? (Hain?)
(To Satish) How can you find out?
Satish (to Jogi): You tell now, how do you know?
Jogi: In the English school they told us.
Satish (irritated): For everything you say 'in English school!' I don't know.

Satish himself noted with irritation that, unlike him, Jogi never said 'I don't know' and made knowledge claims which he attributed to having been a student of an English-medium school. Similarly, in Episode 8.33, Sudhir also felt that he ought to know answers as he had studied in an English-medium school. He claimed he knew them earlier but had forgotten them because he had now joined the government school.

EPISODE 8.33 (CLASS IV)
'Archimedes was a Greek scientist'. Is this true or false?
Sudhir: I don't know. It's not in the book.
How will you find out?

I used to know. We were studying about it in the previous school. We studied English and we knew everything. I came here and I forgot.

The children from LAPS did not believe that Usha, who taught them, could have been educated in the local government school. She said they even asked her how could someone, who had been educated in a government school, be good enough and know enough to teach them?

*

Children frequently depended on asking or being told in order to find out and verify things. We also find that children's asking was not an indiscriminate activity; in deciding who to ask for what, they seemed to be aware of parameters such as cognitive and epistemic competence and trust-worthiness. They were also capable of inference and what Dewey calls 'reflective thinking', which involves presenting, demanding and assessing relevant evidence while evaluating the truth of a knowledge claim (1985b: 182–91).

What emerges along with the realisation that children operate with a rich and elaborated epistemic competence, is the importance of the social dimension of their knowledge and knowledge-related activity. Perhaps knowledge and truth were concerns of individual children constructing and reflecting on their reality and experience; certainly they expressed an excitement about the immediacy associated with knowledge from personal experience. But at the same time, they seemed to be alert to the public nature of knowledge; hence the satisfaction and confidence gained in opportunities to make such individual experience public and shared. Their frequent recourse to asking and telling as the primary ways of finding out and verifying knowledge need not be regarded with dismay. As Welbourne (1993) points out, these are simply a consequence of the children's correct understanding that knowledge is a social thing—it is public and objective—and that it can be had for the asking. Language itself is geared to this 'commoning of knowledge'.[29]

The social context also seems to be a deciding factor in determining epistemic activity. In the peer group, trust in each other's words seems sacrosanct. Enmity and distrust engender a range of epistemically significant activities—argument, assessing evidence and warrants, demonstrating, proving, etc. But overall, in the world shared with adults and those who are older, children seem to be aware of their location within a social hierarchy and the need to behave in a manner commensurate with this location. This is visible in their metacognitive awareness of self and others in the school world. Not surprisingly, the teacher is one of the most important sources of knowledge, and we find that the school space is dominated by 'telling'. Although in response to questions on how they could verify or find out children often said that they could ask their teacher, in practice, children rarely asked them. Welbourne believes that '...[t]he natural climate in which we deal in knowledge is one of mutual respect, mutual give and take. Authoritarianism is liable to set in when, for whatever reason, this mutuality is eroded' (1993: 67). It is uncertain whether for most Indian children such spaces of mutuality are any more 'natural' than the ones of hierarchy. But in any case the school space is structured around authoritarian teachers and there is no mutuality between teachers and children. In this space, knowledge is represented (and experienced) as something to be received from authorities who deserve unquestioning deference and trust. We have seen that the concept of knowledge from verbal testimony itself includes authority and belief. Welbourne argues that the habits of deference and authoritarianism are not consequences of verbal testimony *per se*. And the concern for guarding against these social practices that cripple and corrupt cognition, although rightful, need not require that each person become an intellectual Robinson Crusoe.

We must be concerned with the social organisation of the classroom which seems to invalidate or undermine autonomous activities such as conjecture and inference. In fact, it is the same organisation which also works against verbal testimony functioning as an authentic source of knowledge; children do not feel free to engage with their natural vocation of asking and questioning to dispel ignorance. Although outside the school they are able to judge who and what to believe, to evaluate evidence to decide under what circumstances to believe and to what degree, they do not feel that they can exercise such judgement within the school space. Even when they experience the autonomy of inference, they are careful that this is not interpreted as being in conflict with the teacher's testimony, as this would constitute a challenge to the authority structure of the classroom.

Notes

1. Naturalised epistemology: 'Term due to Quine for the enterprise of studying the actual formation of knowledge by human beings, without aspiring to certify those processes as rational, or proof against scepticism, or even apt to yield the truth' (Blackburn 1996: 225).

2. The term 'narrow' may sound pejorative. Here, it is not used in the sense of a value judgement, where 'narrow' suggests less than good. Here, it is used only descriptively, to refer to the rigour and exactness with which the term will be applied.

3. See, for example, Vygotsky's *Mind in Society* (1978), Rogoff (1990) and Wertsch (1985) for discussions of this perspective.

4. For this reason, Dewey preferred to use the phrase 'warranted assertion' for propositions or knowledge claims. See Haack (1996: 235).

5. This version of the standard analysis is based on Butchvarov (1970).

6. According to this analysis, the notion of false knowledge is incoherent; one can only have false beliefs, descriptions or theories. It may be true that it will rain in the evening, but if Ammu believes this because today is Monday and it rained last Monday, then we would not say that Ammu 'knows'. Her reasons for believing are not sufficient, even though her belief itself may be true. In everyday language, too, we would make a distinction and say: 'Ammu believes... (incorrectly)...'

7. Disembodied, not in the sense of occurring singly, for propositions do often occur together in the form of 'theories', etc., but disembodied in the sense that they are separated from the original utterer and the context in which they were uttered.

8. Issues of who selects, on what grounds and for what purposes are also of interest but are outside the scope of the present enquiry. See, for example, Krishna Kumar's analysis of the failure of Gandhi's Basic Education programme in his essay 'Meaning of progress' (1991:149–87), or Poromesh Acharya on the politics of the language primer *Sahaj Path* in West Bengal (1985).

9. This is notwithstanding the fact that a theory of meaning must contain an epistemological position; also, hermeneutic epistemology (see Hekman 1986 and Baumann 1978) and Wittgenstein's (1958) later work on language communities derive from a theory of meaning.

10. The epistemologist will caution that even if I know that Pilloo refers to her sister, still that does not mean that having heard Ammu, I now 'know' that Pilloo is on the tree—Ammu could be lying or she may have mistaken her friend to be her sister.

11. On the other hand, if I did not know what 'tree' was, I could look up a dictionary and find out. That would be a case of 'lexical misunderstanding'.

12. This is based on speech act theory; see, for example, Searle (1971). Welbourne (1993) goes on to elaborate a fourth type of understanding which he calls 'factual understanding'. All that is known forms a 'fabric of knowledge'. Understanding what we are told/read,

> ... involves receiving it into the web of things already known, and more or less fully appreciating its connections with the rest... [T]he more ramified its connections, the more *significant* a bit of knowledge is, and the more fully it is integrated into the fabric, the better it is understood (ibid.: 50).

It also represents a type of failure of understanding if someone cannot perceive the significance of a bit of knowledge relative to what she/he already knows. Also, if one's background knowledge is thin, then one's understanding may also be thin. How well the new bit of knowledge is integrated into the fabric of existing knowledge is a measure of the quality of the understanding. Factual understanding is prized. It is also not directly transmissible as verbal testimony, as it is a matter of perceiving and appreciating connections; but, as Welbourne also points out, this is different from the point Quinton makes that knowledge degenerates in transmission (ibid.: 51).

13. 'Understanding the speaker when he says...' vs. 'understanding what he says'; 'believing the speaker' vs. 'believing what he says'—these are subtle distinctions denoting different epistemic stances.

14. Welbourne's analysis is in the context of knowledge transmission, hence the third layer of understanding of speech acts is stated differently. Here, I am presenting it as how we will know if the child 'knows', in a sense the teacher/observer/adult is 'receiving' knowledge from the child (although it may not and is unlikely to be 'new knowledge'.) If Ammu heard the teacher say 'the earth is round', then speech act understanding would mean that Ammu must be able to apprehend if her teacher is 'speaking from knowledge'.

15. For a discussion of the *advaita* and *navya-nyaya* views on *sabda* as a source of knowledge see, for example, Datta (1972), Satprakashananda (1974) and Matilal (1986, 1990) for an account which relates it to more recent Western studies in philosophy of language, etc. In Western philosophy, apart from the work on propositions and propositional attitudes by such philosophers of language as G. Frege, S.A. Kripke and W.V.O. Quine, there are few serious treatments of testimony. See, for example, Fricker (1987) and Welbourne (1993).

16. This insight also provided the basis to argue for the truth of scriptural knowledge— these were not the utterances of humans, who are fallible; therefore, as divine utterances they were beyond the question of falsehood.

17. I am grateful to Jane Sahi for drawing my attention Hiriyanna's observation on this aspect of *sabda.*

18. The form of these conversations was akin to Piaget's observation about children's social interaction during parallel play.

19. In *nyaya*, fundamental or simple attitudes are generally doubt or belief. 'Under all normal circumstances utterance of sentences generates occurrent beliefs, i.e., certainties which have knowledge claims.' We do not have a non-committal understanding of what is said prior to this type of certainty. Such an attitude may presumably arise later, when doubt (for whatever reason) has been instilled into the prior certainty. According to Frege, however, it is possible to 'grasp a thought' without judging it to be true or false. So, for example, we may understand the meaning of a compulsive liar's statement but withhold our belief in it. Here, we take understanding to be a basic attitude prior to belief or knowledge (Matilal 1990: 65–66).

20. Propositional attitudes are psychological states towards propositions: e.g., the belief that p, the desire that p, and the intention that p. They are given a central role in folk psychology in the explanation of rational behaviour as an outcome of a suitable belief along with a suitable desire (Blackburn 1996; CREP 2000).

21. Words are mediational while perception is direct. The proverb 'Seeing is believing, hearing is deceiving' brings out the inherent possibility of misinformation through words, and also the epistemically privileging quality of perception.

22. On one occasion, during a conversation with two children from Class IV, when Bhim claimed to know something saying it was written in the book, Naresh clarified, stressing that it was PRINTED (*chhapa*) in the book. This carried the suggestion that something that is printed is far more likely to be true than something that is merely written. Printing seems to suggest a superior authority who has ratified it, while anybody can write.

23. Kripke (1980) has discussed the ontological problem presented by names and the problem of assessing the validity of statements which involve names of things that do not exist. Also see Russell (1959) . This may explain the common observation on the

willingness of people to believe histories which are written as accounts of great personalities.

24. Dronacharya is a character from the epic Mahabharata. Azharuddin is a popular cricketer.

25. In Chapter VI, the section on negotiating boundary control brings out Vipin's privileged position—the frame boundary was weak only for him.

26. See note 7 in Chapter VII.

27. The 'knowledgeable man' in the village community seemed to have a similar social rather than cognitive influence on the actions of others. It seemed to be related to his 'moral authority', derived from making true/believable pronouncements.

28. Sometimes they answered without even comprehending words.

> *The Thar desert is to the west of Delhi. (The statement was read out in English.)*
> Madam, yes.
> *What is 'desert'?*
> Desert? What is 'desert'?

29. Welbourne calls his theory of the transmission of knowledge from person to person the 'commoning' of knowledge, emphasising that the idea of knowledge

> ... is the idea of communicable information, information as to the facts, information which is objective in the sense that it is not dependent on any particular point of view, but is available to any one at all, with the capacity to understand the utterances in which it is embodied (1993: 5).

In other words, the idea of commonable knowledge is the same as the idea of a common, public, objective world.

9

Children's Epistemology 2:
School and Everyday Knowledge

In the last chapter we saw that children were aware of a variety of ways of finding out and verifying things, although asking and telling were the most common. Their arguments were rich in the activities of offering and evaluating evidence. But the space of the school was dominated by the practice of telling and the present form of pedagogic activity did not encourage even asking, leave alone more autonomous practices such as inference. Children were careful not to come into conflict with the authority structure in the classroom. In this chapter, we take up two more areas of study; we begin with an investigation into school science where we will be especially interested in children's understanding of 'experiments'. In the final section we examine the relationship between school knowledge and everyday knowledge.

I
Understanding School Science

The inclusion of science as a school subject is often justified not only for the knowledge of reality that it provides, but also because of its method. According to the foreword of the environmental studies textbooks for Classes III, IV and V, this area of knowledge is expected to encourage children to 'explore the environment, and to participate in different activities so as to enable them to think, to question, to experiment and to seek explanations for different environmental phenomena' (NCERT 1988a). The use of the term 'environment' is a reflection of the re-naming and ostensible integration of science and social sciences into a subject called 'environmental studies' or EVS. The other reason for the teaching of science is its epistemology: 'scientific temper' and 'inquiry', deemed to be fundamental duties in Article 51A of the Constitution of India, are believed to be promoted by the learning of science (NCERT 1988b).

The subject matter: In spite of the umbrella name of the subject *'parya-varan adhyayan'* (environmental studies), there were two separate books subtitled Parts I and II, dealing respectively with areas that could be recognised as 'science' (physics, biology and health/hygiene) and social studies (geography, history, civics). Children's views on the subject matter of science reflected this categorisation which is inherent in the two separate books. One basis on which they differentiated was ontological: 'Science is about plants and trees. *Samajik* (socials) is about *samaj* (society).' The Hindi word *'samajik'* (adj.) itself suggests the nature of its subject matter *'samaj'* (n.) or society. While describing the subject matter of science, children tended to focus on biology. Sometimes, they also referred to hygiene: 'In science they tell us good things (*achchhi-achchhi baten*). About the body and cleanliness' (Navin, Class IV). Even though they did have chapters identifiable as physics in their textbook which dealt with ideas such as energy, force and simple machines, they did not make references to them. But, while talking about the work of scientists, they focused on techno-logical inventions like pumps and spectacles, not hybrid seeds or fertilisers. In spite of the main title 'Environmental Studies', there was nothing in what the children said that suggested that they identified any larger com-monalties between science and social studies, or even that the two repre-sented two different aspects of their environment.

Children also distinguished between science and social studies on epistemological lines.

EPISODE 9.1 (CLASS IV)
Naresh: In science they tell us about experiments (*prayog*). In socials they tell us.
Why not experiments?
We can't do experiments (in social studies).
Why?
These are not matters for doing experiments.

Naresh was of the opinion that the subject matter of social studies did not lend itself to experiments. On the other hand, science was characterised by experiments. Children felt that new knowledge in social studies was got by being told and from reading what was *printed* in books. (Being written wasn't enough. They emphasised that it was printed in books, and so it must be true.) In the case of science, they also referred to '*khoj*' (investigation, research) and '*prayog*' (experimentation) as ways of establishing truth and finding out.

What are experiments?[1]

Experimentation has an important and unique epistemological function in science. Progress in science is closely identified with progress in experimental methods and observation. The status of facts and theories, and their development, rest crucially on experimental investigation and validation. This gives to science its empirical quality. It is therefore significant that the children of the Kasimpur village school identified *prayog* (experiments) as a characteristic of science. I probed further to understand what they meant by 'experiment'.

Don't know: While most children knew that experiments are done in science, they had no idea why. When they had characterised science with experiments, I asked 'what is *prayog*?' or 'why do we do experiments?' Typically, they replied saying '*don't know*'.

> EPISODE 9.2 (CLASS IV)
> *Why (do you do experiments in science)?*
> Dinesh: They are given.
> *Why can't you do experiments in socials?*
> Abhay: They don't make us do them.
> Dinesh: In socials we do question–answers here, and go home and complete them.
> *Can you have science without experiments?*
> Both: No!
> *Why?*
> Abhay: Don't know.

Some children indirectly highlighted the aspect of '*doing something*', i.e., of manipulating materials and observing consequences. But still they were not sure either of what they were doing or why.

Doing something:

EPISODE 9.3 (CLASS V)
In science you do experiments.
Joni: Yes.
Why?
They say 'do this', 'do that'. Tomorrow you come to my house. I will show you an experiment. Take a tumbler. Crush a paper and put it into it.... *(He described the common experiment to prove that air exists and occupies space.)*
Where did you learn it?
Kanta madam did it and showed it to us.
Why did she do it?
Don't know.
What did you learn from it?
Shrugs.

Joni was describing an easy and elegant experiment that suggests that what we think is 'empty' space in fact has something which we cannot see or feel: it occupies space and can exert pressure. The conclusion involves interpreting the unexpected finding of the experiment—that water does not fill up the glass and the paper remains dry. The observation is not self-explanatory. Joni's understanding of the experiment was just the activity, without any interpretation. This *doing* was identified as what constitutes an experiment.

The Class V language textbook had two lessons about scientists: J.C. Bose and Madame Curie. The lesson on Curie talked about the discovery of radium and how useful it is. It also said that she did many experiments in the course of her research (*khoj*). But there was no indication of what kind of activity these experiments could have involved.

EPISODE 9.4 (CLASS V)
How do you think Madame Curie made her discovery (**khoj**)*?*
Vipin: She was interested in science.
Do you think she may have done experiments?
Vipin: May be. Liquid from here to there, there to here.

Vipin's description, 'here to there, there to here', echoed the vagueness in the book about what Curie's experiments may have involved. That experiments are integral to scientific study was known by all children as a linguistic fact. But few children seemed to realise the meaning of this phrase. The word *khoj*, too, creates an ambiguity as the same word is used for 'research', 'discovery' and 'search'. Sometimes, when children spoke about scientists as finding things out by '*khoj*', I wondered if they took this literally to believe that facts (rather than phenomena) already exist, and scientists merely find them.[2]

Inventing something useful: The term *prayog*, which has been adopted as the official, technical term in Hindi for 'experimentation', has a pre-existing meaning—'application'. The word is also commonly used as a verb, '*prayog karna*', which means 'to use'. This linguistic ambiguity, and the description of scientists' activities as '*prayog*', led to another nuance in the meaning of the word: 'bringing something into use': '*Prayog* is making something new. You make something and you bring it into use (*prayog mein late hain*). Then it becomes *prayog*' (Navin, Class V).

EPISODE 9.5 (CLASS IV)
Bir Singh: You know all the things that scientists have made..spectacles, telephone...
Shobhraj: Science is an art (*kala*). The scientists do things from their brain.
What is **prayog**?
Shobhraj: To bring something into use. Scientists have brought things into use, like pumps.

Children were already familiar with the idea of scientists who do experiments and invent useful things. The books also made it a point to tell them how scientific inventions and discoveries aid in mankind's progress. This seemed to suggest that to experiment is to make something useful.

To prove: Though Vipin was vague about the nature of Curie's experimental work, he and a few other children exhibited a keen sense of the epistemological purpose of experiments in their own cognitive activity. When posed with the problem of verifying the hypothesis: 'If you toss a coin 50 times, you will get heads and tails about 25 times each,' Vipin began tossing a coin and keeping track of the results. He then explained to me what he was doing, saying: 'We were doing it to prove something. It was an experiment.'

Only one other child exhibited a similar remarkable clarity regarding experiments. I posed the statement to Naresh: 'If salt water is used to water plants, they will grow well.' I asked him if this was true or false.

EPISODE 9.6 (CLASS IV)

Naresh: I have never heard of such a thing.
How will you find out?
(*In a monotonous voice*): First-we-will-take-two-pots. We-will-fill-one-with...(*he described a control experiment*). Then-we-will-see-the-difference.
Why will you take two pots?
Otherwise how will we know? It has to make a difference. This was a thing from science.
Why do you say that?
It was an experiment we did, to find out.
Why do we do experiments in science?
Because we also want to see if it is so.
But what is given in the book is true, so why do experiments?
We want to see in front of our own eyes. Then we won't forget. And if it comes in the (examination) papers?

Naresh described a control experiment to verify the truth of the claim. His monotonous voice suggested he was repeating something he had memorised. However, this answer was based on his own reasoning. This is another instance of children using the recitation device noted earlier in Chapter VI. In a situation where knowledge is believed to be only received, and memorisation is regarded as the correct way of learning, 'recitation' seemed to convey a sense of 'speaking from knowledge'.

As pedagogic tools: Vipin and Naresh were unique in their sensitivity to the epistemological function of experiments. But even so, they did not think that the experiments in their science textbook had an epistemological function. Experiments seemed to be given in the science textbook for a different purpose: to help students understand and remember.

EPISODE 9.7 (CLASS V)

Why do we do experiments in science?
Joni: Because they are given.
Vipin: To understand and to prove something. Like they have given here: this is to prove that plants grow.
Why was this proved?

Vipin (dismissively): This everyone knows.
So what kind of matters are proved?
Vipin: Don't know.
Can we learn science without experiments?
Vipin: Yes. Those who want to understand will.
Do you learn from experiments?
Never. We never have the need to.

Vipin's dismissive opinion needs to be looked at from the perspective of the treatment of experiments in their science textbook. Experiments given there seemed to have little to contribute to an ongoing enquiry. Facts are stated in the book, e.g., 'All living things grow.' The fact itself is obvious. Then an experiment is described to establish this fact and the same conclusion is drawn. Such a treatment of experiments must have contributed to Vipin's opinion that they did not have any authentic epistemic function in the textbook. So it was reasonable to conclude that they must have been included for some other reason; perhaps to simplify things. Vipin, and others like him who did well in class, did not require such simplification in order to learn: 'Those who are clever can understand without them. When Aunty brings and shows like this, like this, then we remember very well (*pakka*); when we see, then we won't forget' (Krishan, Class V).

There were others who did not in general appreciate the epistemic aspect of experiments, but also believed they were in the book to assist in understanding and memorisation. This was because they believed that 'pictures are also experiments' (Jogi, Class IV). Illustrations were regarded as experiments (and not representations of experiments). So even tables and flow diagrams were pointed out as 'experiments'. Experiments help in understanding 'because we can learn easily through pictures' (Amit, Class V). This typically led to a confusion when I asked if, on this basis, social studies could be regarded as having experiments! The basic contrast seemed to be between what needs to be read and what does not. 'Experiment' seemed to refer simply to a non-text-based, visual or experiential way of conveying information.

For entertainment: Still, children enjoyed the rare occasions when teachers tried to 'do' something, to conduct a simple experiment or demonstrate something.

EPISODE 9.8 (CLASS IV)
Surya Prakash: They do practicals. They need *dhyan* (concentration).

How?
They take a glass and put a candle in it. Then the candle gets extinguished.
Then?
They light it again.
Why do they do such things?
To entertain us (*dil behlane ke liye*). Sometimes they also take us to the TV hall to watch movies (*one of the rooms in the school, which had a television*).

Some of these activities which had unexpected results, like the experiment that Joni described in Episode 9.3, reminded them of magic; these created curiosity, awe and wonder. This seems to have been on Vipin's mind when he told me, smiling wickedly, that with science: 'We can fool people. Like, I will fill a bucket with milk and I'll tell them that I'll do a magic trick so not a drop will fall out. And I'll just say *chhoo-mantar* and spin it round.' But when I suggested that perhaps this activity was a bit like play, Joni (Class V) patiently explained to me: 'Look, I'll tell you about scientists—they search and they find out something (*kuchh khoj nikalte hain*).' He opened his book and turned to the lesson on Madame Curie. 'Look, she discovered radium.' An activity that was pursued by serious adults couldn't be considered mere play.

In Episode 9.9, Sulaiman identified experiments with the matter of verifying truth (through the idea of 'trust'), but for him the activity was still entertainment. The picture he presented brings to mind Richard Rorty's description of knowledge communities as essentially closed linguistic communities (1980). The community of scientists seemed to be basically 'government-paid showmen'!

EPISODE 9.9 (CLASS IV)
Sulaiman: Science is about plants, socials is about population.
How do we get **jankari** (*information/knowledge*)?
We get information only by reading.
And the ones who write, how do they know?
They (re)search (*khoj*) and write.
Why do they do **khoj**?
To see, because they don't trust (*vishvas*).
But isn't it a bad thing not to trust?
No, they just ask each other, in jest (*hansi mazak mein*). They say to each other, do an experiment and show me.

And then?

Then they trust (believe). And they also get entertained (*manoranjan bhi hota hai*).

And do they do it just like that?

Sulaiman laughed and said: No. They get money from the government, so they have to do it on behalf of the government (*sarkar ki taraf se*).

On scientists

Sulaiman's image of the scientist was refreshingly irreverent. For most other children, scientists and science aided in the country's progress. Scientists were people employed by the government to do science. They pictured them as 'good citizens', who did useful things for the country by inventing useful things: 'Like in our country there is gold and silver, they find out. Scientists have made machines. From science they find out' (Ankur, Class IV).

> EPISODE 9.10 (CLASS IV)
> *What does a scientist do?*
> *Neeraj:* Many good things. Like we are poor. If someone steals a necklace from there, then they find out. They take fingerprints and find out.

Even experiments, they believed, helped to distinguish 'what is good and what is bad'. Caught in the ideology of science for welfare, scientists were believed to be employed with pursuits that had moral implications. The logical or epistemological states of 'true' and 'false' were turned into moral states of 'truth' and 'falsehood'.

Experiments in the primary science curriculum

The primary science textbooks contain several kinds of activities for children to do. Some involve making observations. For example:

> Observe small animals such as house lizards, squirrels, puppies, kittens, chickens or any animal found in and around your house. If possible, observe these animals over a period of time. Make a special note whether these animals develop new body parts as they grow. Compare the growth of these animals with that of plants ([Class V] NCERT 1988a: 3).

In some activities, children are expected to do something and see its effect. For example: 'Darken the classroom. Shine a torch light at the animal. How does the animal react to the light?...' (ibid.: 4). Some are based on looking at pictures: 'Look at the animals shown in the picture. Observe carefully their body parts. How do these animals move from one place to another?...' (ibid.: 16). A few can also be regarded as more classic control experiments in which experimental conditions are varied and the conclusions drawn on the basis of the differences observed in the results. For example, an experiment is suggested to investigate and conclude that seeds need both moisture and air in order to germinate. Three cups with seeds are taken; in the first the seeds are kept moist and have air, in the second they are immersed in water and in the third they are not watered. Children are asked to

> ...observe the seeds in the containers for two or three days. Note down all the changes you see at the interval of four to six hours. In which of the containers did the seeds germinate? Note down the conditions in this container. Also note down the conditions missing in the containers where the seeds did not germinate (ibid.: 31).

The meaning that the children of the Kasimpur school gave to '*prayog*' included these dimensions reflected in the textbook. 'Doing things' (activities), pictures and control experiments were all regarded as *prayog*. In addition, there were also the dimensions of inventing or making 'useful things' and magic/entertainment. The pedagogic function—as 'vehicles for understanding' through non-text-based, visual or experiential ways—seemed to dominate over the epistemic function.

In Chapter VIII we saw that, in the concept of learning that prevailed in the school, 'understanding' was not very valued. So it was not very surprising that children did not take even the pedagogic function of experiments and activities very seriously. It was possible to 'understand' and memorise by merely reading the text. In any case, the textbook was full of 'facts' that had to be taken as true by children, basically on trust. The only matters that were subjected to 'experimentation' were those that were almost trivially obvious, and which did not require any persuasion via methodical experimentation or observation. This superficial treatment of experiments in the textbooks for Classes III, IV and V, undermined the 'science-related values',[3] such as critical observation and reasoning, that the books were supposed to promote. The aspect of developing skills necessary for scientific investigation, such as measurement, was completely ignored.

Ramadas et al. (1996: 41) suggest that one of the simple uses of experiments in science in the primary school is to produce a phenomenon and provoke discussion. We saw in Chapter VI, Episode 6.3, that when Nagpal demonstrated an experiment on how to distinguish between types of soils, children were involved and made several kinds of observations. But Nagpal discouraged discussion and the children's comments and observations were kept outside the curricular frame, denying them an active role in knowledge construction.

II
Making Connections

The knowledge acquired in the school did not seem to be integrated into the child's fabric of understanding woven from everyday experiences. The perceived incompatibility between school and everyday knowledge was suggested in the following conversation with Pavan:

EPISODE 9.11 (CLASS V)
For socials do you need understanding or memorising?
Memorising.
Mathematics?
Understanding and memorising.
Language?
Memorising.
Drawing?
That's nothing.
For looking after buffaloes?
Silence.
And growing crops?
Neither. There is no match (*mel*).
Why?
Pavan thought pensively for about two minutes.
I asked again: Isn't there anything to understand or remember?
There is, *ji*.
So why do you say no?
There was no reply... a very long silence.

Pavan declared there was no *mel* (match) between terms like 'memorise' or 'understand', which were used to learn school knowledge, and learning everyday (local) knowledge. In an earlier conversation on how he had learnt to cook and make tea, he had described it as simply happening— by seeing (others do it).

Yet, much of the content of school knowledge, i.e., the curriculum, dealt with things that formed a part of children's everyday local knowledge: plants, animals, the seasons, climate, weather, geography, etc. Did the similarity in content lead to assimilating the one with the other in any manner? The boundary of what can be asked about in a pedagogic/school question was clearly defined to exclude any non-textbook, local know-ledge. This has already been commented upon extensively in the sections on framing in Chapter VI. To explore the connections that may be made, some of the true-or-false statements with which children were presented required them to make connections between everyday/local knowledge and textbook knowledge. Also, in the course of casual conversations, both within and outside the school, whenever there was an opportunity, they were asked questions or queries that required connecting the two arenas of knowledge. It seems that, with very few exceptions, children did not correlate school and out-of-school knowledge. Local/everyday experience was separated from textbook knowledge. The two seemed to function as *separate contexts for thinking.* Reasoning that required moving from one context to the other evoked four types of responses:

Surprise and disbelief: The first type of response was surprise and disbelief that there can be a connection between the two areas. This was usually accompanied with a suggestion that the question being asked was not valid. The Class V students had all read and revised a lesson about the Thar desert in their geography session. I asked them to evaluate the statement: 'The desert is west of Kasimpur'.

EPISODE 9.12 (CLASS V)
Surinder: May be, don't know.
How will you find out?
We will go and see and find out.
It isn't in the book?
No. There is nothing about Kasimpur in the book. How did Kasimpur come into the question?

Surinder was very surprised that Kasimpur was being mentioned in connection with what was otherwise clearly school knowledge. Outside school, too, children made little connection between what they had learnt in school and what surrounded them. Their activities in the course of everyday life did not itself require any such connections to be made. Even when provoked mildly, they showed little interest in doing so, as is illustrated in Episode 9.13. In a recent science class, Joni and Surinder had been studying about storage roots.

EPISODE 9.13 (IN BHARDWAJ'S GARDEN)
Surinder, Joni and Rajkumar were all pulling out canna plants in Bhardwaj's back garden. They had come here after school for tuition. I asked about the fat canna root:
What are these fat things?
(All three shrugged): Who knows... may be a root... who knows. *They did not show any interest.*

Reasoning with local knowledge: The second type of response involved reasoning about known local processes with local knowledge, disallowing any epistemic function, much less an epistemic primacy to school knowledge about the same phenomenon. Generally, they did not seem to have placed Kasimpur in the context of what they had learnt about 'the country'. They disregarded textbook vocabulary[4] in preference to everyday vocabulary while talking about local things. They also used the local understanding of classification and causality. This meant that any contradiction between everyday and school knowledge was ignored.

The facts in textbooks about seeds and germination differed from the local knowledge and beliefs about plants and their growth. I asked the children to say if the following statement was true of false: 'A wheat seed has plumule' (*gehun mein bhroon hota hai*). The response was '*Beej* (seed) is what is sown. We eat *gehun*. It isn't a seed' (Parvinder, Class V). The childern's response was based on the local way of referring to parts of a plant. They classified what is sown as '*beej*' (seed) and what is eaten as '*anaj*' (food grain). By this classification, '*gehun*' (wheat), as it is harvested and eaten, is an '*anaj*'. This classification ran contrary to the classification that formed the basis of the science lesson on parts of a plant.

Children had also learnt in their books that (all) plants grew from seeds. Yet the children who took me through their fields did not believe that weeds grew from seeds: 'They grow on their own from the soil' (Yashpal, Class V). A possible explanation for this is that only seeds of crops were actually seen and sown. And the sowing of crop seeds is an activity which is also an important event, talked about and carefully planned for in the farming calendar.

Kasimpur village does not seem to have entered into the children's considerations of Indian geography and climatology. According to the social studies textbook, India has three seasons. Children of both Class IV and V had learnt this. Yet, when asked to say whether the statement 'There are three seasons in Kasimpur' was true or false, they declared it was wrong: 'No! We have four: summer, winter, rainy and spring' (Satish and Jogi, Class IV); 'Wrong! Winter, summer, leaf-fall (*pat-jhad*), spring' (Pavan, Class V).

EPISODE 9.14 (CLASS IV)
Ashish: Yes. (*He named them.*)
Sulaiman: But in Kasimpur there are more. Winter, summer, rainy and *pat-jhad* (leaf-fall).

While the names of India's seasons given in the textbook were the 'scientific' ones—summer, winter and monsoon—the names the children used to refer to Kasimpur's seasons were the local ones: 'hot', 'cold', 'rainy', 'leaf-fall' and 'spring' (*garmi, sardi, barsaat, pat-jhad, basant*). Even when it was pointed out that they have learnt that in India there are three seasons, they simply shrugged. When I pointed this out to Sulaiman in Episode 9.14, he did not see any contradiction, saying: 'Some villages don't have *pat-jhad*. For them it is three.'

In Episode 9.15, Vikas reasoned that Kasimpur's seasons would be the same as those in the whole of India. Even in the face of his objection, the others insisted on providing the local understanding of seasons as the right answer for Kasimpur.

EPISODE 9.15 (CLASS V)
Vikas: It is the same as the whole of India.
Devendar: In fall (*pat-jhad*), when leaves fall, it is because of the wind.
Ashok: It is wrong. Winter, summer, rainy and leaf-fall.
Vikas: In our book there is nothing like leaf-fall.
Ashok: It is now spring season (*basant ritu*).

Ashok, blithely deaf to Vikas' objection, proceeded to add yet another season from the local calendar, which was not a part of the textbook.[5]

We notice that children had not placed Kasimpur in relation to the rest of the country. This was also true of physical location. All children had learnt about the physical features of the country. Two of the statements I gave them involved reasoning about the physical location of Kasimpur village with respect to the rest of the country:

1. 'Kasimpur is situated in the great northern plains.'
2. 'If we start walking in the western direction, we will reach the Thar desert.'

Apart from two important exceptions which will be taken up later, children showed that they were completely unused to reasoning of this kind, and were confused by it. When they tried reasoning, as in the previous cases, they began with local knowledge and experience and tried to draw out the necessary connection with the general from it. In the following two instances, the children tried to figure out the answer using their knowledge of local directions. Although they did arrive at an answer, this was not based on the class inclusion type of reasoning that the question required. The local directions could not help them locate Kasimpur in relation to the country—at best to locate it in relation to Delhi: 'North, South, East, West...Delhi is in the East, we are in the West...wrong' (Satish and Jogi, Class IV). Pointing out North, South, East, West, Pavan declared: 'Wrong!' (Class V).

EPISODE 9.16 (CLASS IV)
Naresh: No. *(He prompted Bhim):* Now you can tell.
Bhim: No.
How do you know?
Naresh: There is no plain here. There are houses.
Bhim: It is in UP.
Are there no houses in UP?
Naresh to Bhim (emphatically): Now you answer.
Bhim shrugged and did not add anything more.

In this episode, Naresh also failed to locate Kasimpur in India. Based on the description 'great northern plain', he concluded the statement is false as Kasimpur is built up and there is no '*vishal maidan*', meaning large ground in colloquial Hindi.

EPISODE 9.17 (CLASS V)
If we start walking in the western direction, we will reach the Thar desert.
All of them looked blank. Then slowly Ashok said: That is the land of sand (*baloo mitti ka pradesh*).
Vikas: Maharashtra is in the middle. *Continued after a pause:* ...Kasimpur is in Delhi. Delhi is North and large.
Ashok: I don't agree.

As in the earlier question, here, too, children tried to work out the answer starting from an analysis of the local and working outward. Except for Vikas, they were not treating it as a case of syllogistic reasoning based on general statements they had learnt about India, and their knowledge that Kasimpur is a part of India.

Pragmatic considerations and praxis: The statement on the Thar desert brought out another aspect of reasoning about local matters, involving the village and the self. The thinking was dominated and shaped by pragmatic considerations related to acting on the basis of the knowledge, rather than being restricted to a static syllogistic reasoning and simple evaluation of truth.

EPISODE 9.18 (CLASS IV)
Bhim: The desert is in the west of India. We will reach, but it will take five or six days.
Naresh: We have to think. It says... (*He read the sentence again to himself.*)
Bhim: But we will have to take food.
Naresh: Leave the matter of food. Will we reach from *inge* (this side)? (*He pointed in the western direction.*)
How will you find out?
Naresh: We will read in a book.
Bhim: It is written that desert is in the west.
Naresh: It is *printed* in the book... It is in India's west and Delhi is in India, so we will reach.
How did you tell?
Naresh: By reading.
By reading?
Naresh: No, by thinking.

EPISODE 9.19 (CLASS IV)
Sulaiman: This can be. My village is in the west and it is in the desert. But it will take a long time... One or one-and-a-half months. By bus it takes 24 hours.
How can we be sure?
By reading in books.

EPISODE 9.20 (CLASS IV)
Jogi: If we go on a camel, we will reach a serpent and we will have to escape.
Satish: Where did the serpent come from?
Jogi: The desert has serpents.

In the first episode, Bhim was concerned about taking enough food along. In the second, Sulaiman assessed the time it would take to get there. Jogi was thinking about making the journey on camel and the danger of serpents.

Classical syllogistic reasoning: In two of the episodes just reported, Naresh and, to some extent, Sulaiman, showed that they were connecting the two domains of knowledge. But as can be seen from Episodes 9.17, 9.21 and 9.22, only Vikas and Dinesh were at ease with syllogistic reasoning.

EPISODE 9.21 (CLASS V)
Vikas: It is true.
How do you know?
Rajasthan is in the west.
Devendar and Ashok just shrugged.

EPISODE 9.22 (CLASS IV)
Dinesh: True.
How do you know?
Dinesh: Rajasthan is in that direction, and we will reach, and we also have the knowledge of the directions. We understand.
Kasimpur is situated in the great northern plains.
Dinesh: Yes.
Deepak: It's from Punjab to UP.
Dinesh: It's from *samajik*, it is in the map. Haryana also comes in. And Delhi is also coloured.

Especially in reasoning about the great northern plains, Dinesh used clear syllogistic reasoning involving two steps in moving from the general to the particular: all x is y; a is a member of x, so a is y. Such instances of connecting the two areas of knowledge were very rare.

*

Perceptual Positions

Luria (1976) and later Cole and Scribner (1974, 1981), studying cultural variation in the nature of reasoning, found that in oral or pre-literate societies, reasoning was dominated by the local context and by practical considerations. In contrast, those who had been to school used abstract forms of reasoning. Luria gave problems based on syllogistic reasoning to peasants in a Central Asian part of the erstwhile USSR. Some of the problems were based on their local experience. For example: 'Cotton grows where it is hot and humid. In the village it is hot and humid. Does cotton grow there or not?' The non-schooled peasants had no trouble with the first type of problem. They would draw the correct conclusions. But when asked how, they would support their answer on the basis of their experience saying: 'That's the way it is; I know myself.'

Another problem which Luria gave required them to reason about a situation which was not in their experience: 'In the north, where there is snow all year, the bears are white. Town X is in the north. Are the bears white in that town or not?' In response to this problem a typical response would be: 'How should I know what colour the bear was? It was your friend that saw him, ask your friend.' In contrast, those peasants who had some schooling were able to accept the problem on its own terms and draw the logical conclusion. Cole and Scribner felt that the reason for this is not that those peasants who have gone to school have learnt to think in new ways. Rather, they felt that because of school they become more familiar with such syllogistic contexts and settings of discourse.

Textbooks produced at the national level in India are written for children in a wide spectrum of locations. There is an implicit assumption that the content is general and can be 'applied' to local situations. The reasoning of children in the Kasimpur school raises the question, why do these children, who are going to school, reason dominantly in context-bound ways where practical experience and considerations are important? A Piagetian explanation would be that they are still too young for this late-concrete, early-formal operational capability. Another explanation comes by extending Cole and Scribner's framework. This suggests that, on account of the separation of school and non-school knowledge as contexts of thinking, in non-school areas 'traditional', pre-literate forms of reasoning persist. This is not to suggest that pre-literate thinking does not permit syllogistic reasoning, but that such thinking is not in isolation of, but related to, action.

It seems that where school knowledge is concerned, children have a propositional attitude *de dicto*, i.e., as general beliefs which belong to a logical, propositional space, rather than the attitude *de re*, i.e., as specific beliefs of things, on the basis of which we can act.[6] Lewis (1979) points out that book learning can provide us with knowledge on which we act on the world, provided we have something more; we need to be in a position to self-ascribe the property of being in a 'certain perceptual situation'. We can think of the school knowledge as constituting a 'possible world' through its statements and propositions, i.e., a logical, propositional space. What one requires, in addition, to be able to act upon this knowledge, is to know which possible world this is. Locating oneself in relation to this world would make it possible for the statements to be evaluated for truth and to become cognitively significant, providing a basis for action. Lewis argues that this property of self-ascription may be called belief or knowledge *de re*. School knowledge in a strongly framed curriculum is *de dicto*, constructed within the logical space of the school and therefore not in itself carrying the property of self-ascription.

The strong framing furthermore implies that none of the epistemic practices encourage children to locate their own perceptual situation vis-à-vis school knowledge. The truth (or falseness) of school knowledge seems to be within a logical space (of the school world) rather than have any relevance to ordinary space outside the school. So, for instance, they could believe that plants grow from seeds within the school, and yet believe that the weeds they find in their fields do not grow from seeds. The failure at class inclusion in syllogistic reasoning involves relating a general belief from the school world to a particular belief in the ordinary world. A more harsh interpretation is that for the children school knowledge was not propositional at all, although it may have been uttered in the propositional form. Sometimes, the truth or falsity of textbook statements seemed to have no relevance to many of the children who seemed unconcerned even about the linguistic meaning of the sentences they remembered.

The concern for acting in and negotiating the real world seemed to dominate the everyday context, while school knowledge seemed to be only a passive object to be 'put into the brain' by memorisation, perhaps also irrelevant to the real world. In the case of the Kasimpur school, there is much in the school knowledge that can be related to experience outside. Yet the practice of framing does not encourage children to locate themselves vis-à-vis school knowledge. The two arenas of knowledge remain dichotomised, not only experientially but also cognitively.

The concept of knowledge belongs to the real world of belief and action. Schools must create an ethos where this interrelationship is realised. Dewey promoted the project method as a way to integrate the arenas of school and reality (outside the school). He believed that the context of an ongoing enquiry would situate the child epistemically in the course of knowledge construction and provide a perceptual situation, (Dewey 1985b). We may disagree with Dewey and agree with Durkheim that '(Teaching) is not a preparation for action; it is essentially bringing about comprehension, and as far as it is possible, explanation... The teacher (*maitre*) does not address himself directly to the will, but to understanding' (Durkheim 1979: 129–30). But even so, the understanding that we prize most, in which every bit of new knowledge and information is received into a richly woven fabric of interconnections, would have the potential to influence action, whether immediately or in the future. For this, the school must encourage the qualities of openness of mind and concern for meaning and truth.

Notes

1. See Ramadas, J. et al. (1996) for a comprehensive discussion of the role of experiments in school science teaching. The findings of their study of the understanding of primary school students in tribal and urban schools confirms the patterns noted in Kasimpur.
2. My scientist friend Amitabha Mukherjee points out that many working scientists also believe this; the philosophical position is called 'realism'.
3. Science Related Values is a box item printed in the beginning of the primary school EVS textbooks of the NCERT (NCERT 1998a):

Science-Related Values

Be inquisitive about things and events around you.

Have the courage to question beliefs and practices.

Ask 'what', 'how' and 'why' and find your answers by critically observing, experimenting, consulting, discussing and reasoning.

Record honestly your observations and experimental results in your laboratory or outside it.

Repeat experiments carefully and systematically if required, but do not manipulate your results under any circumstance.

Be guided by facts, reasons and logic. Do not be biased in one way or the other.

Aspire to make new discoveries and inventions by sustained and dedicated work.

4. Even in textbook knowledge itself, the focus was so completely on the questions and their answers, that students did not concern themselves with 'minor' matters of not comprehending words or questions or the obviously apparent contradictions in them.

> (In Class IV)
> Naresh read: ' "*Vashpan*" happens all the time...' True!
> **What is vashpan?**
> He shrugged.
>
> (At Geeta and Pavan's home in the village).
> Geeta pulled out her social studies book and came near me. Pavan and she told me: The Earth is round, like a globe. She showed me her book. On one page was a picture of the globe. The opposite page had the Mercator flat projection.
> **How come here it is flat?**
> She shrugged.
> The map of India was coloured. I pointed to it and asked: **Why is this portion coloured and everything else white?**
> Geeta: I don't know, but read here (pointing to the text nearby). It must be given here.

5. It is also interesting that the EVS book for Class IV presents a different number of seasons in two different lessons. In the lesson on why seasons change, which explains the changing seasons on the basis of earth's rotation around the sun, it is stated that there are four seasons. But the chapter on climate in India states that India has three seasons. Just as the children did not locate Kasimpur in relation to India, in this case also, there seemed to be a failure of class inclusion and India was not located in relation to the earth.

6. *De dicto* means of, or concerning, a dictum. *De re* means of, or concerning, a thing. A *de dicto* belief is a belief that a bearer of representative content is true. A *de re* belief is a belief concerning something that has a particular characteristic (CREP 2000).

10
Conclusion

The study of the Kasimpur Boy's Model School represents a first step towards understanding the relationship between the child as knower and 'knowledge'—in society, in the school curriculum and in everyday life. We gazed, with the anthropologist's eye, at the various levels at which the reality of the school is constituted. In the absence of any related previous work that could be built on, the enquiry had to begin with characterising the nature of school experience. The task was difficult because, rather than the esoteric, it involved the mundane, everyday reality of the common Indian school. The scenario was so familiar that in order to observe it, one had to deliberately suspend the tendency to see it through frames of previous knowledge and experience and instead adopt the stranger's frame of reference. The apparently static, oppressive everyday reality of the ordinary government school appears on closer inspection to be akin to a standing (stationary) wave, produced dynamically through the interaction of several waves; a process of constant creation, negotiation and interpretation by teachers and children.

The first part of this concluding chapter draws upon the findings of the study to build a discussion of the schoolchild as a knower and learner; it includes a summary of the findings. The second and final part is based on some of the insights gained in this study, and essays to conceptualise and address issues relating to school reform and the study of education/ schooling.

I
The Schoolchild as Epistemic Subject

What is the nature of the child's construction of school knowledge? In this study the question was answered using the tools of an anthropologist rather than a psychologist. It included a study of the activities and discourse in the community, in the school and in the classroom, which formed the context and mediated the meaning of schooling, education and learning. Clearly, the 'social' cannot be regarded as an 'influence'—as something external to and acting on the process of 'natural' development.

The social character of being

The social nature of the human condition is more profound, and is located in the activity and discursive practices in which humans engage. The reality we construct is a shared one, not only because we live in a community with other humans who also experience the same reality, but also because the process of construction is socially mediated. Dewey recognised that the environment is not a neutral context. He referred to it as 'ethos'. Especially in the education of children, Dewey believed that the teacher must shape the classroom ethos, so that it reflects the community's concerns and engenders enquiry and reflection in certain directions and not in others. However, Dewey visualised the ethos as essentially benign. He regarded the community as a small, spatial unit and all communication in it to be free and face-to-face.

The understanding that emerges from this study is that the individual subject herself may be conceived of as a social product, acquiring an identity and existing as a manifestation of social arrangements. Opportunities for enhancing social status, the experience of power and opportunities to exercise it are important in the construction of self-identity, and in the self-awareness evident in the articulation of 'who we are'. The child learns to be a 'child', and even to be 'a' child, in the context of the social reality he or she shares with care-givers, older and younger siblings and other children. Social processes support and direct decentring from initial infant egocentrism, where the individual–social dichotomy is meaningless. Social and cultural practices, both within the family and in the community, influence the degree to which this dichotomy is actually realised and instituted. What it is to be an individual being, and what an individual can be, are both socially constituted and maintained by the symbols and discursive practices of the community.

Human life is inexorably bound in social practices, symbols, rituals and discourse, so that it is not meaningful to talk about the constitution and realisation of human life outside social complexes. The separation of the natural from the artificial, of where biological and 'natural' processes stop and society 'takes over', is a matter of conjecture. Definitions and boundaries are pushed this way or that, depending on socio-political concerns. It is not easy to claim a privileged status on ontological grounds for either the Rousseauesque modern, romantic positions that plead for allowing children to grow and realise their innate goodness, free of the evil influence of society, or the claim that children are mischievous and must be disciplined and taught things that adults believe are valuable.

Being a 'child' is to play an important role within the institutions of family and school, and also in the larger community. Several times in the previous chapters, we saw how this role provides an orienting framework that informs interpersonal interactions within the family, between teachers and students and in the peer group. The role of child also provides an orienting framework that informs epistemological concerns related to the construction of reality and the relationship with reality constructs already existing in society. For example, *asking* is how children find out and verify truths. But this does not imply that the child is a passive product or object of social processes. On the contrary, children are actively engaged in being and becoming children. They are aware of themselves as 'humans-who-are-not-yet-but-learning-to-be-adults'. The presence of more knowledgeable others in their lives—older children and, especially, adults—is important. Socialisation and enculturation, rather than being tacit processes that do not rise to consciousness, often become intentional activities.

As social constructs, 'child' and 'childhood', and equally, 'adult' and 'adulthood', are categories with socio-historical particularity as regards their domains of reference and their meaning. They are responsive to social change, evolving new orientations and simultaneously providing the channel through which older orientations and purposes continue to act. We see that the basic dichotomy of parent–offspring found in the primary institution of family, along with other traditional and folkloric dichotomies such as guru–*sishya* are extended into the school to constitute the new dichotomy of teacher–taught.

The child as knower

Several times we encountered the idea that in the community of the village and the school, the category 'child' is important as an epistemic entity and an epistemic orientation. As an entity, the 'child' is a human who has not yet achieved adulthood, being recognised as physically, mentally and chronologically separated from the entity called 'adult'. As an orientation, it connotes an incompleteness or variance with knowledge that functional adults of society might have, whether as a student, a devotee, a *sishya*, a seeker or researcher. The usage of the term 'child' is informed by both reference and sense.

As knowers, children are accorded a special place in society. They enjoy mediated knowledge of, and action on, reality, with mediators typically being older children and adults. The role of the child involves entering into mediating relationships, where the construction of reality is a primary concern. The orienting frameworks are not simply 'taken on', but negotiated and co-constructed through interactions with adults and peers. It is in this inheritance, of not only linguistic categories but also of a socially constituted identity and praxis, that human existence is social, and human knowledge, of self and the world, is a social construction. The child is an epistemic subject in this relational sense.

Children and adults: Means and ends

Chapters III and IV explored the meaning of schooling that manifests in children's understanding and which informs their construction of school experiences. The community integrates the institution of school into the logic and structure of its changing economy and employment opportunities. It is from this logic that the community derives the role that the school performs. Children understand the purpose of schooling as one of opening up employment opportunities by providing the means for social mobility. They begin to believe that by becoming literate, learning English and acquiring general knowledge, they will become socially adept and access the world of the 'educated man'—the *bada admi*. This world includes a desk job, steady income and self-respect. In contrast, the world of the illiterate—the *anpadh*—means hard manual work, low pay, insecurity and low status. Within the school, this dichotomy is presented not simply as possible scenarios of future adult life, but as an ongoing commentary on the child's present. The cumulative activity of an individual *all through* the period of growing up leads to the one or the other scenario. Thus, success in adult life acquires a regulating function in all the activities children engage in. Simultaneously, it creates in them an awareness of the self as a human-who-must-grow-up.

Given the special function that school is expected to perform vis-à-vis 'growing up', it seems necessary to recognise two epistemic stances of children. One is with reference to knowledge acquired directly from experience—implicitly or tacitly. The other relates to knowledge acquired through propositions and articulated—involving the metacognitive awareness of knowing that we know. Both kinds of knowledge are constructed. In the first case, children are engaged in constructing knowledge of reality without the explicit awareness of being thus engaged; a situation where they are neither aware of themselves as knowers, nor of the object of knowing, nor the process. For example, in Chapters VIII and IX, we saw that children find it virtually impossible to conceptualise their everyday activities—such as of learning how to cook or to farm—as 'processes of learning'. Certainly, in the process itself, there was no self-aware subject separated from the object to be known; only an ongoing activity, a process, in which the subject, and not necessarily a self-aware one, participated.

On the other hand, the knowledge that the schoolchild as subject (knower) engages with constructing (learning) seems to be, importantly, knowledge *de dicto* (see Chapter IX). 'Learner', 'learning' and 'Learning' (*n*)—i.e., the subject, the process and the object—are all identifiable and separable, recognised and experienced as such by the child himself. As was brought out in Chapter VI on knowledge regulation, all three involve social definition, constitution and sanction. The aims of this learning that were mentioned earlier are important in understanding why it is so. The one that is primary to children (and perhaps also their parents) is gaining entry into, and functioning in, the world of work. The other aim that is important for children, but is not always separable from the first, is acceptability in the adult social world. The last aim, which takes precedence mostly for teachers (and probably also the state) is to become 'good citizens'. All these aims belong to a future, 'adult world', outside the school and the child's present life.

For the entire community, including children and the school, this 'adult world' seems to be more 'real' or significant than the present. This seems to be the primary reason why knowledge and knowledge construction are experienced as *de dicto* and not *de re*. Activities in childhood are believed to ultimately shape destinies in adulthood—but it is the latter, not the former, that seems to be of 'real' consequence. Childhood provides the 'means' towards 'ends' in adulthood; and while means are regarded as connected intimately to the ends, there is still a separation of the two. It is possible to effect this separation because society provides a special institution for it, namely, the school. Schooling marks childhood as a period of preparation, and the completion of school marks readiness to enter the world of work.

In Chapters III and IV we saw that both children and adults seemed to be aware of 'other' realities—such as those of previous times, when one did not need to go to school to learn, or the one in which the illiterate lives. But these realities seemed to be either unworthy or less worthy of realising in the present-day context. As realities, they seem to exist *along* with the one reality which is worth living in. When discussing the perception of the *anpadh* and the 'failures', we saw that children seem to see a certain parallel with their existence as children and these other realities. Those who fail to graduate to the 'adult world' are condemned to be transferred into these other worlds.

'Childhood' in Kasimpur seems to have evolved as a response to the postponement of entry into the world of work. And the epistemic orientation of 'child' also seems to derive from the hiatus that the postponement institutes. The awareness of 'incompleteness' of the child and the need to 'grow up' by acquiring knowledge that is valued in the adult world is one aspect of the orientation. In addition, the logic of selection and distribution of opportunity being defined on the basis of 'individual achievement' rather than 'birth' seems to add a heightened awareness of the 'potentiality' of the child. By being a 'student' in school, the 'child' can acquire the means to become the 'successful adult'.

The child-knower in school

The place of school in the lives of children seems to create in them the awareness of what they consider as a new identity—that of the 'knower'. This is not an identity inculcated in them *after* they enter school; it seems to be an identity they anticipate even as they are growing up, before they have reached school-going age. Also, children are not passive objects of socialisation, but are equally engaged in constructing and realising this identity. They may even actively constitute their passive stance vis-à-vis the adult world, as suggested by their requests to their teacher: 'Guru*ji*, *yaad karvaiye* (make us memorise)'. This is not a general orientation towards all of reality, but specifically towards the symbolic capital that the school seems to be instituted to transmit, or at least make available to all those who are worthy of gaining it.

In Chapter IV we saw that the idea of school in Kasimpur was based on a discontinuity from the everyday reality of the community, and in Chapter V we saw that the members also marked the school as a space distinct from the village. Within this space, adults and children relate with each other and with reality and reality constructs in a way different from outside the school—through the roles of 'teacher' and 'student' and a symbolic universe. The space has an abstract, implicative relationship, not with immediate reality, but the future. The only 'work' that children are really expected to engage in is work that will prepare them for the adult world of work. The school prepares children for this world without their ever having to step into it or deal with it. Experts called teachers 'teach' them abstract skills that are believed to be useful later in the adult world. Schooling is the period when they learn skills and knowledge that they will later apply in the 'real world'.

The fact of the adult–child discontinuity itself is not peculiar to schools like Kasimpur that seem to be geared to the future world of employment. The idea of school, any school, assumes this, and such a discontinuity would be found even when the curriculum is 'child-centred', involving learning about reality and work in more direct ways. The institution of school not only concretises the adult–child discontinuity, but also introduces into the life of the child a ritual marking of 'growing up' and getting closer to the final adult state by moving through a hierarchy of grades or levels over the years. Passage through these grades marks increasing capability to function in adult life, including the world of work. In the case of Kasimpur, the knowledge to be acquired includes social politesse, English and general knowledge, in addition to literacy and numeracy (see Chapter III). The children who are given manual work to do in the school are those who seem to be already showing signs that they will not be able to succeed.

While the adult–child discontinuity seems to be inherent in the idea of school, the pedagogy of the Kasimpur school reflects a specific understanding of the process of schooling. Unlike everyday interactions, where adults are found to play a mediating function in the child's reality construction, the teacher–adult does not play a mediating role between the child (learner) and reality of the workplace or in dealing with the world. If she does mediate at all, it is between the child and an artificially constructed 'learning task', with no direct consequence on any reality apart from the child's cognition. The reality of the school—success in examinations, etc.—is only a symbolic universe that is supposed to be preparation for the 'real world'. But while the world of the school is not the 'real world', it is not 'unreal' like the worlds constructed during play. While actors in the play world know that their actions do not have any impact on reality, the nature of action in school is at least believed to be related to reality in a more complex way. The school is a symbolic mapping of the 'real world'.

Ways of acting in it and success and failure in it (especially as measured by examinations and assessed by teachers) are believed to determine and to be able to predict success and failure in later life in the real world.

The adult, in this case the teacher, and the child, the learner, also now relate to each other differently in the course of handling a task. The focus shifts from succeeding in the task at hand, which often characterises situations in which adults and children work together outside the school. Within the school, the attention is on the extent to which the learner is able to function 'independently'. As we saw in Chapter VI on knowledge regulation, techniques such as the teachering device and interrogation are aimed at turning children into individual subjects, with no access to the scaffolding cognitive assistance that the teacher–adult could provide. An opacity is introduced into the relationship and the two can no longer function together as co-workers. Responsibility for consequences of action, even in symbolic learning situations, now rests solely with the individual learner and is no longer the shared responsibility of consequences of mediated action. In this situation, the learner experiences individuation rather than autonomy.

Pedagogic activity and school knowledge

The whole picture of the epistemic orientation of the 'child' and, by extension, of the 'student' emerges from the pedagogic and discursive practices of the Kasimpur school epistemic community. The identity of the child is structured essentially as an interpersonal condition, primarily realised in the teacher–taught duality, explored in Chapter V. It carries not only epistemological stances relative to these roles, but also the ways of meshing these roles together in the classroom and school community. The authority structure of this essentially epistemic relationship is elaborated and deepened beyond the immediate context of school knowledge to the tacit, taken-for-granted, level. This is done by representing the teacher–taught as parent–child, and other folkloric and traditional relations like patron–protégé and guru–*sishya*. The form and depth of the authority of the teacher over the taught, as revealed in its multidimensionality, is essential to understand how teachers constitute and exercise epistemic authority in matters of school knowledge. 'Knowledge' itself is not an independent variable of pedagogic settings. It is either simply an attribute of the teacher, or a consequence or by-product of relating to the teacher. The most important values in this relationship are discipline and obedience. The most valued way of learning is memorisation–understanding, and even doing experiments, are relegated to a low status, as methods used by those who cannot directly memorise.

These practices suggest that in the school there are normative, structural hierarchies and value congruences, not all of which can be derived from the framework provided by the school as a 'modern' institution. The primary school in most Indian villages is an institution established by the state following its agenda of development through 'modernisation'—a paradigm which recognises education as the most important vehicle through which people may acquire 'modern' rationality. However, once created, this space resonates with voices, images, rituals and practices which bear little or no relation to the modernists' agenda, and in parts even contradict that rationality.

Listening, observing and understanding these voices and practices in Indian village classrooms provides a crucial insight into the universe of meanings that make up school experience. Education researchers and planners, both of curriculum and of examination boards, have accorded to textbooks, the contents of school knowledge it prescribes and the examination system, an external, fact-like status. Kumar (1988) has traced the microprocesses of the present Indian classroom, particularly coercive practices, back to two major coercive instrumentalities of the colonial state—the textbook and the examination. There has been a tendency in Indian educationists to trace the locus of coercive pedagogic practices to prescribed textbooks, the prescribed curriculum and examinations. The extension of this logic seems to suggest that a transfer of control of these to the teacher will result in the realisation of an alternative (more progressive/liberal) pedagogical universe of experience for the child. This is evident in the recommendations of the Acharya Ramamurti Committee report (Government of India 1990) and the Yashpal Committee report (Government of India 1993), in their call for increased teacher involvement in textbook production and examinations.

The textbook and examination alone, however, cannot account for the complete agreement within the community—teachers *and students*—on the norms of good school and classroom practices or on the universe of meanings that inform their activities. The framing of boundaries and the sharing of control of epistemic activity in the classroom emerges from the authority exercised by the teacher over the taught, that extends from the epistemic into tacit, primeval levels. 'Parent–child', 'guru-*sishya*' (Vedic or Bhakti) or 'sir–student' (associated with colonial education) are invoked together to constitute a complex. It is from within this complex that the structural hierarchy and the basis for exercise of control in epistemic matters, which are visible in pedagogic activity, are realised. Pedagogic activity, which at once carries both regulatory and instructional functions, draws all members of the community into the network of power–knowledge relationships.

The knowledge community

The epistemic stances of the child-knower in the Kasimpur school are a reflection of the network of relationships. The relationship with other knowers is in terms of whether they know more or less (rather than peers, who are those who know 'as much'). The very nature of school knowledge, as it is realised in the course of pedagogic communication and activity, carries its regulatory function in it. Pedagogic discourse, especially the 'teachering device', is used to draw every child into a network of knowledge–power relations and to turn every child into both an object and a source of power as they internalise the teacher's eye and keep watch on themselves and each other. The context of learning is far from benign. Prescribed epistemic activities in the classroom, such as 'question–answer' sessions and 'showing that one knows', reveal that the interlocutors are responsive to hierarchical epistemic authority. Children exhibit great sensitivity to accommodating contradiction in order to avoid conflict with authority. Framing of knowledge is primarily teacher-controlled, but in classrooms where the teacher is also from the village, the control is constantly negotiated.

Children's spontaneous epistemic activity is determined, in form and course, by the nature of interpersonal relationships, taking different forms depending on whether it involves friends or enemies. In the everyday context, thinking and reasoning are found not to reflect any of the categories learnt in school and are shaped by local knowledge and pragmatic, praxis-related considerations.

In this complex, verbal testimony operates as the most important source of knowledge for the child. Knowing is activity directed at what is already known by an expert—either a teacher or someone older. The process is relational and realised through interpersonal activity.[1] Asking and telling constitute important activities of knowing and sharing knowledge. An important finding is that although verbal testimony is the most important way of knowing, children are familiar with other ways of finding out and verifying. They also discriminate while asking or being told by more schooled adults and teachers. Children also show a metacognitive awareness of themselves and others as sources of knowledge; they are adept at constituting propositional attitudes in their listeners and deciding whom to ask for what. But, in general, propositions are heard with an attitude of belief, unless there is reason to doubt the credibility of the speaker. There-fore, one rarely hears the articulation of warrants of assertion, unless the speaker is not regarded as trustworthy. In such situations, there is a confla-tion of epistemic and moral matters. Speaking to be heard implies speak-ing the truth, i.e., repeating what is already known to be knowledge.

It is only in the context of the community that knowers can experience the 'objective' and 'public' nature of knowledge. The implication of this membership is not only that members share a common body of know-ledge; it also implies a metacognitive and self-reflexive awareness of each other as knowers.[2] It is such a membership in a knowledge community that makes cooperative action possible. But the community in the Kasim-pur school is competitive rather than cooperative. There is little mutuality between the members. There is an institutionalisation of authoritarian-cum-deferential attitudes. Although children are familiar with more autonomous epistemic practices, they ensure that the prevailing hierarchy is not called into question. The idea of 'what is known' is not yet distinct from what this or that person may know. A denaturing of knowledge in the course of transmission is evident.

School knowledge and action

The child realises himself as a 'knower'—i.e., the metacognitive awareness of the self engaged in the process of knowing—in the specific context of school knowledge, and not as a general orientation to all reality constructs. The operative epistemology in this universe is essentially relational (see note 1). Only within the complex of highly structured relations, whether peer group or hierarchical, do opportunities for the articulation and meas-ures of the realisation of this knowledge arise. These are the only 'reality tests' against which school knowledge is measured. What the epistemic community accepts and makes function as 'true' or 'correct' is accorded the status of knowledge, without any reference to the world outside. These constructs do not form a part of an ongoing enquiry or activity; for ex-ample, children have learnt that one must not play on roads as it is dan-gerous ('Protection from hazards', Class V, EVS, NCERT 1988a), yet in the village they all play on the roads. They have all learnt that plants grow from seeds, yet they believe that weeds do not, etc. In contrast, the concept of knowledge in everyday life is almost overshadowed by pragmatic and praxis considerations.

The Deweyan characterisation of knowledge, which acknowledges the important function of social ratification, would be hard-pressed to accord to such knowledge constructed in the school the status of being 'warranted assertions'. Even the purported usefulness in adult life relates to *adapting* to social situations, rather than to *acting* on the world (physical or social) and undergoing consequences. They do not constitute beliefs on the basis of which one may act.

This discussion suggests the need for a reconsideration of how current education psychology presents the child as knower. What both teachers of young children and curriculum planners must recognise is the importance of the *ethos* of the child. This is an ethos constituted not only by the home and the community, but equally by the activities of teachers and the curriculum itself. The study also shows how these are nested and interconnected psycho-social spaces, including and influencing the ideas regarding the purpose of schooling, the nature of knowledge, knowledge acquisition, knowledge application and the identity of self as knower. The ethos influences, if not determines, the epistemic stances that the learner will adopt in the knowledge community and vis-à-vis school and everyday knowledge. Thereby, it also influences the epistemic practices necessary for constructing knowledge, even from verbal testimony. Constituting the appropriate ethos in the school and classroom is probably the most critical element of curriculum planning.

II
Whither Schooling?

These days it is fashionable to smile at the naïve optimism of the Victorians who believed in the inevitability of progress.... Yet, under the skin, most of us are still, like the Victorians, children of the Enlightenment. We still believe that learning, knowing, understanding, and thinking 'civilize'; that education—the cultivation of human minds and spirits—is the foundation of a good and economically productive society; and that the improvement of education is a means to a better society.

—Ronald Dore 1980: 69

Having had its fill from the water droplet, the cockroach on the kitchen counter resumes its journey. Alive, breathing, still a cockroach.

This study demonstrates that there is much that can be learnt from the school about schooling if we approach it with the eyes, ears and tools of the anthropologist. The small effort represented by this study to engage with this reality and interpret it meaningfully suggests the potential and the scope of the issues and possible responses. What seems routine, mindless, ritual practice reveals itself to be more complexly interconnected and related to the local ethos and socio-cultural situation of the participants— the teachers, the children and the community. It is this fact of the school— that it is 'living' and 'lived in'—that constitutes a challenge to education theory, practice and reform-oriented policy.

The effort in this final section is more difficult than taking on the value-neutral stranger–anthropologist stance within the school—it involves re-entering the educationist's frame. Unlike anthropology, education is necessarily normative. But hopefully, the postponement of the normative frame has allowed us to appreciate better the phenomenon of the government school as an object of social engineering and reform in both its *totality* and *complexity*. Many of the preceding chapters which exposited and interpreted field data also included discussion, reformulation and elaboration of concepts and themes relevant to understanding schooling and learning in the Indian context. These included ethos, cultural capital, pedagogic authority and control, pedagogic device, framing in curriculum, memorisation as learning, links between school and everyday knowledge and verbal testimony as knowledge. Drawn from philosophy and sociology of education, psychology of learning and epistemology, these concepts and themes permit nuances in the analysis and commentary on schooling and the child's experience, which are of interest to an educationist. These nuances suggest features that we must take into cognisance when we plan intervention and change, allowing us to engage with the present reality in a meaningful manner rather than predicating our actions on discounting it or on its radical transformation.

There are several important issues that the study did not raise; for example, the influence of the social–hierarchical structure of the village— both caste and gender—in the school, dropouts and questions related to whose knowledge the curriculum represents. But hopefully it has demonstrated the rich potential of the framework and methodology to investigate such questions. Based on the understanding gained in this study I propose to formulate and discuss some issues which relate to the problem of reform in government schools.

The need for ideas and ideals in education

Ronald Dore describes schooling which is ridden with the 'diploma disease' as '... ritualistic, tedious, suffused with anxiety and boredom, destructive of imagination; in short anti-educational' (Dore 1980: 69). With some exaggeration we could say that this describes schooling in Kasimpur, not as perceived by the participants themselves, but by educationists with university-based, progressive/liberal/modern leanings. The negative connotation of this description may not be shared by local educationists at Kasimpur, although they would agree that the schooling experience is dominated by the overarching concern to pass examinations and interviews, find suitable jobs and exit the rural, traditional set-up.

The orientation towards gaining diplomas and employment is a feature of schooling shared by almost all developing (ex-colony) countries *and* increasingly it also characterises schooling in the developed countries (Dore 1997).[3] In the developed world, the institution of schooling spread and education became universal through a long history of social, economic and political changes, which included changes in childhood socialisation. However, in the developing countries, schools are recent institutions which have come into being and spread with the paradigm of education for employment as the dominant, if not only, basis of their raison d'être. The anti-educational consequences are devastating. Not only do many children experience 'failure' of various forms in school, but even those who succeed are often not capable of using the tools they are supposed to have acquired, such as language expression or reasoning skills, to their advantage, leave alone for creative purposes. There are no myths or ideals (such as the Victorian faith in the liberating role of education) which had supported the historical development of the institution of school in the developed countries, and which continue to give their teachers some vitality.

The perception that education is linked to employment and social mobility, even if undesirable, cannot be wished away. Reforming the school curriculum cannot be made conditional on negating it. The danger is not in accepting the validity of 'schooling is to enable securing jobs' as an aim of education.[4] There is probably more danger in not doing so. The failure to recognise local perceptions of the purpose of schooling would render one's reform efforts irrelevant. The real question is whether we can prevent this from dominating all aspects of, and the entire period of, schooling. Can we engender a wider educational agenda for the common school, co-opting this as one of the aims? We may be cynical about the claims of education and welcome sociological enquiry which debunks concepts such as 'character', 'intelligence', 'cognitive development', 'merit', 'rationality' and 'equality'. Whether we call it 'ideological baggage' or 'philosophical moorings', only a view of education that is supported by a richly elaborated ideational framework which *includes* these concepts can mitigate the tyranny and anti-educational effects of qualification-earning. It can deepen the meaning of school experiences beyond success in examinations and prevent them from becoming ritualistic, tedious and anti-creative. Pending the transformation of society, better-trained teachers would be central to propagating and institutionalising these as 'higher order' aims for schooling, and orienting their own pedagogic practice towards them.

As a matter of fact, the Kasimpur school does already include some 'higher order' aims. When we look into details, the Kasimpur school cannot be taken as a simple, coercive, totalitarian institution that can be directly and easily recognised as harmful and evil. We also realise that the practices which seem ritualistic at first glance, because of their monotony and repetitiveness, are not so. The school and its activities have been integrated 'meaningfully' by teachers, children and the community. We see that, for most of the participants, the activities and practices they are engaged in are supported by 'theories' which they share, derived from a popular, folkloric, indigenous cultural inheritance. This is a framework that supports current pedagogic practices, which include features like deference to the teacher's authority, endorsing strict discipline in the school, memorisation as the way of learning and undermining the value of understanding. The fact that there is a framework is significant and worth comment. It is for this reason that the activities in the Kasimpur school cannot be described as merely ritual performance, oriented to gaining certificates. The teacher and pupil identities are not simply bureaucratic, but draw on older pedagogic traditions. Within the overall orientation to employment, there are also the dimensions of education for moral development and acquiring the marks of 'educated men'. As we recall these aspects of the experience of schooling in Kasimpur, we begin to feel that the spectre of the 'diploma disease' mentioned at the beginning of this section may not be a very appropriate characterisation of the Kasimpur school; although at first sight, it seems to share its features. It is not the result of a unidimensional, schooling-for-jobs theory, but of a multidimensional 'popular' or 'folk' theory, which also includes the idea of education-for-jobs. To the extent that schooling in Kasimpur is not ritual, mindless practice, reforming the school needs more acknowledgement of the framework.

Liberal vs Kasimpur frameworks

The educational potential of a curriculum cannot be realised simply by good strategies, pedagogy and management. It requires a framework that orients teachers and children and on which they can draw for meaning. But many reform efforts, beginning with Gandhi's attempt to tackle 'book-ish learning', do not offer much by way of 'theoretical inputs'. There is much emphasis on getting teachers to do activities and make materials themselves—'learning by doing works better than learning by hearing' is a popular belief. For many trainers, the dramatic surge of interest and enthusiasm among teachers (and children), after even a simple origami workshop and singing rhymes together, seems to be convincing proof that this is what is needed and that more of the same must be given. There is often an implicit disdain and contempt for theory and ideas and a prefer-ence for manual-type, module-based retraining of teachers with tokens such as 'play-way', 'child-centred' and 'joyful'. This substitutes for the liberal perspective. Presenting these as tools for universalising education ignores the complex social history of the universalisation of education in Western countries.

Teachers definitely need inputs regarding 'what' to do with children, but there is also need for inputs on 'why' to do these things and not other activities and learning tasks. 'Play-way' and 'joyful learning' packages, when presented as techniques without the framework they are supposed to be derived from, can also become ritual practice, oriented to gaining certification. When placed in a Kasimpur-like setting, and deriving mean-ing from ideas of childhood and the process of education available there, these could be understood by teachers as methods meant for underpri-vileged children, to be conducted for the first six months to get them used to school. Just as experiments in the science course, presented without any apparent epistemic function, were interpreted as entertainment, so also 'play-way' could be interpreted as having little to do with education itself. This scenario would be quite familiar to education reform activists within NGOs and the government. It is a common experience of inter-vening catalytic agents that the 'quality' of the intervention depends on their presence in the field. Efforts to introduce child-centred practices do not seem to take root easily. Teachers and supervisors for clusters of schools, who are supposed to provide academic support, often do not seem able to creatively interact and come up with new ideas autonomously. In the absence of supporting ideas and theory, child-centred concepts interpreted in the Kasimpur framework could also become superficial, ritualistic and even bizarre. For example, the use of rhymes and songs to make memorising facts easy, quizzes as the way to promote interaction and student involvement in learning, computers to provide students with immediate feedback, and programmed learning as a way to promote teacher and learner autonomy! Equally frustrating is the experience that what seems obviously good for the child's learning and development, such as play and de-emphasising memorisation, are viewed with suspicion by the community and are resisted by teachers.

What we call the 'child-centred' perspective is not just a group of techniques. The techniques are believed to reflect beliefs about the nature of children, the qualities of childhood, the process of learning and the purpose of education—most of which can be traced to a liberal ideology. As I argued in the earlier section of this chapter, these ideas about children, childhood and learning are not ontologically more valid than the beliefs in Kasimpur. The reasons for our espousing these ideals also cannot be on the ground that they are 'more true' to the nature of childhood or the purpose of education. And we have no reason to believe that their validity is transparent, or that we do not need to explain or justify our choices with more deliberate articulation, if not argument, on the significance of understanding childhood, education and growing up in these terms rather than in other terms.

The frameworks in question here—the Kasimpur one and the 'liberal' one—both reflect philosophical–political beliefs and choices. The term 'liberal' is associated more directly with the philosophical–political–economic movement originating in Western Enlightenment, which includes ideals such as freedom, democracy, equality, rationality, humanism, choice and the free market. Although presented as 'universals', these ideals are, in fact, personal, *political* choices and commitments. They can exert an influence, not only through dramatic events in abstract spaces such as 'society' and the 'market', but also in the more tangible social realm of interpersonal spaces in the community, the family and the classroom. The Kasimpur framework, with its emphasis on adaptation rather than transformation, is oriented to maintaining a status quo in social arrangements. The qualities that mark the educated person and the means by which we educate, reflected in the Kasimpur vs. the liberal framework, represent different groups of beliefs about human nature, human agency and human potential.

Questions relating to 'child-centring' or, more accurately, 'liberalising'[5], the Kasimpur framework are inevitable: can it be transformed? Must it be replaced? Are there conditions under which 'liberal' reforms can be grafted onto this framework? Before examining these issues we must first understand the bases on which the two frameworks can be compared. The points I am about to make, regarding comparing and contrasting these frameworks, follow recent writing in development studies and anthropology which questions the tendency to dichotomise the two paradigms:

the 'local'- 'folk'-'traditional'-'indigenous' on the one hand, and the 'scientific'-'Western'-'modern'-'rational'-'dominant'-'liberal' paradigm on the other (Dube 1988; Antweiler 1998; Agrawal 1995). I will use the terms indigenous, folk, traditional and local, mostly interchangeably, to refer to the Kasimpur framework. The terms represent an overlapping set of meanings, with slight variations in emphasis, e.g., 'folk' highlights the rural base and 'local' a limited, geographic area. Similarly, I will be using the terms modern, liberal and humanist interchangeably.[6] The first point to note is that terms like 'local' or 'indigenous' do not have exact references; this is especially clear when we try to apply the terms to a situation like India's which has innumerable cultures, sub-cultures and traditions. The second point to note is that traditions may not be monolithic but may be composed of several strands, even contradictory ones. As Dube noted, the 'traditional' may also share many features of the 'modern' (and vice versa) and may not be antithetical to it. And finally, as Antweiler reminds us, no tradition, not even an indigenous tradition, is static but is dynamic, responding to changes and evolving.

This understanding of the 'indigenous' is the beginning of what may be a more fruitful engagement with the question of 'liberalising' the Kasimpur framework. It requires establishing more continuity with the present reality, which I believe has not been fully acknowledged and to which theory, discourse and activity have been largely unresponsive. Its plurality must be recognised, certain values which are a part of this vast inheritance need to be reclaimed and reconfirmed, even as others are critiqued. There is need to speak a language which is mutually comprehensible, and also to forge links between both frameworks to develop a wider education theory.

Integrating with the present

Liberal ideas in themselves are not absent from indigenous traditions in India. Although the mainstream Hindu tradition, often referred to as the 'great tradition' by anthropologists, seems to be dominated by authoritarian–deferential attitudes in the adult–child relationship and belief in the ignorance of the child, this is not true of other cultural groups, e.g., tribal communities representing 'little traditions'. In my recent work among the Baiga tribe in Chhatisgarh, I noted that children are encouraged to be independent, to explore and to take initiative and responsibility. They are treated as valued members of the community and their creativity and potential are appreciated. Even the 'great tradition' which the teachers in the Kasimpur school seem to be drawing upon, is not a coherent, consistent body of knowledge. In the images, metaphors and stories, one finds a multiplicity of concepts and theories, drawn from both the classical and the folk traditions, coexisting and even contradicting each other, as the examples that follow show. The ones we find in the Kasimpur school are a selection from this corpus.

Alternative ways for adults and children to relate to each other and stories that assert the importance of independent thought and decision-making *in children* are available in folklore and classical literature. There are folk stories which emphasise the importance of autonomy and thinking for oneself, even for children. The Panchatantra stories, which revolve around rational problem solving and practical wisdom, have an explicit pedagogic intention. For example, the story in which a little animal, the rabbit, when faced with a problem in the form of a hungry lion, the king of the jungle, who wanted to eat him, saved his own life by a cunning trick. Stories of unconventional *sishyas* such as Nachiketa and Ashtavakra are also popular. In spite of experiencing the angry disapproval of the father–guru, these students pursued their enquiry defying conventional authority and eventually reaped rewards. The theme of the ideal child as a 'miniature adult', as exemplified by Rama's childhood, is popular. But more complex portrayals of the child's autonomy and wisdom can also be found. For example, the child-god Kartikeya's interactions with his father, Shiva.[7] The interpretation of Krishna's childhood, which was discussed earlier in Chapter IV, exemplifies the complexity and ambiguity inherent in presenting such divine and mythological children as potential role models.

There is also need to recognise values in indigenous traditions that are not usually part of modern, liberal education theory. The understanding of children as valuable and significant members of the adult community is one such value. But this feature, taken for granted in tribal communities, could be undermined.[8] If we uncritically accept the universal validity of liberal–humanist 'truths' on ideal childhood, we will be unable to appreciate the place of work, especially within the family, as an instrument of socialisation and acculturation, enabling children to take on responsibility as a natural part of growing up rather than as a burden in adulthood. So also the value of learning about work through working rather than turning childhood into a period of waiting and preparation. We must be critical of the tendency in the progressive movement to de-skill children and discount their abilities. There is already a danger that these values are being eroded by the idea of childhood without work as a universal ideal, promoted in the strident discourse of many child rights activists in their effort to protect children from exploitative labour. There is equally the danger to childhood independence and freedom on account of the disjuncture and even aggression by the 'great tradition' on the 'little tradition', as is already evident in many rural schools in tribal areas.

Another value is the understanding of a true guru. In traditional discourse, along with the characteristics of the pupil, there are also descriptions of good teachers. Kakar quotes Muktananda as saying:

> A true guru breaks your old habits of fault finding, of seeing sin, of hating yourself. He roots out the negative seeds that you have sown as well as your feelings of guilt. Instead, when you are in his company, you will experience your own divinity. You will never be found guilty in the guru's eye (Kakar 1991: 57).

The import of this attitude in the teacher can be appreciated even more in the context of common Indian government schools. Situated in social set-ups where caste and class divides induce early notions of inferiority, especially in children from dalit and tribal communities, this, 'ambiance of affective acceptance' (ibid.: 57) may be the most crucial aspect of the pedagogical relationship.[9] Even the more conventional stories of guru–sishya, if taken beyond the lesson of obedience to be learnt, suggest the teacher's assessment of and involvement with each individual pupil's abilities and needs. Ironically, modern educational psychology employs descriptions such as 'lack of self-esteem', 'lack of confidence' and 'shyness' as the major reasons for the poor educational achievement of Scheduled Caste and Scheduled Tribe children. Such terms suggest that the problem lies in the personal failure of the children themselves (or their primary socialising experience in the home) rather than in pedagogical failure.[10]

In the context of the teacher's pedagogic functions, one feature of many reform efforts must be commented upon. There is merit in removing the teacher from his authoritarian position in the classroom. But the absence of teacher authority would not be epistemologically valid. The school is an institution concerned with knowledge transmission, and an authority will accrue to the teacher by virtue of his or her knowing more. Roles such as 'friend' or 'facilitator', which are provided to teachers as alternatives to their traditional roles, cannot fulfil the scope of the pedagogic relationship; they can at best only add to the constitutive layers of their identity. The effort should be to ensure that the teachers' authority does not undermine the mutuality and dialogue which is possible within the classroom, rather than to undermine the teacher's authority *per se*.

If the exposition of 'liberal reform' is elaborated and its language is reworked to become more sensitive to these concerns, themes, metaphors and ideas, it may be possible to communicate with teachers and the community more effectively and with more conviction. Although the suggestion may seem facetious at first, stories, metaphors and analogies which have a resonance in the community may be more effective as vehicles for ideas, and more capable of conveying the interconnectedness and significance of child-centredness than only 'rational' discourse. If the teachers' ideational apparatus and repertoire were to be enriched with these other stories, images, symbols, myths and aphorisms, their professional identity could be more robust and their practice could be more autonomous. Engendering the growth of the liberal branches of existing cognitive–cultural frameworks may bear sweeter, more creative fruits, and for longer.

Forging new directions in theory

There are also other links that can be made between both frameworks to forge a wider theory of education—particularly in areas of epistemological exploration, language and communication, and understanding human agency and interaction. This is an area for active, creative and even bold engagement, and not simply one of interpretation. Solutions for modern conditions—and certainly universal elementary education for democratic societies is a modern concern—cannot be 'found'. In the literal sense, you can find only something that is already there. They must be created through reflective involvement with the present reality.

In areas such as the development of reason/rationality, concepts and moral thought, there have already been seminal contributions which help us understand development issues and their implications for curriculum planning and teaching. We need more understanding of developmental issues related to verbal testimony and its epistemologically significant features, such as propositional attitudes, autonomy, trust and discrimination in who and what to believe. In Indian theories of knowledge and knowing, *sabda bodha* and *sabda prama*, i.e., knowledge of meaning and knowledge of facts from sentences, have been important concerns. Although primarily in the realm of spiritual development, these philosophers were concerned with the problem that textual knowledge lends itself easily to cognitively passive and sterile activities such as rote memorisation and attitudes such as deference to authority. Their enquiry provides us with useful concepts and important insights, some of which were drawn upon in this study. In this study, propositional knowledge itself was treated as a 'bloc'. But clearly the statements: (*a*) the Earth is round; (*b*) if you toss a coin 50 times, you will get heads and tails, each, about 25 times; and (*c*) India was colonised by the British, are epistemologically of different genres. How children come to know these, evaluate evidence, verify their truth, and integrate them into their understanding, may be the subject of future research. It is also important to study children's response of belief in propositions that have proper names occurring in them; their epistemic stance to historical texts would depend on this. The television as a source of knowledge, coloured by the popular, everyday attitude of 'seeing is believing', is also important to examine.

It will benefit current curriculum efforts, government or otherwise, to note the explicit concern in the *Nyayasutras* for an epistemologically authentic stance in learning and in the relationship between teachers and learners. This includes elements such as a concern for truth, for the learners' need and potential to make knowledge their own, and for the importance of the idea of agency, even in the child, for ownership of mental knowledge episodes.[11] The *Nyayasutras* emphasise the importance of doubt for enquiry, but along with this include the necessity for a purpose as opposed to idle curiosity (Matilal 1986: 74). Such a theory of knowledge was the basis of Dewey's educational philosophy and also informs progressive ideas of education. The categorisation of forms of debates mentions, first, *sandhyaya*—'a form of debate to be held between the teacher and the students or between friendly philosophers, where each participant is a seeker after truth (*tatva bubhutsu*). There will be defeat or censure (*nigraha*), but with no animosity' (Matilal 1986: 84).[12] Children's mistakes, which are often turned into weapons for damaging their sense of self-worth, can instead be valuable experiences for learning a discipline, provided this is the teacher's intention, that the students know it to be so and that they trust their teacher.

There is need for curriculum research and planning (including textbook production) to seriously address the issue of how to ensure that school knowledge can become warranted assertions for the child. This was most recently addressed by the Yashpal Committee (Government of India 1993). The committee concerned itself with why there is lack of genuine learning in school and why children are being burdened by voluminous information to memorise. The report pointed out how textbooks, poorly conceptualised and written, leave children with no epistemic control over what they are being taught. Historical facts are presented with no indication of how they have been arrived at. In science, experiments are given along with their results. Mundane generalisations of the world masquerade as 'simple knowledge' for children. School knowledge, as presented in text-books, lacks authentic epistemic basis or function.

Overall, the stance of the school is towards the future, not present reality. The strong framing of the school curriculum is predicated on the belief that the present reality outside the school is not worthy of engagement. Both these constitute adverse conditions for children to locate themselves vis-à-vis school knowledge and make connections between the school and the everyday/out-of-school. Sometimes, one encounters the suggestion that the very separation of school and out-of-school knowledge is anti-educational, and that there should be no framing. I believe that while weak framing is important for effective learning, the absence of any frame would be incompatible with the idea of the school. The idea of the school as a specialised community of knowers engaged with knowledge transmission—teaching and learning—implies the presence of a frame. A weak frame makes it possible for learners to actively participate, take initiative and construct, or co-construct, knowledge—a process of reconstruction or, in Vygotskian terms, a 'scaffolded' learning. This is not a process of independent creation. It carries the sense of objective measures or standards and the experience of 'public', 'shared' knowledge. This is important for the realisation of the possibility of shared, joint action, and also the economy and efficiency of the knowledge production process.

Reflecting the concern over the discontinuity between school and everyday/local knowledge, the Acharya Ramamurthi report (Government of India 1990) and the Yashpal Committee (Government of India 1993) called for including local knowledge in the school curriculum. The findings of this study suggest that the nature of the discontinuity itself must be analysed before suggesting ways of establishing a continuity. School and local knowledge may be each constructed to serve different purposes, possess different social worth and be realised in essentially different epistemic modes. Even if schools derive their curricular content from local experience, the two may remain epistemologically separate for the child. The debate will have to include local perceptions of the purpose of schooling and school knowledge and also the social and economic status and function of local knowledge. The idea of specialised instruction in spaces such as the school does include the expectation that it will be concerned with transmitting knowledge that cannot be learnt in the course of everyday association in the community and the family (Dewey 1916: 81). The urban setting where children are more cut off from a range of interactions with community and nature has increased the expectation that schools must respond to this depletion of the child's environment; this includes both the middle-class child and the child living in an urban slum. But the school in a rural area would need to respond to different concerns posed by the environment. At the same time, there is the function the school has of communicating value through the selection of knowledge that it does include in the curriculum. It would be naïve to presume that there would be more integrity in educational experience if the local community made the curricular choices which involve epistemological, sociological and pedagogical considerations.

We need to remain alive to the questions of how to make school knowledge 'real' for students and how to engender a multilayered weaving of their understanding. Along with 'local knowledge', the *epistemic function* performed by 'work' in Gandhi's Basic Education and 'enquiry' in Dewey's curriculum for schools, could be taken up for serious attention. These ideas need to be researched and studied, not as historical artefacts that are assessed for ideological reasons or 'reasons of failure', but as important conceptual constructs of curriculum theory. Exploring and understanding the significance of work and enquiry for the construction of knowledge will help prevent curriculum planners from falling into solution traps such as allocating one period in the timetable for 'socially useful productive work' (SUPW) or 'activities', or the recent 'art of healthy and productive living' (!).

It is interesting to note that even traditional, indigenous pedagogic practitioners were critically aware of the need and potential of the listeners to make knowledge their own, and of the role of a critical, reflective and active stance with debate, argument and questioning. The emphasis on these qualities in teaching and learning need not be regarded as 'foreign' and contrary to 'Indian' values such as respect for the teacher and trust. On finding that these issues were being debated more than a millennium, even two millennia, ago, we need not feel despondent that all we seem to be doing is reinventing the wheel. It does not mean that they had found the answers which we lost on account of the compulsions of history. Or that they had arrived at a pedagogically sound system which we will do good to revive. Or even that we are more privileged than, and superior to, other societies where the debates are not as old. I believe that the existence of these debates, concerns and articulations suggest a deeper truth about the pedagogical enterprise when it is deliberate and reflective rather than habitual.

Notes

1. The operative epistemology of students is also essentially a relational one, bound with the metacognitive awareness of both the self and of others as knowers. The following is an attempt at the axiomatic formulation of three of the operative relations.

   If 'p' is a proposition that functions as knowledge in a community, such as 'plants produce their own food', and A and B refer to subjects, then:

   1. A can claim to know that p, provided that B is satisfied that A knows that p. This, of course, means that A must believe that B knows. A need not know that B knows. Belief is enough for A to accept B's verdict regarding his own knowledge. Usually, A is a student and B the teacher or quasi-teacher.
   2. If A claims to know that p, then B can claim a superior epistemic status if he can establish/prove that A does not know that p, even without additionally establishing that he himself knows that p.
   3. A can claim to know that p if A states that p in a gathering of people and nobody challenges it, and p is accepted by the gathering as appropriate. The term appropriate is used here deliberately to emphasise that the acceptance of p is because it is appropriate in the social context of the gathering and that its acceptance is not determined by reflection on its truth value.

2. According to Welbourne (1993: 27), the knowledge community is created by acts of 'commoning knowledge'. This is not simply a community created by members who are epistemically independent of each other. Where x and y are members of a community and p is a knowledge proposition, then:

Firstly	x knows that p and y knows that p,	members are epistemically independent of each other.
Secondly	x knows that y knows that p and y knows that x knows that p,	asking and telling can operate.
Finally	x knows that y knows that x knows that p and y knows that x knows that y knows that p,	here cooperative action is possible, facilitates conversation and intelligent action.

3. Also see papers in *Assessment in Education* (1997).
4. However, it would be valid for the school to actively seek to undermine this principle through its hidden curriculum. The widespread demand for schooling as established by the PROBE report (1999) notwithstanding, the expectation that schooling will lead to employment is beginning to seem unrealistic. Even in interior villages, one encounters educated, unemployed youth clothed in 'pant-shirt', with transistor at the ear to maintain a tenuous link with 'another reality', wandering about looking for people 'like themselves' to talk to, unwilling to do manual work. This scenario prompts questions regarding the future of schools: How much longer will the school be able to survive as a valid, relevant institution? Having transformed social reality irreversibly and having

created a permanent niche for itself in relation to childhood, will it survive by reinventing itself with a new meaning? Will it become a ground for marking time for large numbers of children who have 'failed'? Or to keep the city safe by keeping these children 'off the roads'? Will it simply become dysfunctional?

5. Although it may be more accurate to say 'liberalising' the framework rather than 'child-centring' it, I hesitate to use the former as the intention may be misinterpreted. 'Liberalisation' is a term too strongly connected with the present political agenda of globalisation which, in fact, is antithetical to many 'liberal' values.

6. Following from and responding to the dichotomisations made by developmental theorists, Dube (1988) uses the terms 'traditional' and 'modern' and Agrawal (1995) uses the terms 'indigenous' and 'scientific'; Antweiler (1998) presents a good discussion of the varieties of terms used in both positions.

7. See Ram-Prasad (nd) for an interesting discussion of the portrayals of the childhood of Rama, Krishna and Kartikeya.

8. It is difficult to overcome the sense of despondency at how the village school and modern education erodes this value. The school represents not simply an intrusion into the so-called 'child's world', as is the case with schooling in non-tribal areas. The intrusion and the disjuncture is with the community and its world-view. In contrast, the Kasimpur school, although marked by discontinuities with the community, is in fact ideologically continuous with the community.

9. In his description of the nature of the teacher, Samkara first mentions the attributes of compassion and sympathy (Alston 1989: 268).

10. Jane Sahi points out that the dimension of 'parent–child' in the teacher's identity may also be an advantage as it includes a benevolent, supportive interest in the student. This is absent in the purely bureaucratic–institutional professional identities of teachers in developed countries (personal communication). A recent contribution to education psychology, Rogoff's work on cognitive apprenticeship (1990), draws extensively on the mother–child interaction in a traditional Guatemalan village community.

   The experience of the Kasimpur school suggests that, in fact, women teachers are not very willing to be 'motherly' although the men teachers seem to be 'fatherly'. This contradicts the popular assumption that having women teachers in primary schools is necessarily good. It seems that children are freer with teachers who are from the same village. It is possible that the societal stereotype of women as mothers is so strong that women in the professional arena feel compelled to be more like the stereotypical distant male figure of authority.

11. This is different from the independence of the knower which is the basis of Piagetian child-centred pedagogy and which places the teacher–adult in the role of co-enquirer or facilitator.

12. The other two forms of debate which the *Nyayasutras* mention are *jalpa* and *vitanda*. *Jalpa* is held between equals, i.e., two rival parties; here the goal is victory, which may not coincide with the establishment of truth. The debate is akin to a game and strategy is important. *Vitanda* is characterised by the lack of any attempt to prove the counter thesis (Matilal 1986: 85–86).

Appendix A:

A Note on the Theoretical Framework

Most of the theory which guided the study, shaping questions, the fieldwork and the analysis and interpretation of data, has been woven into the main chapters of the book. As is evident from the many sources I have drawn upon, the landscape of the study of interrelationships between society and knowledge is vast and multidisciplinary. The contours began being shaped by sociologists of knowledge, beginning with Mannheim (1954), or perhaps earlier with Marx's notion of ideology[1] and Durkheim's *The Elementary Forms of the Religious Life* (1965). The symbolic interactionist–phenomenological school of sociology of knowledge and study of everyday reality, using the method of ethnography, drew upon Mead (1964) and Schutz (1962, 1970), and was shaped by the contributions of Berger and Luckmann (1966), Goffman (1959) and Blumer (1969). This influential approach gave a new direction to sociological studies in education in the 1970s. More recent contributions from post-Kuhnian (Kuhn 1970) studies in the sociology of science[2] have more definitely introduced the dimension of power.

Particularly since the 1970s, cultural and development psychologists building on the work of Vygotsky (1978) have contributed new dimensions to the study of knowledge and knowledge transmission in society, with ideas such as 'mediated action' and 'distributed cognition'.[3] A third area from where there have been important, new contributions is epistemology. Feminists such as Belenky et al. (1996) have re-problematised concepts of knowledge and truth by asking such questions as 'what counts as evidence for me?' And 'how do I know what I know', and have included the possibility of relating the nature of truth and knowledge to the way we see the world and ourselves as participants in it. Freire's praxis philosophy (1974) links practices of knowledge to societal structures and opportunities. There has been a renewal of attention to argumentation, verbal testimony and authority.[4]

In negotiating this vast multidisciplinary terrain, with a plethora of terminologies, approaches and conceptions, I was guided closely by a group of convictions and concepts regarding human agency, the nature of knowledge and the nature of society and social interaction. In this note I will briefly discuss only those features which I regard as key to my 'social constructionist' framework: a theory of knowledge, best stated by John Dewey; a perspective on the child derived from Jean Piaget; and a conception of society and social interaction as elaborated by Peter Berger and Thomas Luckmann, and Burkart Holzner.

School knowledge presents two problems for first-person conceptions of the knower, of knowledge and of the process of knowing. One is on account of its being an essentially social process, 'situated' and involving the interplay of individuals with each other and with cultural artefacts such as the textbook. The other problem is because of the character of school knowledge itself; it is codified and available as 'knowledge' in the form of facts, statements and theories, existing 'objectively' as the object of learning. This aspect, which dominates and characterises the Indian classroom, presents not only a sociological, but also an epistemological challenge.

As a student of education, the questions asked in this study regarding the child's condition as a knower both in society and in school—constructing knowledge of reality through her own inquiry and also in interaction with 'objectified' knowledge taken from society's corpus of 'known truths'—began to take shape while reading Dewey's theory of knowledge and knowing, and the function of knowledge in society. His epistemology was modelled on the 'method of science', where inquiry leads to the formulation of 'warranted assertions' on the basis of which one can act upon the world.[5] As inquiry is situated in a world that is also social, the theory permits the recognition that the social dimensions of establishing truths and acting upon them need not be prejudices or extraneous factors, but are integral to knowledge processes in society. He accepted Pierce's definition that '(t)he opinion which is fated to be ultimately agreed to by all who investigate is what we mean by truth, and the object in this opinion is the real' (1958:138). This was the basis of the pragmatists' insight that for knowledge claims to be established and to function as truths in society, they need social ratification in addition to other kinds of warrants. Pierce prepared the ground for a phenomenology of truth in pointing out that in society, beliefs are constituted not only by 'the method of science', but also methods such as tenacious clinging to existing beliefs and reference to authority (ibid.). Dewey recognised that these different methods did not constitute differential concern for truth; nor did their differences relate to the issue of which methods are more proof against false beliefs. The choice was more a matter of how truths function in society and direct men's lives (Dewey 1985a). It was important, in the context of this study of an Indian school, to admit the validity of the notion of knowledge as received, and then begin to notice the epistemic features of the pedagogic activity within which this view of knowledge is constituted. It prepared one to look at knowledge and truth as categories with both sociological and philosophical import and influencing life (in the school) on both counts.[6] At the same time it was apparent that Dewey's conception of the social milieu, relying primarily on either intuitive or more cultural aspects, was not sophisticated enough in matters of how it is organised, how it functions or the dimension of power.[7]

Two important Piagetian ideas are a part of the framework. One is the perspective that children are 'active'; that they act upon the world purposefully, based on their understanding, rather than simply react or respond, and their construction of the world grows as a consequence of this interaction.[8] The recognition of the intentionality and agency of humans, including children, is key in constructivism. It is an important aspect of Dewey's praxis epistemology and also underlies the phenomenological–social interactionist approach. The second conviction, also derived from Piaget, is that the talk and actions of children, even very young ones, can reveal the often only implicit frameworks of their understanding: their theories of themselves, the world and their place in it.[9]

There is a well-recognised inflexibility inherent in Piaget's theory in its present form, which limits it in providing concepts and tools to understand knowledge construction in everyday, social contexts.[10] Within cognitive and developmental psychology, the emerging paradigm of 'cultural psychology' or 'action theory' has developed on Vygotsky's insight into the importance of interaction, the social milieu/context and language in constituting cognition.[11] It provides elegant ways of conceptualising the 'situated' nature of cognition and learning. I drew on only a few key ideas such as 'mediated construction' and 'negotiating control' while interpreting data. In the present study, the study of the social milieu and context was shaped, not by this paradigm, but by symbolic interactionism and phenomenology. This is partly because the study is not about children's cognition in general, but particularly about school knowledge and knowing/learning it within the school institution. But more importantly, the choice was determined by the existence of a tradition of studying the school and school learning in the sociology of education, established by studies such as Lacey (1970), Woods (1979), Young's *Knowledge and Control* (1971), the 'Schooling and Society' course of the Open University (see Hammersley and Wood 1976) and Cosin et al. (1971).[12] In particular, Keddie's (1971) empirical study of teaching in British classrooms, Esland's (1971) proposal to study teaching and learning, not with, but *as,* the organisation of knowledge and Bernstein (1971) on curriculum knowledge, were suggestive of the potential of this tradition for the present study.

In the interactionist–phenomenological approach (Mead 1964; Schutz 1962, 1970 and Berger and Luckmann 1966), the everyday world is treated as meaningful to the human actors who participate in it and share it intersubjectively. The individual has a dialectical relationship with society, acting upon it on the basis of his or her subjective understanding and simultaneously being shaped by it. In this approach there is an interest in the subjective point of view. The approach suggests that the study of day-to-day activities and discourse in the school, the classroom and the village (relating to children and education), could reveal the meanings and structures on the basis of which teachers and children interact with each other, recreating life in school everyday, and organising and regulating the transmission of knowledge. This could be analysed to understand the epistemic functions—the constitution and regulation of children's identity and activity as knowers, and the nature of knowledge constructed. In particular, the study drew on the concepts of 'social roles' and 'frames of reference' as elaborated by Berger and Luckmann (1966) and Holzner (1968),[13] and the latter's contribution of the idea of 'epistemic community'.

In this social–constructionist approach, each person is seen as approaching the environment, in which he or she moves from his or her social setting, with a limited and specific repertory of frames of reference or orientations. Social roles may be thought of as frames of reference or theories in terms of which role occupants deal with situations which come their way. Each role also implies an epistemological position which sensitises the occupant to certain aspects of encountered reality and desensitises him or her to others. For instance, in the role as allopathic physician, the role occupant is not interested in the kinds of dreams the patient reports. A role also implies employing certain ways of evaluating the validity of reality constructs in preference over certain others. Thus, while a priest may consider consulting oracles on the matter of a cosmic event, an astronomer may resort to the telescope and mathematical calculations. Holzner also proposes that through specific roles, society regulates access—limits and distributes the chances of access—to different types of environments, including actual situations and physical environments.[14]

Holzner's conception of 'epistemic community' (1968: 60–71) was particularly useful in understanding the institution of the school. An epistemic community is a social arrangement which maintains a similar epistemology— e.g., that of science, or of religious groups. There is a meshing of similar role orientations, unified by a common epistemology and frame of reference. All members, in their capacity as members, agree on 'the' proper perspective for the construction of reality. The conditions of reliability and validity of reality constructs are known, and applicable standards are shared. Holzner points out that the establishment of shared frames of reference is a delicate process. Not only is there need for value congruency, but also for power arrangements in the exchanges of the interaction processes which sustain the shared perspective once it is established, or influence its acceptance in the first place. These structures of power regulate the frames of reference and the allocation of situations to the members; all members within a community need not be equal. The relationship of the community with the surrounding society is also a matter of importance to its members, to control the flow of information and maintain its distinctiveness. Members are also often concerned with maintaining a boundary around the epistemic community: to demarcate members and non-members is an important concern of all its members.

The combination of Dewey, Piaget and phenomenological interactionism may seem eclectic; there is little cross-referencing in the literature in each of these 'schools'. But when read together, they complement each other in many ways. Mead's profound influence on Dewey aligns his notion of social milieu and society with that of the interactionists. Similarly, Berger and Luckmann recognised the parallel between their theorising and Piaget's conception of interactionism in reality construction. Both Dewey and Piaget share a praxis theory of knowledge. This framework informed the present study explicitly, as is evident by the references in the main text, but mostly implicitly, guiding the direction of fieldwork, data collection, analysis and interpretation. The fieldwork methodology, which is elaborated in Appendix B, was also based on this. The theoretical inputs that went into specific themes of exploration, e.g., curriculum framing or verbal testimony, have been incorporated into the main text. The framework would benefit from more sharpened tools to conceptualise the operation of power and the influence of larger societal structures on the microcosm of the school, and also from the inclusion of a historical perspective. These are areas for further work.

Notes

1. See extracts of Marx's 'A contribution to the critique of political economy' (pp. 181–82) and 'The German Ideology' (pp. 178–80), reprinted in Cosin et al. (1971).
2. For example, Latour (1987) and the 'strong programme' which draws on Durkheim. See Bloor (1981) for a statement of the paradigm.
3. See, for example, Wertsch (1985), Rogoff (1990), and Lave and Chaiklin (1993).
4. In addition to the renewed interest in the Indian philosophical approaches, e.g., the *Advaita* and *Nyayasutra* (Matilal 1986, 1990), there is also renewed interest in this within dominant Western philosophy, e.g., Fricker (1987) and Welbourne (1993). Since Whorf (1956), the philosophy of language has also contributed to the under-standing of the interplay between culture and cognition.

5. See, for example, his *Logic: The Theory of Inquiry* (1938) and the more readable *How We Think* (1985b).

6. That is, their cognitive significance as reality constructs, forming belief, acquiring a moral force and influencing action.

7. Foucault (1980, 1984) is more aggressive on the relationship of truth with power, and argues that each society has its 'regime of truth', where truth is understood as a system of ordered procedures for the production, regulation, distribution, circulation, and operation of statements.

8. See Piaget (1954, 1971).

9. This was an important aspect of the methodology of the present study (see Appendix B). See Inhelder and Matalon (1960) for a detailed discussion of the methodological significance of this stance.

10. For a discussion of the problems inherent in Piaget's conception of the social and his structuralism, see Sarangapani 1999b. Russell (1978) tries to develop the social aspects of Piaget's theory, observing that children's development includes being cognitively socialised into a public system of criteria of truth, of which responsibility, causal dependence, useful worth, etc., are aspects. The notion of validity, which is central to Piaget's conception of knowledge, is not abstractly acquired by the child, but in the presence of others which whom she interacts. Accommodation need not be simply adjustment to 'reality', but to the way the world is experienced by others.

11. See note 3 above.

12. For detailed discussions of the theory/approach, see the work of these authors. For a study of an Indian school which follows in this tradition, see Thapan's *Life at School* (1991).

13. Holzner's *Reality Construction in Society* (1968), like Berger and Luckmann's (1966) better known *Social Construction of Reality*, is derived from Schutz's phenomenology.

14. In the present study, I was not able to fully explore this important dimension of role definition and distribution.

Appendix B:

On Fieldwork

The ethnographic study of children's knowledge construction in social contexts required, first of all, identifying a common school and community for study. I planned on choosing a village that had already been studied so that I could take advantage of the anthropological and sociological data and insights already available. I decided to choose a village near Delhi, and surveyed the ICSSR catalogues of village studies to locate possible field sites. From the 1980s onwards there were no significant studies listed. Of course, the villages were all referred to by pseudonyms, but from the description it was possible to find their approximate location on a map. Some of these villages have since come within the city limits of the growing metropolis of Delhi. Not speaking the local dialect—Haryanvi—was a disadvantage, but as standard Hindi is comprehended everywhere, and is also the official language for school, I felt that this problem could be over-come. Proximity to Delhi also seemed an advantage because I could return to the University from time to time, to use the library and to keep myself from being overwhelmed by the field.

Another concern was that the village should have a *functioning* primary school—a school with a full teaching staff strength where classes are held regularly and where there is teaching–learning going on, so that children do interact with the knowledge in textbooks. This seemed to be a more difficult problem. I had visited several schools of the Municipal Corporation of Delhi (MCD) within the city in connection with a previous research study and had often found the teachers lounging outside their classrooms, drinking tea and gossiping, leaving student monitors to manage the class. I was apprehensive about schools in the villages. The schools of rural Delhi are under the jurisdiction of the MCD education directorate. I consulted a senior ex-employee of the MCD, who was familiar with the status of various MCD schools, while making a choice. His advice was to choose the Boys' Model Primary School at Kasimpur Village (KBMS). The headmaster of this school was a state awardee teacher and very dedicated to his job. This was a working school, and there would be no trouble gaining entry into the school as the headmaster was known to him personally.

Kasimpur sounded ideal. It had been studied in the 1960s and 1970s (Mann 1979). There was a slight hesitation as, though it continued to be a village, the government had designated Kasimpur a census town; and the school there was not co-educational but a boys' school. I decided to first visit the school and meet the headmaster. The village was quite easy to reach—connected directly by bus to Delhi, on the GT Road, about an hour away from the University. It was the beginning of October. The journey was quite pleasant: we passed several villages and fields with yellow mustard in bloom.

The headmaster, Mr Satpal Singh, was very cordial and modestly proud of his well-maintained school. On being congratulated on his state award, he gave a short speech on how important it is to be a teacher and work for the good of the nation by making children good citizens and teaching them good values. He seemed quite pleased that his school might be chosen for a research study. He was not curious about the exact nature of the work. All the same, it was important to provide him formally with details of the study—the duration and the nature of data collection.

The government school system in India has a tradition of inspection to ensure that schools maintain standards. This is usually an evaluation of teachers on the basis of a spot assessment of children's knowledge—through an oral quiz or by observing a classroom. School classrooms are generally exposed to observation only at times of evaluative inspection. In pre-Independence times, these evaluations could result in several punitive measures, including a reduction in the teacher's already low salary. Under the MCD a bad evaluation could lead to transfer to an inconveniently located, 'bad' school, where the teacher would spend more time in commuting and which would offer fewer possibilities for additional income through private tuition. Given this context, it is to be expected that normal classroom routines are disrupted and new routines enacted for the purpose of inspection. It was important to impress upon the headmaster that this study was not an evaluation of the school or the teachers, so that my presence would not alter their usual pedagogic practices.

Mr Satpal Singh said that, unlike the nearby villages, Kasimpur also had some private, English-medium schools. The original research design had included studying a private school attended by children of 'higher' socio-economic status, for comparative purposes. This was a point in favour of locating the study in Kasimpur. The size of the village was still a concern.

I spoke to the MCD zonal officer at Narela and also to Mrs Parcha, the head-mistress of an MCD school, who I met by chance in the bus.

Mrs Parcha informed me that other MCD schools, like the one she worked in, did not have a full staff strength or even proper drinking water facilities, while the Kasimpur school, because it was a model school, got priority attention of the Directorate. The zonal officer was also quite certain that the Kasimpur school would be most suitable for the study. The village was more conscious than others of the importance of education; it had a primary girls' school, though it was not a 'model' one, and senior secondary schools for both boys and girls. It even had a Delhi University degree college nearby. The grounds and buildings of the Kasimpur school certainly looked far better in comparison to other local schools. The choice was made. Formal permission to work in the school was obtained from the zonal office. Fieldwork began soon after Diwali in November 1992 and continued till May 1993.

The process of observation

Blumer (1969) has used the metaphor of 'lifting veils' to describe the dialectical development of observation and frameworks of understanding of the field-worker in the course of fieldwork. This metaphor carries the sense of pene-trating barriers in the process of seeking information; it captures the experience of some researchers of the exercise of restrictions and censorship within the community. This is the sense that one gets in Thapan's description of fieldwork in an elite school (1991). I experienced no such barriers in the course of my fieldwork. I was quickly and easily accepted into the community, though the process of figuring me out continued all through the period of my fieldwork. The effort was not to 'lift veils' but to 'submerge oneself' in a hermeneutic endeavour of placing psychological processes of knowledge construction and meaning-giving in a sociological framework.

The evolving dialectic of field observation and theoretical frameworks continued through the period of fieldwork and afterwards helped structure the landscape of the child's social world. It threw into relief aspects that bore on the questions being asked, also augmenting and altering them. This I regard as a distinctive feature of the method *because* I was working primarily with young children and they mediated my interactions with the rest of the community.

In the course of fieldwork, observations were made in three different schools: the major portion was in the Kasimpur Boy's Model School (KBMS). In addition, the Little Angels Public School (LAPS) and the Government Girls' Primary School (GGPS) were also observed. The principals of three other private schools in the village were met and interviewed. Several village people, elders, and adolescents as well as children were visited—I interviewed some formally and informally interacted with many more. Various arenas of life and experience were entered into, not all at once, but in a succession of stages. Familiarity in one extended and provided a bridge into another.

I will take up matters of method in the chronological sequence as they arose in the course of fieldwork. The first part will be devoted to being a researcher at school. The second part will describe observation of village life. Finally, aspects relating to interacting with children, both from the perspective of observation and of investigating the attribution of meaning and truth, will be discussed. As Srinivas (1976) and Dube (1955) have done before, I use the narrative style in order to convey a sense of the entire field experience as it unfolded, and to provide a feel of the personalities of the subjects of the study.

A researcher in school

It seemed possible that one could travel daily to the school from the University and postpone taking up residence in the village until later. On my first day in school, I soon realised that the headmaster Mr Singh had not told the teachers anything about me. In fact he seemed a little surprised to actually see me there, as he seemed to have forgotten about the earlier visit. It seemed wise to again clarify the nature of the work—that I would be sitting in the classrooms, observing teaching–learning and talking to children. From the start, the curiosity of teachers and students had to be handled. In ethnography, the participant–observer herself also enters into symbolic interactions with members of the community. Her identity and intentions, as construed by the members of the community, have a strong bearing on what they will permit her to observe and interact with. Previous experience and knowledge had prepared one for a few dangers from which to safeguard in the presentation of self to the teachers and children.

The teachers: The first aim was to ensure that the teachers did not feel threatened by my presence and were able to continue with normal teaching practices and other routines. Introductions with students were postponed until the teachers had been met and were acquainted with my research purpose. The purpose of being in the school was specifically stated as aimed at learning about students for my PhD at the University of Delhi. The study had nothing to do with them as teachers and was not connected with the MCD.

The teachers and other adults in the school—the *chaprassis*—asked several questions to acquire the information they wanted to construct my identity. They quickly confirmed their suspicion that I was from South India. They inquired about family, place of residence, caste and marital status. Most questions seemed to be aimed at gauging where we stood with respect to social hierarchy. They speculated that my schooling must have been in English. They wanted to know: Why was I doing a PhD? How did I support myself? What sort of job would I get after my PhD? It seemed an over-qualification for a PGT (i.e., a postgraduate/high schoolteacher), perhaps I would become a lecturer? Being from South India proved to be an asset. The teachers did not know much about the south, and didn't have too much more to ask about my family. All the questions were answered honestly, with the exception of playing down family economic class. The reason is that previous experience with government schoolteachers suggests that in professional arenas, they will resort to very deferential behaviour with those who they believe are socially better placed than them.

Most of this information was shared with them individually or in small groups on the school grounds during the first few days of my visit. The younger teachers, when they saw me outside, made it a point to meet, exchange greetings and talk to me. On one occasion, they asked me if I was about 25–26 years old. I confirmed their guess, at which they nodded to each other saying they had calculated right. This confirmed my suspicion that they discussed me, and my presence in their school, amongst themselves.

There was a deliberate attempt to show teachers that I was more interested in spending time with children. They wanted to know—why young children and not older students? I told them that I liked working with young children. They seemed impressed that I had travelled all the way from South India to Delhi to live alone and study. They declared this must be some 'good' work; perhaps on the basis of this study there would be some recommendations about how education for young children could be improved.

'IQ' is one of the most important psychological inventions that has entered into everyday discourse as a 'scientific' explanation of student achievement. In most BEd programmes, IQ, along with other psychological measures for ability and achievement, is presented as the scientific basis for all observed student phenomena, and as the basis for making curriculum and pedagogical choices. Education research revolves around testing and measurement. In response to the stated interest in children, the five younger teachers in the school, who were also graduates with BEd degrees, all assumed that I was there to study the IQ of village children. It seemed to confirm their belief that the village children have a low IQ. On the very first day, two of the young male teachers rolled their eyes knowingly, smirked and declared that I would find a lot in this school.

The young woman teacher of Class IV, too, was sure I was there to study IQ. On my first visit to her classroom, she reeled off the names of eight children, ordered them all to come to me and asked me to 'check' them. I was a bit taken aback by this, and a little anxious that the children may think of me as some kind of inspecting authority. I quickly clarified that I didn't want to talk to children like this, and asked the children to go back to their places. Later, when I spoke to her, she seemed disappointed that I was not going to assess IQ and soon lost interest in trying to understand what I was doing in the classroom.

In spite of the overall goodwill towards my intentions that the teachers had construed, in the first week at school it was necessary to actively establish credibility and also safeguard my place as researcher in the school community. The fact that I was not administering tests on children, and seemed to be 'hanging around', could have led to the feeling that they could take advantage and use me as a spare hand. Despite my upper-caste status and proficiency in English, the fact of being a woman, together with the low status attached to people working in primary education, and with no obvious institutional role or access to authority, made me more prey to such treatment. One day, when a few of the teachers of the school were absent, the headmaster of the school suggested to the teacher in charge of substitution that I could be given charge of a class to mind. I asserted my identity as researcher and made it clear that I was obliging them by minding the class for just one hour. I also clarified that I would not do it for the whole day, as I had to do the work I was there for. The headmaster and other teachers got the message that as a researcher, I would not take charge of the classes of absentee teachers. Much later in the course of my fieldwork, I had to deal once more with the problem of the status of women in the Jat community and tackle the over-familiarity of two of the young male teachers.

From the very beginning, all the teachers had been informed that the objective of visiting their classes was not to observe them, but the children. Still, they seemed relieved when they learnt that observations would be restricted mainly to the two sections of Classes IV and V. The four teachers involved were initially conscious of my presence and I felt they were putting on the act of the 'good, conscientious teacher' for my benefit, though Nagpal of Class IV seemed least affected. I made no effort to hide my notes from their curious gaze. Krishna Kumari, a Class V teacher, came up after her lesson, took the observation book from me and checked what had been written. She even seemed a little disappointed that merely the proceedings of the class had been recorded with no evaluative comments. She must have shared her finding with other teachers. After that, they became less concerned about my note-taking. They did not seem disturbed by my moving around the room, sitting among the children, looking into their books and even talking to them when they were supposed to be doing individual work.

Later, when I began talking to children, the teachers sometimes offered to leave the class so I could talk to the children more freely. Sometimes, it did both the children and me good to let their teachers have a break. But on a few occasions I had to insist that the teachers take charge of their class and not go away, ostensibly to oblige me.

Though initially the teachers seemed to be grappling with social considerations such as caste and educational background, later on it was the relationship I had developed with all the children that they puzzled about, and in some way respected. Several of them commented upon the fact that the children held me in affection and that I spent a lot of time making paper toys for them. All of them had been keen on explaining to me how they were forced to take up jobs as primary schoolteachers though they were cut out for better things in life. I, on the other hand, seemed to not only give a great deal of time and attention to children from all castes and classes, but also seemed to enjoy relating to them much more than spending time with adults. Though educating children was supposed to be regarded as a noble duty, still, in their milieu, the primary schoolteacher's job was a very low status job. It didn't seem to make sense that I should be going out of my way to speak to children. They respected what they saw as an eccentric streak.

The children: In a situation where the child's primary experience of the adult is as a figure of authority, I knew I had to be very careful about managing and shaping the experiences on which children would base their construction of my identity. I would have to present myself as an adult with whom they interacted in the school, but neither as a teacher nor an inspector. It was important that they did not regard me as someone who would evaluate and assess them. Suspending pedagogic communication and entering into simple communication depended on this. I took opportunities to reiterate to teachers, within hearing range of the children, that I was not here to evaluate them. I emphasised that I was here just to see how things are done, to talk to people, and not to test anything. No report would be written. When one of the teachers enquired if a book would be written, I confirmed the possibility.

There was a concern that the teachers would unwittingly turn me into some kind of inspector, an authority figure for the children. Nagpal (Class IV) and Bhardwaj (Class V) seemed to be inclined to use a stranger observer in the classroom as a bogeyman to get children to comply. In the presence of children, under the cover of humour, I asked them to please not scare the children, that I was not there for any evaluation purpose. It was all right for the children to believe that I was interested particularly in them, but not that I was a figure of authority akin to their teachers.

The children soon figured that I was there especially to get to know them better. They were not used to being the focus of attention of any adult and at first were a bit embarrassed when answering questions about themselves. Though some of them quickly opened up to the attention, many others usually twisted, glanced and smiled at each other and stammered out responses. They were excited and curious about my presence in the school and that I was not a figure of authority. Though I was an adult, I was not going to check or discipline them. When they found that I was in fact willing and interested in conversing with them and getting to know them better, they grew much bolder and every morning after assembly, as they filed past on their way to class, they would shout, inviting me to come to their class. They also checked my marital status and decided on the appellation of '*didi*' (older sister), rather than 'aunty', for me.

The children also had questions about me: where I came from and why I was visiting their school. Most of them decided that I was also a student doing a '*master-ni*' (f) course (teacher training course), perhaps based on the speculation of their parents or older siblings when they went back with reports about me and my activities. Some of them also believed I was going to write a book about them, a conjecture they confirmed by asking me and by looking into my notes.

They were all very curious about the book in which I made notes, observing at once that I wrote in both English and Hindi. I made no effort to hide the book or the activity of recording from them, so that they would get used to it. They could even look in the book when they felt like it. They were surprised, excited and puzzled that what they and their teachers said and did were noted down. Later, they sometimes instructed me to write down what they were saying. Some of them asked me what would be done with these notes. The answer I provided was rather innocuous and meaningless; I said I would be discussing these with my teacher, and he would tell me what to do. But they seemed to accept this quite easily. After the first few weeks, they were less curious about the notes and rarely looked in to see what was being written. But even later, whenever they expressed an interest, I let them see what had been written. They seemed to be at ease, and were amused that I noted even their absurd antics and play.

They were also curious about the book they believed I was going to write—a book about them. 'What will you call it?' one of them asked. I asked him if he had any suggestions. He said that it should be named after whichever word comes in it most often; 'Like if the word "plants", "plants", "plants", comes again and again, then the lesson is called "plants"' (Ajay, in the village).

Other schools: In addition to KBMS, classes in a private, English-medium school—the Little Angels Public School (LAPS)—and the Government Girls' Primary School (GGPS), which was not a 'model' school, were also observed. LAPS was run by a Keralite entrepreneur couple. On the first visit to the school, Mr Thomas agreed to let me observe his classes. He was very conscious of being an outsider in the village, and of his fluency in English. He had a very poor opinion of the villagers. He also seemed to have a very poor opinion of students, of education, or higher education on the whole, and made disparaging remarks about how PhDs are about useless matters and get written by simply copying and cooking up results from here and there. He wanted to see my interview schedule and asked what I would be 'proving' and what my hypothesis was. When I told him I had none, that my observation method was that of the ethnographer's, he was sceptical. In any case he allowed me to observe the classes in his school, but continued to make critical observations about PhD scholars and about the villagers. He, too, was very surprised about the fact that I had no intelligence tests to administer. After three months of observation, he abruptly asked me to stop, saying that I was disturbing the children in his school. (I had taught them also how to make paper birds.)

LAPS was completely financed by the fees that were collected from the students. The school was the oldest private school in the village. But the enrolment in the school had come under great threat in recent years with two fairly big public schools coming up near the village. This was of great concern to Mr and Mrs Thomas. Perhaps on account of my friendly relations with most of the villagers and his schoolteachers, and the children's obvious pleasure in my presence, Mr Thomas felt that I may start my own school or tuition business.

My experience with the GGPS was very pleasant. By the time I went to speak to the headmistress of that school for permission to observe the classes in her school, I had spent five months in the village and had lived there for two months. I was a familiar figure by then and some of the students of the school knew me through interacting with me in the village. Obtaining permission was easy. However, in this school, teachers were far more casual about teaching. I found that they often left their classes to the student monitors to manage and teach.

The study represents a departure from dominant research methodology in education in India. As such, there has been no serious anthropological study of *common* schools in India. Earlier studies, such as Thapan (1991) or Srivastava (1993), are anthropological studies of elite, special schools. In such schools, not only are unconventional roles for researchers understood, but also, they have institutional spaces for members who are neither teachers nor students. The field experiences of the common school, which were presented in this study, are therefore significantly different. The assumptions about the role of a researcher in the school, which is informed by the universe of examination and evaluation in which the school exists, come into play in the presence of the anthropologist researcher, whose behaviour does not conform to such expectations. The negation of this role and an active effort to establish credibility for the role of ethnographer was an important aspect of fieldwork.

Observing village life

Knowledge about the village was gathered from various sources. Apart from observations and speaking with people, data were also gathered from other records. Mann's (1979) study of the village, the study of similar villages by Lewis (1958) and Rao (1971), provided a great deal of information on the basic culture and social organisation. In addition, there were data to be accessed from records. The local ration shop records provided a good idea of the actual population of Kasimpur, including the migrant labour, as opposed to the figures that the censuses gave. The block office that was located in Kasimpur had information on ownership of agricultural assets, and some land holding and cropping data. The Census of Delhi had separate data on Kasimpur from 1971 onwards (Government of India 1971, 1981, 1991). The data from the latest 1991 Census were also available from the central census office. The *Tehsildar*'s office in Tis Hazari, Delhi, was not able to provide details of land holdings as the records were sealed and with the courts, on account of the extensive litigation in land-ownership matters.

The school was on the outskirts of the village. I ventured into the village after about a month's observation at school, when I was familiar with the children. I had no introductions to people in the village. It seemed that one would need some valid reason to be entering the village. The children provided access to their homes. Initially, I literally invited myself to the home of Navin of Class V. He was clearly excited but also embarrassed at the prospect of my visiting his home. Fortunately for me, his mother and sisters were curious about me and kept up a conversation. (Having brought me to his home, Navin himself quickly vanished.) His sisters told me a great deal about themselves, their family and the village. They seemed to enjoy having someone to talk to and invited me to come again.

After this first visit, it was easy to enter the village and visit children's homes. When they saw me walking through the *galis,* children would excitedly call and invite me in. My fame as the *didi* who makes '*chiriya*' (bird) from paper had also spread in the village among the children. I took to carrying old newspapers in my bag. Walking through the streets, I would hear children saying to each other or calling after me: '*Didi, chiriya.*' Whenever I heard this, I would stop, pull some paper out of my bag, make origami cranes and show the children how to make them fly. The villagers began to see me as a friend of their children, who had something to do with the school. They would sometimes stop me on the street and enquire after me, or about me. I sometimes overheard them talking as I passed them, describing me as 'so-and-so's *didi*, from the school'.

The excitement children exhibited when I gave them birds or cardboard 'clappers', and the patient attention I gave them, must have led the villagers to believe that I was interested in and given kindly towards their children. They were benevolent towards me and welcomed me into their homes. Children also began to frequently invite me to their homes. I always took up their invitations and visited them. I chose to deliberately walk through the *churha* and *chamar* sections of the village. Soon, these children too began calling out to me as I passed by. I also agreed to teach one of the children's sister some English to ensure that I could return to the area more freely.

I don't believe the villagers quite figured out what I was there for. One day when I was in the village with a group of children, an old woman, whose grandson studied in KBMS, stopped to talk to me.

EPISODE B.1 (IN THE VILLAGE)
You come to the school every day, don't you?
Yes.
Do you teach there?
No.
Does the government pay you?
Not really, I get some money to study.
So you do a *naukari* (job)?
No.
She comes with the schoolchildren everyday, she must be a *chaprassin*. (*The old woman exclaimed, to no one in particular.*)

Questions about why I was spending time with the children and what kind of job I would get after I completed my studies continued all through the period of my interaction with the villagers.

Two months later, in the beginning of January, I took up residence in a house near the school, outside the traditional village. This was made possible through an acquaintance who was married into one of the families in the village. It was now more easy to visit children's homes and spend more time in the village. It was also possible to observe more arenas of the children's life-world: their activities over the weekend, early in the morning and late at night. As I had to go into the village for provisions and other necessities, this made me a more familiar figure and my presence in parts of the village, like the *shani bazar* (weekly market held on Saturday), less odd.

During this period, I visited some homes more often than others and developed deeper ties with them. The understanding of the village ethos was informed a great deal by the long conversations with these villagers, both native and migrant, over many cups of tea and meals at their homes. I tasted a variety of *rotis* and *khichris* cooked on dung, coal, wood, kerosene and gas stoves. In addition to conversations with the families of children, I conducted more lengthy interviews with some men and women who were regarded as prominent members of the village community. Their names were suggested by the *gram sevak* (village worker) and other villagers. Most of these people, both men and women, had seen me in the village and had already some idea of my interests and business. In these interviews, no special effort was needed to get them to voice their opinions. They seemed only too willing to hold forth and moralise on childhood, education and social change in the village. Both Dube (1995) and Roy and Srivastava (1986) have commented on this style of discourse among adult villagers. These interviews were generally quite open, without much need for focusing. I made notes and occasionally asked them to elaborate on some aspect or other.

Communicating with children

The focus on the child required a renewed sensitivity to methodological matters. The more important aspects of fieldwork arose in the context of ethnographic work with young children. Communicating with children, which involved opening up and making sense of a universe of activity and discourse, was exciting and challenging. During class hours I mostly observed. I spoke to the children in the classroom in between lessons, during the long spells of non-teaching and independent-work time, when they were supposed to do copy-writing or memorise something. The children seemed to quickly grasp that I was a non-teacher adult who was willing to give them her undivided attention.

Existing research methods of studying children do point to the need for flexibility in dealing with children, but none of them prepares one for the predicament of the ethnographer in a classroom of 30 children. The first few days when they were alone with me, the children began entertaining me with songs, riddles and dances. I needed some way to interact with children without their having to resort to entertaining me. I also felt that as they were young (9–12/13 years old), it would not be easy to sit around and chat with them without making them feel they were being interviewed. We did not have enough shared or common experiences which could form the basis of such casual interaction.

Joan Tough (1977) used a puppet to carry on conversations with children; it was the puppet which asked children questions and to whom the children spoke, explaining themselves. This seemed more suited to younger children who play with dolls and not the age group I was working with. The Piagetian clinical interview gets the conversation going by having an activity to provide a context and direction for verbal interaction (Inhelder and Matalon 1960). I had planned to use activities at a later stage of the fieldwork to gather more specifically epistemic data. I decided to use non-pedagogic activities from the start, to provide the basic contour of interaction within which a conversation could be evolved. I began bringing old newspapers with me and making origami flying cranes and other toys out of throwaway materials for them. Many of the toys were based on the folk toys and low-cost designs in books by Arvind Gupta (1989) and Sudarshan Khanna (1992). The emphasis was on things that they could make themselves and which we could do together.

Soon we were spending a great deal of our spare time together making toys and chatting. They began bringing and showing me other toys they made and teaching me how to make them. They opened their schoolbags and showed all the things they brought with them to school—the coloured wrappers they found in some workshop, the cigarette packets they had collected, the pictures of Gods they kept and prayed to before a test, the colourful advertisement cuttings and even the taboo comics they read. They invited me to watch and explained to me their play and games. They talked a lot and willingly talked to me about themselves. They allowed me to participate in their conversations, and even question them and pursue things they had said.

I don't believe I ever ceased to be an adult for them, and in their interactions with me they did not treat me as a child. Rather, they treated me as an adult who wanted to know them better. Negotiating this non-traditional adult role, which allows children's discourse to be as unconscious of hierarchy as possible, was a constant issue. Anthropologically-styled research in Western countries, such as the work of Tough (1977) or Rogoff (1990), have little to say about this issue, possibly because hierarchy in adult–child relationships is not as much a feature of those cultures. I asked the children questions about things they didn't even consider questionable, and on matters they took for granted. They were patient with my questions and stupidity in understanding what they said. They allowed me to probe their minds and shared with me their understanding of the world, which they would not normally have ever articulated or vocalised to anyone.

Later, during the period of fieldwork, it seemed that the class monitors stopped playing their role when their teachers were out of the class. Instead, they would start talking with me, and allow the class discipline to deteriorate. On one occasion, the headmaster walked into one of the sections of Class V which had grown quite noisy. He scolded them, and also told me that he had hoped I would keep them quiet. I did not want the expectations of teachers to alter the free communication I now enjoyed with the children. I resorted to a mildly teasing tone and pointed out to the headmaster that I was not their teacher. Later, in private, I apologised to him, saying that for the research it was important to allow the children to do whatever they felt comfortable with. He said he understood the point. One of the Class V children also remarked that when I was around, their teacher, Bhardwaj, beat them less, so they took the opportunity to be cheeky.

Enquiring into the child's construction of knowledge, there was need to access children's discourse and thinking about knowledge and school experience. At the beginning of fieldwork, the main interest was in the epistemic aspects of children's knowledge—both school and everyday, and the extent to which school knowledge is assimilated to everyday knowledge and experience. I had planned to interview children in the clinical interview style used by Piaget in his work on *Play, Dreams and Imitation* (1951). For this, I planned to pose factual statements to them, first asking them to comment on their truth and then get them to elaborate on the criteria they were using for warrants. I also had plans of getting them to speak about the things they learnt in school and to listen for references to factual statements and assertions in casual conversation, to assess and investigate aspects of natural epistemics, assimilation and knowledge application.

Upon entering into the school, it became clear that there was much more in their experience of school knowledge than epistemic matters related to the textbook. 'Pedagogy, curriculum and evaluation considered together constitute the three message systems through which formal educational knowledge can be realised; in this sense they constitute a modern epistemology' (Goodson 1988: 28). One would have to impute meaning to the discourse of the epistemic community of which the child is a member, on education and learning. Such data were not available through simple ethnographic observation; they were too much a part of the taken-for-granted, natural attitude. I wanted children to speak about '*bade admi*', 'failures', 'what schooling is meant for', 'memorisation' as opposed to 'rote learning' and 'understanding', 'discipline' and many other such concepts that organised their experience of school and school knowledge. It was in terms of these concepts that they gave meaning to their activities in the school and identified with the tradition of becoming educated.

For this, one had to be on guard so that when such ideas came up in the course of conversation, they were followed up and additional questions were asked to probe the idea further. The course of conversation was therefore always unpredictable. For example, one afternoon, Pavan (Class V), who had finished his mathematics examination early, came out to play near me and I asked him about how he had prepared for this examination. This developed into an investigation of the difference between memorisation, understanding and rote learning. It then moved on to considering what kind of learning occurs in everyday contexts, in relation to non-school related knowledge. In such conversations, children often answered in single-word sentences, and also often with silence.

It was not possible to converse with many children in such naturally occurring one-on-one situations. School normally kept them busy all through the day and for such conversation it would have been necessary to take the child out of the class individually. On the few occasions that I did try this, the children became tongue-tied and uncomfortable about being singled out. They usually turned very quiet, which gave the whole conversation a very forced, stilted air. The other 'problem' was that practically it did not seem possible to carry out such one-on-one conversations. When in conversation with one child, other children would come up and collect around at the slightest opportunity. To shoo them away made the child being interviewed feel even more uncomfortable and conspicuous.

But this turned out to be an unexpected asset. I began interviewing groups of children. Such interviews became more akin to conversations and took away the pressure of being interviewed and answering. These conversation between and among children provided a lot of unexpected avenues and ideas. There was also the advantage that they interpreted things to each other, 'explaining', and making overall comprehension better. When they contradicted each other, argued or became persuaded, many epistemic matters came to the fore. The conversation reported in Episode B.2 illustrates this. I was leading the children's initial spontaneous question about states of matter to get them to theorise about change of state:

EPISODE B.2 (CLASS V)
Joni spontaneously asked the question, in a general knowledge testing mode. There was a sense of challenge inherent in the asking: What substance is both solid and liquid?
Vipin (immediately): Water-ice and water.
What about iron?
Ashok: Impossible. It can form crystal—not liquid.
How does ice become water?
Surinder, Vipin, Ashok: It melts. It heats up and melts.
So can't iron also melt if we heat it?
Only Vipin said: Maybe it can. *The others were quite disbelieving.*

The genre of questions being asked was unfamiliar to the children, though the content was not. Some of the questions were about their studies in school: why did they study the things they did, not about farming? How was it that their grandparents had not studied and yet they had managed to earn a living? They answered with some hesitation and showed quizzical pique at the kind of questions I asked. The matters involved seemed too obvious, a part of the world they simply took for granted. It is quite likely that none of them had thought of even asking such questions before I posed them—or that it was even possible to ask such questions. With varying degrees of readiness, they came out with answers when asked.

In most conversations of this kind, which were not casual but instigated by me, we would reach a point where I got the feeling the child or children were willing to go with me thus far and no further. The genre of questions seemed to be too removed from their everyday experience of questions for them to stay engaged for very long. They would grow tired of pursuing the topic, explicating, differentiating and elaborating. Usually they would show signs of getting a bit tired or would go quiet. With some children it happened earlier than with others. But when it did happen, it seemed wise not go on.

To assess epistemic matters related to school and everyday knowledge, more focused interviews were used. These were conducted in the latter half of the fieldwork, in keeping with the overall anthropological approach. They were conducted not only with children individually, but also in pairs and in small groups of children. Apart from a few children each time, the composition of the rest of the group was generally not fixed and children would join and leave as they wished. From their school science and social science textbooks and from general matters, several factual statements had been constructed. For example: 'The earth is flat', 'Kasimpur is situated in the Gangetic plain', 'The whale is the biggest fish'. Several such statements were listed on a sheet of paper. A list of some of these statements is included at the end of this appendix. They would read each statement out in order. Then I would ask them to tell me if it was true or false (*sahi ya galat*) and also ask them to tell me how they knew. If they said they didn't know if it was true or false, I would ask them: 'How will you find out?' These interviews were generally easier to conduct. The children also seemed to enjoy answering these questions and figuring out the answer in each instance.

Apart from these interviews, I also had extensive conversations with children outside the school, while accompanying them back home or in the fields around the village where they played. I also talked to three of the children on a half-day outing when we took a walking trip to the railway line about 7 km away. Generally in their homes, they did not have much opportunity to speak to me, as there were other older people around who assumed primacy.

On the whole, the children's answers and conversations with them indicated their faith in the scheme of things that currently obtain in society. Their answers did not appear to be a verbalisation of some previously articulated knowledge. At the same time, they did not seem to be simply off-the-cuff; there was an overall coherence.

Handling data

I always carried a notebook with me in the field and extensive direct observations were recorded in it chronologically, as they occurred. The observations included events, people and conversations. As far as possible, verbatim transliteration of interviews, dialogues and conversations were recorded in process, or soon after, using a rough shorthand. More details were filled in almost immediately after, or late at night when I returned home. Every few days, all the data were transcribed from the versions recorded in the field notebooks into discursive accounts, using a word-processor. Details of location, setting, people and conversations, along with both verbal and non-verbal information, were filled in. Later, when I began staying in the village, this was done on my weekly visits to the University. The records were entered day-wise. This helped review observations. In the process, questions and themes for further enquiry emerged. This activity also simultaneously prepared the data for analysis.

When fieldwork was complete, the first step towards analysis was to divide up each day's observations into shorter 'episodes'. Each 'episode' roughly represented a single 'theme', 'idea' or 'event'. It could be the whole or a segment of a conversation or event. Each episode was supplied with a code for reference. For example, 'ep85d4-2, B-VB' means the 85th episode of observations made on 4 February (1993), in the Boys' school, Class **VB**. The code **G** was used for Girls' school, and **LAPS** for the private school. Locations in the village were noted as such. All the episodes was printed out on separate slips of paper.

Every episode was first summarised. Then, about 70 key words and key phrases were used to categorise the episodes into themes, such as 'discipline', 'teacher–pupil relationship', 'why schooling'. A single episode could have more than one key word. Both word processor 'search' commands and mechanical regrouping were used to gather together the episodes themselves. After this, the episodes under a common theme were grouped for closer analysis.

The process of analysis was carried out in two main phases. In the first, which lasted about a year, time was spent alternately between analysing the data and extensive library work to study the related literature and explore themes. This helped to identify and focus on sub-themes, shades and nuances, and interpret the data. Later, the processes of writing and reading were interspersed with work that was not related to the thesis. The process of analysis and interpretation continued all through the process of writing—from the preliminary rough drafts to the final form. At each reworking, including the preparation of this manuscript, interpretation was sharpened and more connections were made.

Sample of true-or-false statements

Every statement was read out individually. Children were asked to say if it was true or false, how they knew, and if they did not know, to say how they would find out:

1. All new plants grow only from seeds.
2. The earth is four-cornered.
3. Some plants grow shorter day-by-day.
4. If you toss a coin 50 times, you will get heads about 25 times and tails about 25 times.
5. The Thar desert is to the west of Kasimpur.
6. Wheat has a plumule.
7. Archimedes was a Greek scientist.
8. If you start walking in the western direction, you will reach the Thar desert.
9. The Angel fish is the smallest fish in the world.
10. The Tulsi plant can survive for 10 days without water.
11. Plants flower and fruit better if we give them fertilisers.
12. Kasimpur has three seasons.
13. There are three pots, each with a different type of soil. Water is poured in all three.

	I	**II**	**III**
	Water flows through fast.	Water stays on top.	Water flows through slowly.
A says	sand	clay	loam
B (gury*ji*) says	clay	loam	sand

Who will you believe? Why?

14. Diesel is mixed with petrol and used in aeroplanes as fuel.
15. Malaria disease is spread by bad air.
16. Kasimpur is situated in the Great Northern Plains.

Glossary

The glossary gives the meaning of many Hindi and Sanskrit words which are employed in the main text, and also some technical terms particular to the Indian context. Many of the episodes appearing in the text include the teachers' and children's own words. As translations of these are included there, they are not listed here. I have used an informal, hopefully intuitive, spelling while rendering the Hindi and Sanskrit words in the Roman script. In the list provided here, I have added the use of a diacritical mark on 'a': 'ā' is to be pronounced as in the word 'ask' and 'a' is to be pronounced as in the word 'arithmetic'.

āchārya	teacher
ādarsh	model
advaita	philosophy of non-dualism
anāj	food grain
anpadh	illiterate
Ārya samāj	Hindu Reform Movement founded by Dayanand Saraswati in the 1870s
asāmi	tenancy rights for cultivation
athgāma	eight-village unit
bābu	clerk
badā ādmi/bade ādmi (pl)	big man
badhai	carpenter/carpenter caste
bājrā-khichdi	gruel of coarse grains
bāl sabhā	assembly/gathering of children
balishtā	childishness
bālvritti	childlikeness
baniā	merchant–trader caste
basti	typically lower income housing locality

beej	seed
bhakti/Bhakti	devotion/religious movement from the medieval period onwards, where devotion was emphasised over the performance of rituals etc.
bhāshā	language
bol-chāl	speech-walk, generally referring to character/etiquette
brahman	transcendent, absolute reality
brāhmin	priest/priestly caste
buā	paternal aunt, father's sister
buddhi	intelligence, 'brains' in colloquial English
bus addā	bus stop/bus terminus
chāchā	paternal uncle, father's younger brother
chamār	leather worker/leather worker caste (Scheduled Caste)
chanā	gram
chaprāssi/chaprāssin(f)	office boy
chārpāi	wooden cot
chaupāl	an open paved area in a village, traditionally a meeting place for men
chipi	tailor/tailor caste
chulhā	hearth or cooking stove, usually made of clay
churhā	sweeper or scavenger caste (Scheduled Caste)
dādi	paternal grandmother
dalit	term used to refer to oppressed low castes, also see *harijan,* Scheduled Caste
Dassera	ten-day festival, usually occurring in October, before Diwali
dhābā	roadside eatery/hotel
dhyān	attention, concentration
didi	older sister
dimāg	brain
durrie/durries (pl)	large, heavy woven carpet (also dhurrie)
gali	narrow lane, alley
ganit	mathematics/arithmetic
ganvār	rustic

gāyatri mantra	an important and sacred verse from the *Rig Veda*, praying for an enlightened mind/understanding
ghāghrā–shirt	ankle-length skirt and long blouse traditionally worn by women in North India
gher	manger
gotra	non-localised patrilineal clan
grām sevak	village worker (a government post)
Green Revolution	term used since the late 1960s to describe a change in agricultural practices based on the use of hybird seeds and fertilisers, etc., in several parts of India, primarily with development aid from the United States of America
guru	teacher
gurukul	place where the guru lived with his disciples
gyān	knowledge
harijan	'God's people'—term used by Mahatma Gandhi to refer to the untouchable castes, *also see* dalit
harit-krānti	'green revolution', *see* Green Revolution
Jai jawān, jai kisān	'Hail soldier, hail farmer.' A slogan coined in 1965 by Lal Bahadur Shastri, then Prime Minister of India
jajmān	patron, usually higher caste group, receiving a service
jajmāni	patronage, system of economic exchanges interlinking caste groups typical of rural North India
jalebi	ring like sweet, fried and dipped in sugar syrup
jānkāri	information, general knowledge
Jāt	cultivator caste
jhoota	ritual pollution associated with food and eating (including vessels)
ji	a tag often appended with names, signifying respect
kabaddi	game popular in North India, requiring two teams and no equipment

kachchā	raw/unripe/earthen sun-dried construction/ temporary
kāmin	worker, usually lower-caste group, providing a service
kharif	rainy season crop
khoj	search, research
kho-kho	popular game in North India
kumhār	potter/potter caste
lakh	one hundred thousand
lāl dorā	'red line', urban land limits
laukic (adj.)	of the people
likhāi	(hand)writing
lilā	play
mā–bāp	parents/mother–father
mahaul	environment/surrounding
māmā	maternal uncle, mother's brother
man	mind
mandi	market
mazdoor	labourer
MCD	Municipal Corporation of Delhi
moksha	liberation
motā dimāg	fat/thick head/brain
nāi	barber caste
namaste	traditional Indian greeting
naukari	service
nawāb	noble man
nyāya	a Indian school of logic founded by Gotama, about two millennia old
padh lenā	to (be able to) read
padhāi	studies/education/lessons/schooling
padhā-likhā	educated
padhnā	to read/to study
pakkā	ripe/baked bricks and cement construction/ permanent
paryāvaran adhyayan	environmental studies
pat-jhad	leaf-fall (the name of a short season before spring, not autumn)
pehchaan	identity/recognising marks
pir (pihar)	woman's father's home
pradhān	headman

pramā	true and certain knowledge
pramāna	means of knowledge, testimony
prayog (n)	experiment
prayog karnā (v)	application, to use
pujā	worship
rābi	winter crop
ratnā (v)	to memorise
roti	a type of unleavened bread
saag	any green leafy vegetable
sabda	word, verbal testimony
sabda bodha	knowledge of meaning
sabda pramā	words expressing true and certain knowledge
sabda pramānam	verbal testimony (also see *pramana*)
salwār–kameez	trouser–shirt like dress traditionally worn by Punjabi and Jat women
samajhnā	to understand
sāmājik	social, also shortened version for social studies
sāmājik sāstra	social studies, also often shortened to *samajik*
samjhaanā	to cause understanding, i.e, to explain
samosā	savory–pastry stuffed with curried potatoes and fried
sāri	common dress of Indian women
sarkār (n)/sarkāri (adj)	government/of the government
sāstra (n)/sāstric (adj)	religious and philosophical texts, such as the Vedas, Upanishads, *brahmasutras,* etc.
savāl	question
Scheduled castes/tribes	Particular castes, races or tribes specified by presidential orders issued under the provisions of Article 341 of the Constitution of India. These groups are regarded as meriting special privileges in view of their oppressed position.
seekhnā	to learn
sikshā	education
sishya	disciple
sloka	verse
soch(n)/sochnā (v)	thought/think
solgāma	sixteen-village unit

surya namaskār	Hindu salutation to the sun
tapas	a rigorous system of self-discipline
tāt patti	long, narrow, woven jute mats
tāu	paternal uncle, father's older brother
tehsildār	government functionary (lower level) responsible for records
teli	oil crusher/oil crusher caste
Upanishad/Upanishadic	philosophical texts of the Vedas/pertaining to the Upanishads
Veda/Vedic (adj.)	ancient sacred texts of the Hindus/pertaining to the Vedas
vidyā	learning/education
vidyārthi	student
vigyān	science
yaad karnā (v)	to memorise

Bibliography

Acharya, P. (1985). 'Politics of Primary Education in West Bengal: The Case of *Sahaj Path*', in S. Shukla and K. Kumar (eds.), *Sociological Perspective in Education: A Reader*, pp. 314–27. Delhi: Chanakya Publications.

Agrawal, A. (1995). 'Dismantling the Divide Between Indigenous and Scientific Knowledge', *Development and Change*, 26: 413–39.

Allen, R.T. (1987). 'Because I Say So: Some Limitations Upon the Rationalisations of Authority', *Journal of Philosophy of Education*, 21(1): 15–24.

Alston, A.J. (1989). *Samkara on Discipleship* (Vol. 5: A Samkara Source-book). London: Shanti Sadan.

Anderson, J.R. (1995). *Learning and Memory: An Integrated Approach.* New York: John Wiley and Sons.

Antweiler, C. (1998). 'Local Knowledge and Local Knowing: An Anthropological Analysis of Contested "Cultural Products" in the Context of Development', *Anthropos*, 93: 46–94.

Assessment in Education. (1997). 'The Diploma Disease Twenty Years On', *Assessment in Education: Principles, Policy and Practice.* 4(1).

Avalon, A. (ed. and intro.) (1982). *Sarada Tilaka Tantram.* New Delhi: Motilal Banarsidass Publishers.

Barnes, B. (1986). 'On Authority and its Relationship to Power', in J. Law (ed.), *Power, Action and Belief: A New Sociology of Knowledge?* pp. 180–95. London: Routledge and Kegan Paul.

Baumann, Z. (1978). *Hermeneutics and Social Sciences.* New York: Columbia University Press.

Belenky, M.F., N. Rule Goldberger and **J.M. Tarule.** (eds.) (1996). *Women's Ways of Knowing: On Gaining a Voice.* New York: Basic Books.

Berger, P. and **T. Luckmann.** (1966). *The Social Construction of Reality: A Treatise in the Sociology of Knowledge.* London: Penguin Books.

Berne, E. (1963). *The Structure and Dynamics of Organizations and Groups.* New York: Ballantine Books.

Bernstein, B. (1971). 'On Classification and Framing of Educational Knowledge', in M.F.D. Young (ed.), see below, pp. 47–69.

——. (1977). *Class Codes and Control, Volume 3: Towards a Theory of Educational Transmission.* Second edition, Ch. 6: 'Class and Pedagogies: Visible and Invisible', pp. 116–56. London: Routledge and Kegan Paul.

Blackburn, S. (1996). *Oxford Dictionary of Philosophy.* Oxford: Oxford University Press.

Bloor, D. (1981). 'The Strengths of the Strong Programme', *Philosophy of Social Sciences,* pp. 254–72.

Blumer, H. (1969). *Symbolic Interactionism.* Englewood Cliffs, N.J.: Prentice-Hall.

Bourdieu, P. (1986). 'Forms of Capital', in J.G. Richardson (ed.), *Handbook of Theory and Research for the Sociology of Education,* pp. 241–58. New York: Greenwood Press.

Bourdieu, P. and **J.C. Passeron.** (1970). *Reproduction.* Paris: Editions de Minuit.

Bruner, J. (1985). 'Narrative and Paradigmatic Modes of Thought', in E. Eisner (ed.), *Learning and Teaching the Ways of Knowing. Eighty-fourth Yearbook of the National Society for the Study of Education,* pp. 97–115. Chicago: University of Chicago Press.

Butchvarov, P. (1970). *The Concept of Knowledge.* Evanston, Illinois: Northwestern University Press.

Byres, T.J. and **R. Crow.** (1983). *The Green Revolution in India.* Milton Keynes: Open University.

CREP. (2000). *Concise Routledge Encyclopedia of Philosophy.* London: Routledge.

Cole, M. and **S. Scribner.** (1974). *Culture and Thought: A Psychological Introduction.* New York: John Wiley and Sons, Inc.

——. (1981). *The Psychology of Literacy.* Cambridge, Mass.: Harvard University Press.

Cosin, B.R., I.R. Dale, G.M. Esland, D. Mackinnon and **D.F. Swift.** (eds.) (1971). *School and Society: A Sociological Reader.* Second edition. London: Routledge and Kegan Paul, in association with The Open University Press.

Datta, D.M. (1972). *Six Ways of Knowing.* Calcutta: Calcutta University Press.

De Castell, S. (1982). 'Epistemic Authority, Institutional Power and Curricular Knowledge', *The Journal of Educational Thought,* 16(1): 23–28.

Dewey, J. (1916). *Democracy and Education.* New York: The Free Press.

——. (1938). *Logic: The Theory of Inquiry.* New York: Henry Holt and Co.

——. (1957). *Human Nature and Conduct.* New York: The Modern Library.

——. (1985a). 'The Problem of Truth', reprinted in J.A. Boydston (ed.), *How We Think and Selected Essays 1910–1911 (Series title: John Dewey: The Middle Works, 1899–1924, Vol. 6),* pp. 12–68. Carbondale: Southern Illinois University Press.

——. (1985b). *How We Think,* reprinted in J.A. Boydston (ed.), pp. 177–356.

Doise, W. and **G. Mugney.** (1984). *The Social Development of the Intellect.* Oxford: Pergammon Press.

Dore, R. (1980). 'The Future of Formal Education in Developing Countries', in J. Simmons (ed.), *The Educational Dilemma,* pp. 69–76. Oxford: Pergammon.

——. (1997). *The Diploma Disease: Education Qualification and Development.* Second edition. London: Institute of Education, University of London.

Dube, S.C. (1955). *Indian Village.* London: Routledge and Kegan Paul.

——. (1988). 'The Cultural Dimensions of Development', *International Social Science Journal,* 118: 505–12.

Durkheim, E. (1965). *The Elementary Forms of the Religious Life.* New York: The Free Press.

——. (1979). *Durkheim: Essays on Morals and Education.* W.S.F. Pickering (ed. and intro.). London: Routledge.

Edwards, D. and **N. Mercer.** (1987). *Common Knowledge: The Development of Understanding in the Classroom.* London: Routledge.

Esland, G.M. (1971). 'Teaching and Learning as the Organization of Knowledge', in M.F.D. Young (ed.), see below, pp. 70–115.

Foucault, M. (1979). *Discipline and Punish: The Birth of the Prison*, Part 3, Ch. 3: 'Panopticism', pp. 195–230. New York: Vintage Books.

——. (1980). *Power/Knowledge: Selected Interviews and Other Writings*. C. Gordon (ed.). New York: Pantheon Books.

——. (1984). 'Truth and Power', in P. Rabinow (ed.), *The Foucault Reader*, pp. 54–75. New York: Pantheon Books.

Frege, G. (1993). 'On Sense and Reference', in A.W. Moore (ed.), *Meaning and Reference*, pp. 22–35. New York: Oxford University Press.

Freire, P. (1974). *Pedagogy of the Oppressed*. New York: The Seabury Press.

Fricker, E. (1987). 'Epistemology of Testimony', *Proceedings of the Aristotelian Society*, Supplementary Volume. London.

Garvey, C. (1977). *Play*. Cambridge, Mass.: Harvard University Press.

Goffman, E. (1959). *Presentation of Self in Everyday Life*. Harmondsworth: Penguin.

Goodson, I. (1988). *The Making of Curriculum: Collected Essays*. London: Falmer Press.

Government of India. (1971). *1971 Census: District Census Handbook–Town and Village Directory, Delhi*. New Delhi: Census of India.

——. (1981). *1981 Census: District Census Handbook–Town and Village Directory, Delhi*. New Delhi: Census of India.

——. (1986). *National Policy on Education–1986*. New Delhi: Ministry of Human Resource Development, Department of Education.

——. (1990). *Towards an Enlightened and Humane Society: NPE, 1986–A Review*. Report of the Committee for Review of National Policy of Education (NPE), 1986, under the chairmanship of Acharya Ramamurthi. New Delhi: Government of India.

——. (1991). *District Census Handbook, Delhi: Part XII–A & B*. New Delhi: Census of India.

——. (1993). *Learning Without Burden*. Report of the National Advisory Committee appointed by the MHRD to suggest ways and means to reduce the academic burden on schoolchildren, under the chairmanship of Yashpal. New Delhi: Department of Education, Ministry of Human Resource Development.

Graubard, A. (1974). *Free the Children: Radical Reform and the Free School Movement*. New York: Vintage Books.

Gupta, A. (1989). *The Toy Bag/Kabad Se Jugad*. Bhopal: Eklavya.

Haack, S. (1976). 'The Pragmatist Theory of Truth', *British Journal of Philosophy of Science*, 27: 231–49.

Hammersley, M. and **P. Woods.** (eds.) (1976). *The Process of Schooling: A Sociological Reader*. London: Routledge and Kegan Paul in association with The Open University Press.

Hekman, S.J. (1986). *Hermeneutics and the Sociology of Knowledge*. Cambridge: Polity Press.

Hiriyanna, M. (1993). *Outlines of Indian Philosophy*. Delhi: Motilal Banarsidass.

Holzner, B. (1968). *Reality Construction in Society*. Cambridge, Mass.: Schenkman.

Hoskin, K. (1979). 'The Examination, Disciplinary Power and Rational Schooling', *The History of Education*, 8(2): 135–46.

Inhelder, B. and **B. Matalon.** (1960). 'The Study of Problem Solving and Thinking', in P. Mussen (ed.), *Handbook of Research Methods in Child Development*, pp. 421–55. New Delhi: Tata McGraw-Hill.

Inkeles, A. and **D. Smith.** (1974). *Becoming Modern.* Cambridge, Mass.: Harvard University Press.

Johnson, A.G. (ed.) (1995). *The Blackwell Dictionary of Sociology.* Cambridge: Basil Blackwell.

Kakar, S. (1981). *The Inner World: A Psychoanalytical Study of Childhood and Society in India.* Second edition. Delhi: Oxford University Press.

———. (1991). *The Analyst and the Mystic.* New Delhi: Viking.

Kalyan. (1953). *Balakank* (Annual Issue on Childhood) 27(1). Gorakhpur: Gita Press.

———. (1988). *Sikshank* (Annual Issue on Education) 62(1). Gorakhpur: Gita Press.

Keddie, N. (1971). 'Classroom Knowledge', in M.F.D. Young (ed.) see below, pp. 133–60.

Khanna, S. (1992). *The Joy of Indian Toys.* New Delhi: National Book Trust.

Kripke, S.A. (1980). *Naming and Necessity.* Cambridge, Mass.: Harvard University Press.

Kuhn, T.S. (1970). *The Structure of Scientific Revolutions.* Second edition. Chicago: The University of Chicago Press.

Kumar, K. (1988). 'Origins of India's Textbook Culture', *Comparative Education*, 32(4): 452–65.

———. (1991). *The Political Agenda of Education: A Study of Colonialist and National Ideas.* New Delhi: Sage.

———. (1996). 'Agriculture, Modernisation and Education: the Contours of a Point of Departure', *Economic and Political Weekly*, 31(35–37): 2367–373.

Lacey, C. (1970). *Hightown Grammar: The School as a Social System.* Manchester: The University of Manchester Press.

Lannoy, R. (1971). *The Speaking Tree: A Study of Indian Culture and Society.* London: Oxford University Press.

Latour, B. (1987). *Science in Action: How to Follow Scientists and Engineers through Society.* Cambridge, Mass.: Harvard University Press.

Lave, J. and **S. Chaiklin.** (eds.) (1993). *Understanding Practice: Perspectives on Activity and Context.* Cambridge: Cambridge University Press.

Lewis, D. (1979). 'Attitudes De Dicto and De Se', *Philosophical Review*, pp. 513–43.

Lewis, O. (1958). *Village Life in Northern India.* New York: Vintage Books.

Luria, A.R. (1976). *Cognitive Development: Its Cultural and Social Foundations.* Cambridge, Mass.: Harvard University Press.

Mani, V. (ed.) (1996). *Puranic Encyclopaedia.* Delhi: Motilal Banarsidass.

Mann, R.S. (1979). *Social Structure, Social Change and Future Trends: An Indian Village Perspective.* Jaipur: Rawat.

Mannheim, K. (1954). *Ideology and Utopia: An Introduction to the Sociology of Knowledge.* London: Routledge and Kegan Paul.

Matilal, B.K. (1986). *Perception: An Essay on Indian Classical Theories of Knowledge.* Oxford: Clarendon Press.

———. (1990). *The Word and the World: Indian's Contributions to the Study of Language.* Delhi: Oxford University Press.

Mead, G.H. (1964). *The Social Psychology of George Herbert Mead*, A. Strauss (ed. and intro.). Chicago: The University of Chicago Press.

Memmi, A. (1967). *Colonizer and the Colonized.* Boston: Beacon Press.

Mills, C.W. (1970). 'Language, Logic and Culture', in L.L. Horowitz (ed. and intro.), *Power, Politics and People: The Collected Essays of C. Wright Mills*, pp. 423–38. New York: Oxford University Press.

Mookerji, R.K. (1989). *Ancient Indian Education: Brahminical and Buddhist.* Delhi: Motilal Banarsidass.

Mulay, S. and **G.L. Ray.** (1973). *Towards Modernisation: A Study of Peasantry in Rural Delhi.* Delhi: National.

Myrdal, G. (1968). *Asian Drama: An Enquiry into the Poverty of Nations.* Harmondsworth: Allen Lane.

Nanda, B.N. (1992). 'Pedagogy and Prescription in Highland Orissa: The Role of Teachers and Doctors in Tribal Development'. Unpublished paper presented at the Comparative Education Conference. New Delhi: Jamia Millia Islamia.

NCERT. (1988a). *Exploring Environment, Books I, II and III* (for Classes III, IV and V, respectively). New Delhi: NCERT.

——. (1988b). *National Curriculum Framework for Primary and Secondary Education: A Framework.* New Delhi: NCERT.

——. (2000). *National Curriculum Framework for School Education.* New Delhi: NCERT.

Nieuwenhuys, O. (2000). 'The Worst Forms of Child Labour and the Worst for Working Children: The Child Labour Issue, Exploitation and the Question of Value'. Unpublished paper presented at the International Conference: Rethinking Childhood. Bulletin No. 3, pp. 41–52. Bondy, France: IRD and AGIDs.

Passeron, J.C. (1986). 'Theories of Socio-Cultural Reproduction', *International Social Science Journal,* 110: 619–29.

Peirce, C.S. (1958). *Charles S. Peirce: Selected Writings,* P.P. Weiner (ed.). New York: Dover Publications.

Peters, R.S. (1966). *Ethics and Education,* Ch. 9: 'Authority and Education', pp. 237–65. London: Allen and Unwin.

Piaget, J. (1951). *Play, Dreams and Imitation.* London: Routledge and Kegan Paul.

——. (1954). *The Child's Construction of Reality.* London: Routledge and Kegan Paul.

——. (1971). *Biology and Knowledge.* Edinburgh: Edinburgh University Press.

Polanyi, M. (1958). *Personal Knowledge.* Chicago: The University of Chicago Press.

——. (1969). *Knowing and Being.* M. Grene (ed.). Chicago: The University of Chicago Press.

PROBE Team. (1999). *Public Report on Basic Education in India.* New Delhi: Oxford University Press.

Ramadas, J., C. Natrajan, S. Chunawala and **S. Apte.** (1996). *Role of Experiments in School Science,* Diagnosing Learning in Primary Science, Part 3. Bombay: Homi Bhabha Centre for Science Education.

Ram-Prasad, C. (nd) 'Promise, Power and Play: Conceptions of Youthfulness and Forms of the Divine'.

Rao, M.S.A. (1971). *Urbanisation and Social Change: A Study of a Rural Community on a Metropolitan Fringe.* New Delhi: Orient Longman.

——. (1991). *Reader in Urban Sociology.* New Delhi: Orient Longman.

Rogoff, B. (1990). *Apprenticeship in Thinking: Cognitive Development in Social Context.* New York: Oxford University Press.

Rorty, R. (1980). *Philosophy and the Mirror of Nature.* Oxford: Basil Blackwell.

——. (1991). *Objectivity, Relativism and Truth: Philosophical Papers, Vol. 1.* Part I: 'Solidarity or Objectivity', pp. 21–34. Cambridge: Cambridge University Press.

Roy, R. and **R.K. Srivastava.** (1986). *Dialogues on Development: The Individual Society and Political Order.* New Delhi: Sage.

Russell, B. (1959). *The Problems of Philosophy.* New York: Oxford University Press.

Russell, J. (1978). *The Acquisition of Knowledge.* New York: St. Martin's Press.

Sarangapani, P.M. (1998) 'The Construction of Identity and Knowledge in an Indian Village Primary School'. Unpublished paper presented at DHIIR Conference: Creating the Future, The Use and Abuse of Indian Role Models, University of Cambridge.

———. (1999a). 'The Child's Construction of Knowledge' in T.S. Saraswathi (ed.), *Culture Socialization and Human Development: Theory, Research and Applications in India,* pp. 85–122. New Delhi: Sage.

———. (1999b) 'Piaget's Theory: Going Back in Order to go Forward'. *Indian Education Review* 35(2): 1–27.

———. (2000). 'Self in Relation to Work: Perceptions of Children in a North Indian Village'. Unpublished paper presented at the International Conference: Rethinking Childhood. Bulletin No. 2, pp. 13–28. Bondy, France: IRD and AGIDs.

Saraswati, B. (1972). 'Traditional Modes of Learning in Indian Civilization', in S. Sinha (ed.), *Aspects of Indian Culture and Society,* pp. 153–69. Calcutta: The Indian Anthropological Society.

Satprakashananda. (1974). *Methods of Knowledge.* Calcutta: Advaita Ashrama.

Schutz, A. (1962). *Collected Papers Vol I: The Problem of Social Reality,* M. Natanson (ed.). The Hague: Martinues Nijhoff.

———. (1970). *On Phenomenology and Social Relations: Selected Writings.* H.R. Wagner (ed. and intro.). Chicago: The Chicago University Press.

Searle, J.R. (1971). 'What is a Speech Act', in J.R. Searle (ed.), *The Philosophy of Language,* pp. 39–53. Oxford: Oxford University Press.

Shah, A.M. (1998). *The Family in India: Critical Essays.* Hyderabad: Orient Longman.

Singh, K.S. and **S. Manoharan.** (1993). *Language and Scripts in Peoples of India, National Series Vol. IX (Anthropological Survey of India).* Delhi: Oxford University Press.

Singh, Y. (1986). *Modernization of Indian Tradition.* Jaipur: Rawat Publications.

Srinivas, M.N. (1976). *Remembered Village.* Delhi: Oxford University Press.

Srivastava, S. (1993). 'Citizens and Others: Post-coloniality and National Identity at an Indian Public School'. Unpublished PhD dissertation, University of Sydney.

Thapan, M. (1991). *Life at School: An Ethnographic Study.* Delhi: Oxford University Press.

Tough, J. (1977). *The Development of Meaning.* London: George Allen and Unwin.

Vaidyanathan, T.G. (1989). 'Authority and Identity in India', in 'Another India' *Daedalus,* Fall, 118(4): 147–69.

Vygotsky, L.S. (1978). *Mind in Society: The Development of Higher Psychological Processes.* Cambridge, Mass.: Harvard University Press.

Weber, M. (1968). *On Charisma and Institutional Building.* S.N. Eisenstadt (ed. and intro.). Chicago: The University of Chicago Press.

Welbourne, M. (1993). *The Community of Knowledge.* Hampshire: Gregg Revivals.

Wertsch, J.V. (ed.) (1985). *Culture, Communication and Cognition: Vygotskian Perspectives.* Cambridge: Cambridge University Press.

Whorf, B.L. (1956). *Language, Thought and Reality.* Cambridge, Mass.: MIT Press.

Willis, P. (1976). 'The Class Significance of School Counter-Culture', in M. Hammersley and P. Woods (eds.), see above, pp. 188–200.

Wilson, P. (1983). *Second Hand Knowledge: An Inquiry Into Cognitive Authority.* Westport, Connecticut: Greenwood Press.

Wiser, W. and **C. Wiser.** (1971). *Behind Mud Walls: 1930–1960*. Berkeley: University of California Press.
Wittgenstein, L. (1958). *Philosophical Investigations: The English Text of the Third Edition*, G.E.M. Anscombe (ed. and trans.). New York: Macmillan Publishing Company.
Wood, D. (1986). 'Aspects of Teaching and Learning', in M. Richards and P. Light (eds.), *Children of Social Worlds: Development in a Social Context*, pp. 191–212. Cambridge, Mass.: Harvard University Press.
Woods, P. (1979). *The Divided School*. London: Routledge and Kegan Paul.
Young, M.F.D. (ed. and intro.) (1971). *Knowledge and Control: New Directions for the Sociology of Education*. London: Collier Macmillan.

Index

future of, 54, 91; and illiteracy/the illiterate, 57, 91; and moral character, 78; and playfulness, 78, 92; social class of, 96–98; stigma of, 91–92; typification of, 73, 92–94
family, 32–33, 68, 103–4, 240, 255, 257; joint, 32; relations within, 33–36; role of women in, 33–35
fantasy and magic, 40, 76, 182–83, 225
father. *See also* parents, mother; 's authority over child, 34–35, 63, 111, 112; 's occupations, 36, 50, 51, 54–55
fieldwork, 15, 16, 20, 30, 189–90, 265, 271–87; with children, 19, 31, 63, 265, 267–68, 281–85; at school, 41, 44, 126–27, 146, 274, 278–79; with teachers, 68–70, 274–76; use of toys, 19, 278–80, 282; in the village, 19, 20–22, 24–25, 30, 31, 279–81
folktales, folklore/folkloric, 80, 83, 90, 117–18, 195, 246, 253, 256, 257
Foucault, M., 162n
frames of reference, 117, 120, 239, 259
framework(s), 14, 15, 73, 74–75, 80, 120, 124, 183, 189, 235, 242, 247, 251, 273; Kasimpur vs liberal, 253–56
framing, 125, 139, 237, 251, 261; boundaries, 247; epistemic authority in, 132–36; in textbook culture classroom, 127–32, 140, 161, 248; weak and strong boundary, 127, 132, 136–38, 236, 261

Gandhi, M.K., 254, 262
Gayatri Mantra, 42, 83, 114, 115
general knowledge, 60, 68, 152, 155, 171, 172, 242, 245
girl-child, girls, 62, 110; attitude towards education of, 29
Green Revolution, 25, 29
guru, 86, 90, 112, 258; as knower, 112; obedience to, 85–86; as parent, 112; *–sishya* relationship, 83, 90, 109, 112–15, 118–19, 241, 246, 247, 258; teacher as, 112–15; true, 258
gurukul, 114

harijan bastis, 21, 280
Haryanavi, 58, 104, 271
Hindi, 49, 58, 65–66, 104, 171, 271

Holzner, B., 14, 101, 121, 266, 268
home and school; cultural discontinuity, 61, 104; linguistic boundary, 61, 104
humour, 105, 110, 111, 277

IQ, 95, 98, 109, 119, 275
identities, identity, 80, 87, 102, 119, 146, 147, 160, 161, 179, 240, 242, 259; of child/learner, 78, 119, 157; of a good student, 90–91, 117, 120. *See also* model student; of teacher, *see* teacher, identity of
ideology, 265; of childhood, 14, 73–75; of education, 14; liberal, 255; of mobility, 55
ignorance, 74, 75, 150, 214, 256
illiterate, illiteracy, 58, 79, 80, 91, 97, 111, 175, 200, 244; stigma of, 58, 66, 78, 80, 174, 179
India/Indian, 72, 91, 114, 164, 176–78, 214, 251, 256, 259; family setup, 109, 111; liberal ideas, 256; concept of self, 91
inference; knowledge formation through, 188–89, 207, 214, 218; vs testimony, 202–5, 207, 251. *See also* sources of knowledge
intelligence, 78, 81, 139, 164, 173–76, 252
interpersonal relations, 33, 210, 211
interrogation, 148, 150–52, 246
interviews, interviewing; children, 190, 281–85; in groups, 189, 284; critical, clinical, 184, 281, 283

jajmani system, 24, 29, 30, 31, 37n
jankari (knowledge), an object of education, 60–61. *See also* general knowledge, quizzing
job opportunity, *see* employment, *naukari*
job security, 50. *See also* desk-job, employment, work
joyful learning, 13, 180, 254. *See also* playway

Kalyan, 73–74, 76, 87, 90, 91, 114, 118
kinship, 29, 33
knower/s, 147, 157, 160, 182–84, 209, 239, 241–42; child as, *see* child, as knower; meta-cognitive awareness of, 243, 249

About the Author

Padma M. Sarangapani, an independent researcher, is currently Associate Fellow at the National Institute of Advanced Studies, Bangalore. She was the recipient of the Indira Gandhi Memorial Fellowship (1999–2001). During her doctoral studies at the University of Delhi, she spent a year at Tufts University as a Fulbright Pre-doctoral Fellow and a Dudley Wright Fellow (1992–93). Dr. Sarangapani's teaching experience includes teaching mathematics and science to high school students in Hyderabad and Bangalore and establishing the Department of Elementary Education at Jesus and Mary College, University of Delhi. She was involved with developing the Bachelor of Elementary Education Programme of the University of Delhi and course content for teaching primary mathematics at the Indira Gandhi National Open University, New Delhi. She continues to be engaged with research, writing and teaching.

Her research interests include the anthropological study of learning and childhood, curriculum studies, mathematics and science education, and teacher education.

DATE DUE